# An Introduction to South Asian Politics

This introductory textbook provides students with a fundamental understanding of the social, political, and economic institutions of six South Asian countries: Afghanistan, Bangladesh, India, Nepal, Pakistan, and Sri Lanka. It adopts a broad theoretical framework and evaluates the opportunities and constraints facing South Asia's states within the context of democracy.

Key features include:

- An introduction to the region.
- The history and political development of these South Asian states, including evaluations of their democratic trajectories.
- The management of conflict, economic development, and extremist threats.
- A comparative analysis of the states.
- Projections concerning democracy taking into consideration the opportunities and constraints facing these countries.

This textbook will be an indispensable teaching tool for courses on South Asia. It includes pedagogical features such as political chronologies, political party descriptions, text boxes, a glossary, and suggestions for further reading. Written in an accessible style and by experts on South Asian politics, it offers students of South Asian politics a valuable introduction to an exceedingly diverse region.

**Neil DeVotta** is an Associate Professor of Political Science at Wake Forest University. His research interests include South Asian security and politics, ethnicity and nationalism, and democratic transition and consolidation. He is the author of *Blowback: Linguistic Nationalism, Institutional Decay, and Ethnic Conflict in Sri Lanka* (2004) and the editor of *Understanding Contemporary India, Second Edition* (2010). He is currently at work on *From Civil War to Soft Authoritarianism: Ethnonationalism and Democratic Regression in Sri Lanka* (Routledge, 2017).

This engaging and nuanced volume provides a comprehensive and balanced survey of the region and countries of South Asia. The well-researched and written "state of the art" chapters make this an indispensable resource for students, researchers, and laypersons.

**Shalendra D. Sharma**, *Professor in the Department of Politics,*
*University of San Francisco, USA*

*An Introduction to South Asian Politics* provides a timely assessment of democratic development in the region. Neil DeVotta has assembled a group of experts who each provide an excellent account of their case. As well as providing comprehensive background coverage the chapters are leavened by perceptive insights based on the authors' specialist research. Readers will get a solid understanding of how the states of South Asia are changing and how they are integrated at the regional level.

**Andrew Wyatt**, *Senior Lecturer, University of Bristol, UK*

# An Introduction to South Asian Politics

Edited by Neil DeVotta

Routledge
Taylor & Francis Group

LONDON AND NEW YORK

First published 2016
by Routledge
2 Park Square, Milton Park, Abingdon, Oxon OX14 4RN

and by Routledge
711 Third Avenue, New York, NY 10017

*Routledge is an imprint of the Taylor & Francis Group, an informa business*

*British Library Cataloguing in Publication Data*
A catalogue record for this book is available from the British Library

*Library of Congress Cataloging in Publication Data*
A catalog record for this book has been requested

ISBN: 978-0-415-82278-7 (hbk)
ISBN: 978-0-415-82279-4 (pbk)
ISBN: 978-1-315-67130-7 (ebk)

Typeset in Times New Roman
by Cenveo Publisher Services

Dedicated to the memory of

Jalal Alamgir
(1971–2011)

# Contents

# Boxes and table

## Boxes

## Table

# Contributors

**Prakash Adhikari** teaches political science at Central Michigan University. His research lies at the intersection of comparative and international politics, focusing particularly on armed conflict, forced migration, and transitional justice, with a regional focus on South Asia. He has done extensive fieldwork in Nepal funded by the National Science Foundation. He has published in *International Studies Quarterly* and *Journal of Conflict Resolution* and presented his research at various national and international conferences.

**Neil DeVotta** is an Associate Professor of Political Science at Wake Forest University. His research interests include South Asian security and politics, ethnicity and nationalism, ethnic conflict resolution, and democratic transition and consolidation. He is the author of *Blowback: Linguistic Nationalism, Institutional Decay, and Ethnic Conflict in Sri Lanka* (2004) and editor of *Understanding Contemporary India, Second Edition* (2010). He is currently at work on a book titled, *From Civil War to Soft Authoritarianism: Ethnonationalism and Democratic Regression in Sri Lanka*.

**Jason Kirk** is Associate Professor of Political Science at Elon University in North Carolina. He previously taught at Virginia Military Institute and the University of Pennsylvania. He is the author of *India and the World Bank: The Politics of Aid and Influence* (2011). His articles have appeared in *India Review*, *Foreign Policy Analysis*, and other journals. His research and teaching interests encompass India's democratic politics, economic reforms, international relations, and role in global governance.

**Mahendra Lawoti** is a Professor in the Department of Political Science at Western Michigan University. He is a regular contributor for the *Kathmandu Post* and Kantipur dailies, an article editor for *Sage Open*, a board member of the Midwest Conference on Asian Affairs, and advisor to several non-profit organizations in Nepal and the United States. His research covers democratization, political institutions, ethnic politics, and socio-political mobilizations in Nepal and South Asia. He has authored, co-authored, edited, and co-edited 10 books and published numerous book chapters, opinion pieces, and journal articles in *Asian Survey, Commonwealth and Comparative Politics, Democratization, Himalaya*, and *Journal of Democracy*.

**Anas Malik** is Associate Professor of Political Science at Xavier University, Affiliated Faculty with the Workshop in Political Theory and Policy Analysis at Indiana University since Spring 2012, and author of *Political Survival in Pakistan* (2011). His research interests are in political economy, political Islam, and development, and his current research project considers polycentric governance and political Islam with respect to constitutional challenges in Pakistan.

**Ali Riaz** is University Professor and Chair of the Department of Politics and Government at Illinois State University. He previously taught at universities in Bangladesh, England, and South Carolina. He also worked as a broadcast journalist at the British Broadcasting Corporation (BBC) World Service in London. His research interests include Islamist politics, South Asian politics, community development, and political economy of media. He is the author of *Faithful Education: Madrassahs in South Asia* (2008); *Islamist Militancy in Bangladesh: A Complex Web* (2008); *Unfolding State: The Transformation of Bangladesh* (2005); and *God Willing: The Politics of Islamism in Bangladesh* (2004). His recently edited volumes are *Religion and Politics in South Asia* (2010) and *Political Islam and Governance in Bangladesh* (2010). He is the editor of biannual journal *Studies on Asia* and has also served as a consultant to various international organizations, including the UNDP, DFID, SSRC, and BTI.

**Vikash Yadav** is an Associate Professor of Political Science and the Chair of the Asian Studies Department at Hobart and William Smith Colleges in Geneva, NY. He is the author of *Risk in International Finance* and has authored or co-authored essays in the *Middle East Review of International Affairs*, *Asian Affairs*, *World Economy*, and the *Journal of Development Studies*. He frequently teaches courses on the Politics of South Asia, the Politics of Afghanistan, Globalization, the Politics of Development, and a seminar on the Discourse of Failed States. His current research is on issues of sovereignty, security, and identity in South Asia, with a special focus on India's grand strategy in Afghanistan.

# Acknowledgements

This book is primarily designed for undergraduates studying South Asia, although it is bound to inform even the most seasoned scholar interested in the region. Its release was delayed by over a year to account for Bangladesh's general election (January 2014), India's general election (April and May 2014), Afghanistan's presidential election (April and June 2014), and Sri Lanka's presidential election (January 2015). That makes the volume as up to date as it can be, and I thank my fellow authors for being willing to make the necessary revisions. Edited volumes have landed many a friendship on the rocks. That this project progressed seamlessly is a testament to its collaborators' professionalism.

This book has also benefitted from the support of Dorothea Schaefter, Jillian Morrison, and Rebecca Lawrence at Routledge, and I thank them for their input, kindness, and patience.

In 2011 the South Asia academic community lost Jalal Alamgir, a solid scholar whose best work was ahead of him. This book is dedicated to his memory.

# Abbreviations

| | |
|---|---|
| AAP | Aam Aadmi (Common Man) Party |
| AL | Awami League |
| ANA | Afghan National Army |
| ANAAC | Afghan National Army Air Corps |
| ANP | Awami National Party |
| ANP | Afghan National Police |
| AP | Andhra Pradesh |
| APF | Armed Police Force |
| BBS | Bodu Bala Sena (Buddhist Power Force) |
| BJP | Bharatiya Janata (Indian People's) Party |
| BNP | Bangladesh Nationalist Party |
| BNP | Balochistan National Party |
| CAS | Ceylon Administrative Service |
| CCS | Ceylon Civil Service |
| CEC | Chief Election Commissioner |
| CHT | Chittagong Hill Tracts |
| CNC | Ceylon National Congress |
| CPA | Comprehensive Peace Accord |
| CPB | Communist Party of Bangladesh |
| CPI (M) | Communist Party of India (Marxist) |
| CPN (M) | Communist Party of Nepal (Maoist) |
| CPN (M) | Communist Party of Nepal (Marxist) |
| CPN (M-L) | Communist Party of Nepal (Marxist-Leninist) |
| CPN (UML) | Communist Party of Nepal (Unified Marxist-Leninist) |
| CTC | Ceylon Tamil Congress |
| CTG | Caretaker Government |
| DDC | District Development Council |
| EC | Election Commission |
| EPDP | Eelam People's Democratic Party |
| FP | Federal Party |
| GDP | Gross Domestic Product |
| ICT | International Crimes Tribunal |
| IOJ | Islami Oikya Jote |
| INC | Indian National Congress |
| ISAF | International Security Assistance Force |
| ISI | Inter-Services Intelligence (Pakistan) |

| | |
|---|---|
| JI | Jamaat-e-Islami, also known as Bangladesh Jamaat-i-Islami |
| JP | Jatiya Party |
| JRB | Jatiya Rakkhi Bahini (National Defense Force) |
| JSD | Jatiya Samajtantrik Dal |
| JUI | Jamiat Ulema-e-Islami |
| JUP | Jamiat Ulema-e-Pakistan |
| JVP | Janatha Vimukthi Peramuna (People's Liberation Front) |
| JHU | Jathika Hela Urumaya (National Sinhalese Heritage Party) |
| KWP | Kirat Workers Party |
| LTTE | Liberation Tigers of Tamil Eelam |
| MQM | Muttahida Qaumi Movement |
| NAM | Non-Aligned Movement |
| NATO | North Atlantic Treaty Organization |
| NC | Nepali Congress |
| NDA | National Democratic Alliance (coalition led by the BJP) |
| NDC | Nepali Democratic Congress |
| NGO | Non-Governmental Organization |
| NL | National List |
| NNC | Nepali National Congress |
| NSP | Nepal Sadhvawana Party |
| OBCs | Other Backward Classes |
| PA | People's Alliance |
| PDPA | The People's Democratic Party of Afghanistan (Communist). |
| PKLNF | Pallo Kirat Limbuwan Rastriya Manch (Pallo Kirat Limbuwan National Forum) |
| PML | Pakistan Muslim League |
| PPP | Pakistan People's Party |
| PTI | Pakistan Tehreek-e-Insaaf |
| RNA | Royal Nepalese Army |
| RSS | Rashtriya Swayamsevak Sangh (National Volunteer Organization) |
| SAARC | South Asian Association for Regional Cooperation |
| SCUD | A mobile ballistic missile produced the Soviet Union. |
| SLFP | Sri Lanka Freedom Party |
| SLMC | Sri Lanka Muslim Congress |
| SNTV | Single Non-Transferable Vote |
| SSAB | State Services Advisory Board |
| SSDB | State Services Disciplinary Board |
| TDP | Telugu Desam (Telugu Land/People's) Party |
| TMVP | Tamileela Makkal Viduthalaip Pulikal (Tamil Eelam People's Liberation Tigers) |
| TNA | Tamil National Alliance |
| TPLF-G | Tarai People's Liberation Front (Goit) |
| TPLF-J | Tarai People's Liberation Front (Jwala Singh) |
| TRS | Telangana Rashtra Samithi (Telangana Self-Rule Association) |
| UNHCR | United Nations High Commissioner for Relief |
| UNP | United National Party |
| UPA | United Progressive Alliance (coalition led by the INC) |
| UPFN | United People's Front Nepal |
| VOA | Voice of America |

# 1  An overview

*Neil DeVotta*

South Asia is an exceedingly diverse region with a long and complex history that the colonial experience further complicated. If the subcontinent's partition and the disputed borders between India and Pakistan and Pakistan and Afghanistan have ensured tense relations among these states, stark poverty and conspicuous income disparities, rampant corruption, malgovernance, democratic regression and breakdown, and insurgent and separatist conflicts combine to create challenging domestic political environments throughout the region as well. Indeed, it becomes all the more clear why South Asia is going to be even more important going forward when one considers: the radicalization of Hindu extremists in India and Muslim extremists in Pakistan, Afghanistan, and (to a degree) Bangladesh; India's economic rise and its potential to become a great power; China's increased influence in South Asia and the tensions this is creating between India and the region's smaller states; and the threat of nuclear war between India and Pakistan. This book, by focusing on India, Pakistan, Afghanistan, Bangladesh, Sri Lanka, and Nepal, seeks to provide students a deeper understanding of the domestic politics within South Asian countries even as global power shifts from western states to countries in Asia in an increasingly multipolar world.

Given that their historical antecedents, complicated relations among and between the different states in South Asia and beyond, and varied modes of governance have influenced each country's political systems and structures, this book evaluates the opportunities and constraints facing South Asia's states within the context of democracy (i.e. suggesting that the countries in the region are experiencing different stages of democratic politics ranging from democratic transition to democratic deepening to democratic regression and that this state of flux conditions the politics within each country and their relations among each other and the wider world). In doing so, the chapters pay special attention to each country's institutions and how these institutions succeed or fail to promote democracy.

Adopting a democratic prism to analyze the region's domestic politics makes sense given that all six countries currently practice and seek to consolidate democratic governance. A consolidated democracy is achieved when all major stakeholders in a country accept that free and fair elections are the only way to change governments. From this standpoint, India can be said to be the region's only consolidated democracy—although India's vibrant democracy gets juxtaposed with troubling malgovernance. Pakistan, Bangladesh, and Nepal seek to consolidate democracy, but weak institutions and fractured polities have prevented them from reaching this vaunted stage. Sri Lanka, having regressed from a commendable liberal democracy to an illiberal democracy, was heading in an authoritarian direction when a new government promising significant democratic reforms was elected in 2015. Afghanistan may qualify as a failed state (depending on one's definition of a failed state); yet the country's attempts to create democratic institutions have ramifications for its people and the region. Its inclusion in this volume is especially pertinent given the recent American involvement in the country and, consequently, the increased interest it holds among American students.

South Asian states face a democratic paradox in that the region's people value democracy even as they deal with malgovernance. While many reasons can be attributed to bad governance, what is clear is that democracy in such a milieu cannot be taken for granted, for even the most robust democracies can get undone when people lose faith in governing institutions. Pakistan is a case in point, given how the military on multiple occasions has manipulated elected leaders' political failures to usurp power. With South Asia facing multiple crises ranging from intrastate and interstate terrorism to separatist conflicts to communal violence, it is understandable why the region's countries have experienced both democratic gains and democratic regression.

In the chapters that follow, each author focuses on the respective country's history and political development; institutions, political parties, and elections; how it has managed conflict; its economic development and contemporary political economy; regional/international relations; and opportunities and constraints. This framework makes for easier cross comparisons and highlights the similar and different challenges facing these countries.

The chapter on India by Jason Kirk first provides an overview of the country's post-independence history, dividing its political development into two broad periods and treating the late 1970s and early 1980s as a turning point. The first half of this history explains the initial dominance of the Congress Party, and the second half discusses new patterns of political mobilization, using the narrative frame of "Mandal and *mandir*" to capture two particularly important trends of caste-based identity parties and the rise of political Hinduism (Mandal was the chairman of a landmark commission to "identify the socially or educationally backward," and a *mandir* is a Hindu temple). The chapter discusses the growing importance of sub-national politics and trends toward language- and region-based parties. It surveys major changes in India's political economy and development policies from the early Nehruvian mixed economy to the post-liberalization period. An analysis of India's approaches to managing conflict also considers Hindu-Muslim relations, separatist movements, and the significant Naxalite insurgency that traverses many less developed districts in central and eastern India. It further surveys India's international relations—focusing especially on Pakistan, China, and the United States—and considers opportunities and constraints facing India in its emergence as a leading Asian and global power.

The chapter on Pakistan by Anas Malik examines Pakistan's political development by looking at certain pre-Partition facets and briefly comparing India's early experience. It pays special attention to the challenges of managing conflict between elected and unelected institutions, the tendency of political parties to have a parochial rather than integrative basis, and election outcomes in Pakistan that have reflected these divides. The chapter reflects on Pakistan's regional and international relations, particularly its enduring rivalry with India, its variable and sometimes contradictory alliance with the United States, its interests in Afghanistan, as well as the geopolitical challenges arising from the Iranian revolution, the Soviet invasion of Afghanistan. Malik evidences how all this has allowed politicians and their challengers to pursue political survival and ascendancy within the context of political Islam.

Ali Riaz's chapter on Bangladesh discusses the developments in that country since its inception in 1971 with due reference made to significant eras—populist authoritarianism (1972–75), military dominance (1975–90), representative democracy (1991–2006); unsuccessful reform (2007–08), and democracy redux (2009–present)—so as to capture the country's struggles with representative democracy. It also discusses the strengths and weaknesses of the country's economy within the context of its increased integration with the global economy and the impact of growth on poverty. Furthermore, it covers the country's relations with India and Burma and its involvement in regional and global institutions. Finally, the chapter highlights the successes of the past four decades and addresses the challenges facing Bangladesh in the years ahead.

The chapter on Sri Lanka discusses the development of political institutions during the pre-independence and post-independence periods, considers how ethnocentric politics helped compromise democracy, and specifies the ways in which the Mahinda Rajapaksa government that ruled from November 2005 to January 2015 especially undermined institutions and pushed the island in an authoritarian direction. The chapter also covers Sri Lanka's relations with India and China and the opportunities and challenges facing the island as it reverts to a more democratic dispensation following the ouster of the Rajapaksa government.

The chapter on Nepal discusses how the country has been struggling to consolidate a democratic political system for more than half a century and the challenges it has faced to create a constitution, which is a country's most important institution. It discusses the reasons for the failure of democracy in Nepal and evaluates its prospects for democratic governance. The chapter discusses Nepal's political development and subsequent trajectory by taking into consideration the roles played by the now-deposed monarchy, the country's ethnic diversity, and regional and global opportunities and constraints.

Finally, Vikash Yadav's chapter on Afghanistan explores the causes behind the rapid erosion of democratic practices and institutions in Afghanistan since the Taliban's overthrow and discusses how the underlying political economy and social divisions in Afghanistan have historically limited the state's capacity and autonomy while fostering dependence on regional and great powers for external assistance in multiple failed projects of "modernization." Although the state is more present in the lives of Afghans than before the Saur Revolution of 1978 and subsequent civil war periods, the chapter discusses why state institutions remain weak, porous, and personalized. This has led to a parliament that is often deadlocked and marginal to governance as political parties continuously fracture on the basis of personality rather than ideology and a state that is unable to contain social conflicts. Yadav argues that the inability of this embattled state to achieve a monopoly on the legitimate use of violence increases the salience of ethno-linguistic identity and threatens regional stability.

The Trends and Prospects chapter builds on the individual chapters to highlight the opportunities and constraints facing the South Asian region and the individual countries covered in the book. It partly discusses India's influence in the region while also paying due attention to China's increased involvement in South Asia and how this stands to impact domestic politics and international relations of the countries covered in the book.

# 2 India

*Jason Kirk*

India is old. Humans have inhabited its subcontinent for 7,000 years. Around 2600 BCE, a sophisticated civilization—larger than ancient Mesopotamia—emerged in the Indus River Valley, centered on the cities of Harappa and Mohenjo-Daro. Its five million people achieved civic and technological feats unknown to their Bronze Age contemporaries, but its greatness would be long unknown after its demise around 1300 BCE (probably through climate change, migration, and intermingling with another people, the Aryans of Central Asia). The Indus Valley Civilization was rediscovered through excavations only in the early twentieth century, by which time India had passed through many ages, from the Vedic to the Mughal, to become part of the British Empire. Today, the Indus ruins are in Pakistan—a young state, born in the Partition of India when Britain withdrew in 1947.

India is also young. The "sovereign democratic republic," as it was proclaimed in the Preamble to its 1950 Constitution, is an institutional feat without precedent. Never before had all of India been brought under a single, unified territorial state and central government. Even during the formal British Raj (Rule) from 1858 to 1947, a third of India's territory had remained in more than 500 princely states.

Nor had the world seen such an experiment as democracy on the scale of post-1947 India. It embraced universal suffrage for all men and women over 21, so that more than 175 million were eligible to vote in the first general election in 1951–52. Around 85 percent of Indians in 1951–52 could not read or write, yet voter turnout was 60 percent.

Average life expectancy was 40, but press reports tell of voting by "a 110-year-old-man in Madurai who came propped up on either side by a great-grandson, [and] a ninety-five-year-old-woman in Ambala, deaf and hunchbacked" (Guha 2007, 154). At such advanced ages, they had beheld both the beginning and the end of formal British rule.

India's huge population and only gradually abating population growth—now an average 2.5 births per woman—have made each successive general election there the largest in world history. In 2014, two-thirds of eligible voters turned out, besting the previous record set 30 years earlier (in a sympathy wave that followed the assassination of Prime Minister Indira Gandhi in 1984). Of almost 815 million Indians who voted in 2014, fully 100 million were added just since the previous election in 2009. Over nine phases of voting, 11 million election officials were deployed across more than 935,000 polling stations, bearing 1.7 million briefcase-sized electronic voting machines that utilize a symbol-based interface, since as many as 287 million voters are illiterate (Ford 2014). An independent, technically expert Election Commission manages this epic feat. Candidates ritually complain to the news media about its decisions, but this only serves to illustrate its intended insulation from more direct forms of political pressure.

As India's population nears 1.25 billion, there are more than 600 million under age 25, and 70 percent of the population is under 40. In contrast—and like the octogenarian prime minister who left office in 2014, Manmohan Singh—four out of five Indian politicians are over 70, older than the republic itself (Kumar 2009). As *The New York Times* reports, there is a "startling four-decade gap between the median age of India's people and that of its government officials... Among the world's major countries, India has the youngest population, and the oldest leaders" (Mustafi 2012).

Recently, this demographic disconnect has been a subtext to protests over everything from official corruption, to freedom of speech, to the treatment of women in a society with persisting patriarchal and chauvinist elements. Corruption—the use of public office for private gain—can entice public servants of all ages. But when many of the same personages and parties have been on the scene for so long, the image of a sclerotic system—ill-suited to tackling abuses, providing good governance and addressing twenty-first-century problems—is hard to shrug off.

In 2011, a movement led by the 74-year-old Anna Hazare—but with mostly young and urban supporters—pressured the Indian government to enact a major anti-corruption law. Hazare undertook hunger strikes and courted arrest, tactics that hearken back to Mahatma Gandhi's leadership in the Indian freedom struggle. Then in late 2012, the anti-corruption movement spawned the Aam Aadmi (Common Man) Party (AAP), which won office in the Delhi state election just a year later. Its leader, Arvind Kejriwal, 45, served as the state's chief minister for just 49 days before resigning to lead a national campaign for 2014. Only four of the AAP's 434 candidates won parliamentary seats, but its meteoric rise may portend more urban voter mobilization ahead (historically, elections have been decided in rural India).

Outside the electoral process, the young-versus-old tension has manifested in showdowns involving freedom of speech. In 2012, police arrested a 25-year-old cartoonist named Aseem Trivedi on charges of sedition and "insulting national honor" when he published two anti-corruption pieces, one replacing the three noble lions of India's national emblem with three rapacious wolves, and the other depicting the Parliament building as a toilet bowl (Singh 2012). As fate would have it, two months later, an 86-year-old former cartoonist turned political boss died in Mumbai, sparking another incident. Bal Thackeray's right-wing Shiv Sena party has held a controlling influence in India's largest city since the 1990s, both in and out of power (the man himself never held public office). When a 21-year-old woman took to Facebook to criticize the city's virtual shutdown for the old don's funeral, she was arrested by police, as was another woman who merely "liked" her comment on the social media site (Parmar 2012). Charges against cartoonist Trivedi were dropped, and the two women in Mumbai were released, but the incidents lent themselves to a narrative of growing disaffection among the young—made more urgent by the slowing of India's recently lively economy.

Finally, in December 2012, global news media were gripped by the gruesome story of a gang rape in New Delhi that led to the death of a 23-year-old young woman. The incident (and several others) set off massive demonstrations in cities across India, compelling the central and state governments to announce new protections for women. Kiran Bedi, a former police officer, told America's CNN that the case highlighted the need for major reforms across Indian law enforcement, still largely governed by the Indian Police Act of 1861. Human rights advocates argue that the Act, which the British adopted after a major 1857–58 rebellion, makes law enforcement more accountable to politicians than to the public

(Daruwala, Joshi, and Tiwana 2005). "It's a tsunami call, the way the new young generation has taken to the streets," Bedi said ("India Rape Case" 2012).

So India is old, and so are many of its leaders and laws; Indian voters are young and energetic, but increasingly estranged; Indian elections are enormously large, with the 2014 election the most epic yet. It was also an historic election, resulting in an unprecedented margin of victory for the Bharatiya Janata Party—the first time a party other than the Indian National Congress has secured a parliamentary majority and formed a government without the need for coalition allies.

## History and political development

When the East India Company arrived in India at the dawn of the seventeenth century, British merchants encountered a patchwork of regional authorities controlling coastal trading stations. The Portuguese had established a presence already; the Dutch and French would follow. The British set up trading posts and forts in Surat, Madras, Bombay, and Calcutta, gradually eclipsing other Europeans and even the Mughal court at Delhi. In 1757, East India Company forces defeated the last independent Nawab of Bengal and his French allies in the Battle of Plassey, a major milestone in British ascendancy.

The Company's policies had a significant impact on Indian society. In Bengal, it implemented a form of indirect taxation, corrupted from the Mughal practice, which relied on middlemen called *zamindars*. The zamindars were originally local revenue collectors with strong enforcement powers, which the British mistook for European-style landed gentry since their offices passed hereditarily. Beginning in the 1790s, these collectors were given formal land rights, entrenching them as a powerful and potentially oppressive landlord class and leaving a legacy that some Indians still refer to as "feudalism" (though the *zamindari* system differed from historical feudalism in Europe). Similar arrangements existed under other names across north India. An alternative *ryotwari* system was enacted elsewhere—especially in the south—in which the Company collected revenues directly from peasant cultivators (*ryots*).

Exactly a century after Plassey, the Company's control over much of India was challenged in the Indian Rebellion of 1857–58. It started when Indian *sepoys* (soldiers) in the service of the Company were outraged to learn that a new rifle cartridge casing, which had to be bitten open, had been greased with the lard of cows and pigs—sacred to Hindus and unclean to Muslims, respectively. Disgruntled local princes backed the revolt in an attempt to roll back British power, and the conflict went on for more than a year, bankrupting the Company. With so much at stake economically for Britain, the Crown and British government assumed direct control over India following this so-called Sepoy Mutiny. It was the nineteenth century version of a private firm having grown "too big to fail."

Famously, it has been said, "the British Empire was acquired in a fit of absence of mind" (Seeley 1922 [1883]). But this airy notion understates the calculated manner in which the British maintained control. A divide-and-rule strategy played up rivalries among various groups. This was evident in the construction of the Indian Civil Service: the recruitment of mainly upper-caste Hindus into this bureaucracy, and into the colonial courts, led to their overrepresentation in the emergent middle class and fostered resentments among the much larger numbers of lower-caste Hindus, not to mention Muslims and other non-Hindus.

The events of 1857–58 notwithstanding, the seeds of India's nationalist movement can be traced more directly to the founding of the Indian National Congress (INC) in 1885.

Originally, the INC—also known as the Congress Party, or simply "Congress"—was set up to work with, not against, the British government. Its founders were Indian and Anglo-Indian liberals who expressed faith in British democracy and loyalty to the Crown. (Exactly 50 years earlier, Lord Thomas Macaulay had famously envisioned in his Minute of 1835 "a class of persons, Indian in blood and colour, but English in taste, in opinion, in morals, and in intellect"; the early INC was just such an assemblage.) The party "sought by resolutions made at its annual meetings to rouse the British conscience to certain inequities of British rule and to the justice of Indian claims for greater representation in the civil services and in the legislative councils at the Center and in the provinces" (Hardgrave and Kochanek 2008, 42).

The INC was part of a broader flowering of associations in late nineteenth century India, reflecting deeper cultural awakenings. Exposure to Western liberalism and Christian teachings spurred reform and revivalist movements, especially among Hindus. While the INC emerged as the main conduit for political appeals to the British, its moderate leadership, headed by Gopal Krishna Gokhale, came under pressure from radicals led by Bal Gangadhar Tilak, a Hindu Maratha revivalist who the British denounced as "the Father of Indian Unrest." In speeches and articles in self-published English and Marathi journals, Tilak called for struggle and *swaraj* (self-rule) rather than the "self-deception of constitutional cooperation" (Hardgrave and Kochanek 2008, 43).

In 1905, the British viceroy, Lord Curzon, partitioned Bengal province into a Hindu-majority west and Muslim-majority east. Ostensibly, this was to facilitate better administration, but the move was also meant to strike a blow to Indian nationalism in its eastern epicenter of Bengal. It backfired. Opponents of the division, mainly Hindu, organized boycotts of British goods in the first Swadeshi (Self-Sufficiency) Movement, which helped to mobilize larger numbers of Indians into the political arena. The Bengal partition also led to the founding of the Muslim League in 1906 at Dacca (now Dhaka, Bangladesh) by Muslim elites seeking to present a united position on rights for the community, particularly in education.

The Bengal partition stood for only six years, and protests against it led to expanded Indian representation in the central and provincial legislatures. But the British also accepted the Muslim League's demand for a separate electorate, meaning that only Muslims could vote for candidates for certain "reserved" seats (117 of 250 total) in the provincial assembly. This concession was meant to check Hindu dominance, but it led to tensions between the INC and the League.

### The nationalist movement under Gandhi

Mohandas K. Gandhi is the figure most often associated with India's freedom struggle, and for good reason: no other leader did as much to transform the nationalist cause into a mass movement, or to harness together the discordant agendas of determined leaders from different segments of society. Gandhi was born in 1869 into a Gujarati *Bania* (merchant caste) family in princely Porbandar on India's west coast, where his father served as chief minister. He studied law in London and led a civil rights movement for Indians in South Africa before returning in 1915 to India, where he became active in the INC and traveled widely to understand the lives of ordinary people.

Gandhi applied the strategy of *satyagraha* (soul force), or nonviolent civil disobedience, to protest injustices of British rule. In 1918, he led a campaign in famine-stricken Champaran, Bihar, where landlords compelled poor cultivators to grow indigo instead of subsistence crops. He launched a wider *hartal* (general strike) in 1919 to protest the Rowlatt

Act, enacted during the World War, to repress "public disturbances" and effectively ban public assembly.

Inspired by Gandhi's call, thousands of Sikhs, Muslims, and Hindus assembled in an enclosed public square—the Jallianwallah Bagh in Amritsar, Punjab—in defiance of the ban to protest the arrest of two local leaders. On orders from Brigadier-General Reginald Dyer, 50 Indian Army soldiers fired at them without warning. (Armored cars bearing machine guns were mercifully unable to maneuver through the narrow passageway to the garden.) At least 379 Indians were killed—including women, children, and the elderly—and 1,100 or more were injured. A ratio can be figured to gauge the deliberateness of Dyer's "lesson": only 1,650 rifle rounds were expended.

News of the Amritsar massacre spread widely. While an official commission later condemned the incident, and Dyer was relieved of command, it had been the rawest display of British dominance. It shocked "the nation," as India was beginning to see itself. Upon news of the tragedy, the great Bengali poet Rabindranath Tagore renounced his British knighthood. In his letter to the viceroy, Lord Chelmsford, he wrote:

> The time has come when badges of honour make our shame glaring in the incongruous context of humiliation, and I for my part wish to stand, shorn, of all special distinctions, by the side of those of my countrymen who, for their so called insignificance, are liable to suffer degradation not fit for human beings.
>
> (Bhattacharya 2011, 134)

Tagore's choice illustrates the particular anguish that Anglicized Indians confronted, unable to reconcile the British ideal with the cruelty of British rule. Gandhi himself remarked that Tagore's renunciation might have been too hasty. Still, it reinforced the bond between them: Tagore had been the first to call his friend and debater *Mahatma*, or Great Soul, in 1915 (Bhattacharya 2011, 134).

Gandhi eventually came to believe that India had to divest itself of British affectations, root and branch. His vision was different than that of earlier INC moderates, in that he gave up faith in Western institutions and believed that *swaraj* should mean an essentially stateless society, radically decentralized, with self-rule in every village. Moreover, in his all-encompassing philosophy, "self-rule" also required that every *individual* should cultivate capacities of self-assessment, self-purification, and self-reliance. A simple loincloth became his trademark, though he recognized that few others were ready to embrace such asceticism. But in a less austere form, his campaign for the use of *khadi* (homespun cloth) became an integral part of the nationalist movement—so much so that to this day, most Indian politicians wear modern variations on the tradition.

Gandhi was a devout Hindu, but his spiritual ecumenism and political acumen led him to pursue unity over communalism. Hundreds of thousands of Indians, across faiths, joined in non-violent campaigns to immobilize the administrative and economic machinery of British rule. In such a charged atmosphere, there were also sporadic outbreaks of violence, and in 1922, when a mob attack on a police station in the town of Chauri Chaura killed two dozen officers, Gandhi temporarily halted the movement.

Gandhi had a special genius for rendering abstract concepts such as "self-rule" in symbols that ordinary people could understand, as in his 1930 Salt March to protest the British monopoly and tax on salt. He led followers on a 240-mile (390-kilometer) march to the seaside and gathered crude salt in defiance of the law, rekindling the civil disobedience movement and drawing worldwide attention to the nationalist cause.

An important British concession came in the Government of India Act of 1935, which offered limited provincial autonomy and expanded the voting franchise fivefold to cover 30 million people, one-sixth of the adult population. Not all of the Act's quasi-federal provisions were fully implemented, and the central government retained discretionary powers subject only to British Parliamentary oversight. Even so, the 1935 Act had a lasting influence on the Indian Constitution of 1950.

But despite Gandhi's leadership, nationalist unity did not last. The principle of separate electorates for minority communities was a key point of contention. Not only did the Congress and Muslim League clash over this, but there was also a personal rift between Gandhi and Bhimrao Ambedkar, a learned leader of "the Untouchables" who advocated this right for his community too in view of historical injustices it had endured. Gandhi led his own effort to uplift these marginalized people, calling them *Harijans* (Children of God) and exhorting his fellow Hindus to remove "the stain" of Untouchability from their rites and traditions. But Ambedkar held a profoundly different outlook from Gandhi toward Hindu civilization, which he later wrote was "a diabolical contrivance to suppress and enslave humanity" (Ambedkar [1948] 2008, 7), and toward the traditional village, which was "a sink of localism, a den of ignorance, narrow mindedness and communalism" (Hardgrave and Kochanek 2008, 131).

Gandhi argued that to separate the Untouchables from the broader body politic would be to divide Hindu society itself, and he undertook a fast while serving jail time in 1932 to counter Ambedkar's proposal. Ambedkar accepted a compromise that gave up the separate electorate demand, but still set aside reserved seats for Untouchable candidates (within the overall Hindu allotment). As an architect of India's Constitution, Ambedkar later shaped the post-Independence institution of reservations for Untouchables, now known as Scheduled Castes (see below). He is revered among the Scheduled Castes, whose self-conception as *Dalits*—the "ground down," "crushed," or "oppressed"—has left Gandhi's "Harijan" a rather discredited paternalist relic.

In the end, though, it was the differences between Congress and the Muslim League that proved most irreconcilable. The League first put forward the idea of a state for India's Muslims in 1930, but its leadership was not united behind the idea—which in any case did not necessarily mean a separate nation-state, but possibly a sub-national state within an Indian federation—and the League did not carry broad popular support until the late 1930s, as many Muslims continued to identify with Congress. But in 1940, League president Mohammad Ali Jinnah argued that Hindus and Muslims comprised two separate "nations," and the demand for an independent Pakistan began to harden. Jinnah was a Westernized lawyer-politician, not a Muslim fundamentalist. But he had been deeply unsettled by provincial elections in 1937, which the INC swept, with the Muslim League failing to win anywhere.

World War II proved a turning point for Britain's position—and for that of the League, as well. During the First World War, moderate Indian nationalists had been loyal Crown subjects, expecting the British to reciprocate with significant concessions. Instead, they had faced repression. Now, in 1939, INC leaders condemned the viceroy's declaration of war for India, saying that if India were to join the fight against fascism, it must do so as a free and equal nation. The INC's elected members in the provinces resigned their seats. The British suggested that independence could be discussed after the war, but maintained that no proposal unacceptable to Muslim leaders would be considered. Rejecting alternatives such as "limited dominion" status, Gandhi and the Congress leadership launched the Quit India campaign in August 1942, demanding total independence. They spent most of the war in prison while Jinnah cooperated with the British and consolidated support for the idea of Pakistan.

The war placed Britain under great financial strain, and a new British government was elected in the general election of 1945, ousting Winston Churchill and the Conservative Party. Led by Clement Attlee and the Labour Party, it resolved to liquidate the empire. In the Shimla Conference of 1945 and Cabinet Mission of 1946, last-ditch efforts at a compromise between the INC and Muslim League failed to produce an agreement for a unified India. Under the hurried direction of Lord Louis Mountbatten, the final viceroy, Britain finally did "quit" the subcontinent in the summer of 1947. The independent states of India and Pakistan were born, the latter in two non-contiguous territories to the west and east of India (partitioning Punjab and re-partitioning Bengal).

The "full measure" of Partition's costs would be taken in the harsh light of days to come. The image of a peaceful transfer of power must be set against the recognition that Partition was a catastrophic trauma. The border settlement was announced haphazardly, and in the fearful chaos that ensued when Muslims fled India, and Hindus (and, in Punjab, Sikhs) fled Pakistan, thousands were raped and beaten, perhaps a million were killed, and some 10 to 12 million were displaced from their homes. It was the largest sudden mass-migration in world history, executed under appalling conditions.

Within three months of Independence, India and Pakistan would be at war. Within six months, a Hindu zealot would assassinate Gandhi, and in just over a year, Jinnah would be dead of tuberculosis—leaving for others the tasks of building the new states they left behind.

## Institutions, parties, and elections

The product of three years' work by a Constituent Assembly of more than 300 persons, India's Constitution went into effect on January 26, 1950—a day first marked as "Independence Day" exactly 20 years earlier, when the INC adopted a resolution calling for independence. (That this took place in Lahore, which went to Pakistan in 1947, is one of the many ironies of Partition.) The date is now commemorated as Republic Day in India, with a grand parade in New Delhi.

Here we can only scratch the surface of this rich and detailed document—the world's longest constitution. Its Preamble proclaims India to be a "sovereign socialist secular democratic republic." Below, we will survey formal institutions of the Indian state that give expression to the constitutional vision. First, we consider dimensions of Indian social organization that have led many observers to regard the durability of the democratic republic as defying long odds. In fact, India's extreme heterogeneity leads historian Ramachandra Guha to describe it as an "unnatural nation" (2007, 1), and many skeptics have doubted that India could be held together at all, much less under representative democracy. Even a onetime INC president, Subhas Chandra Bose, remarked in 1941, "After the end of British rule in India there must be a dictatorship. No other constitution can flourish in the country" (Hay 1988, 313).

### The sociocultural context of Indian democracy

The most politically salient cleavages in Indian society are those involving *language, religion, caste* and *class*. In addition, *tribe* is an increasingly distinct identity, with the marginalized *Adivasis* claiming aboriginal lineages outside of Indo-Aryan culture. As Guha explains, these "axes of conflict operate both singly and in combination" (2007, 1). At the same time, identities evolve, and may be malleable to political appeals.

## Language

A case in point is language. Before the Raj-era polarization of Hindus and Muslims, the term *Hindustani* was used to describe an amalgam Hindi-Urdu spoken across much of northern India. Over the Delhi Sultanate and Mughal periods, Hindustani developed as court Persian and Turkic languages mingled with the Delhi dialects of Hindi. The developing lingua franca could be written in either a Perso-Arabic script (favored for official use) or in the Devanagari script (used for classical Sanskrit, and similar to scripts used for other Indo-Aryan languages such as Bengali, Marathi, Gujarati, and Punjabi).

But as Hindu-Muslim tensions grew in the nineteenth century, a sense of difference developed. Hindi became associated with Hindu culture, while "Urdu" began to connote a separate language spoken by Muslims (though the connotations were essentially constructed). Gandhi and other syncretists tried to revive Hindustani; Nehru described it as a "golden mean" between Hindi and Urdu (Guha 2007, 130). But such sentiments receded in the politics of Partition.

After Independence, the issue of language led to sharp debates in the Constituent Assembly. Some demanded that Hindi should be India's national language. Others argued that this would discriminate against the majority who did not speak it, especially South Indian speakers of Telugu, Tamil, Kannada, and Malayalam—all Dravidian languages, and separate from the Indo-Aryan family. Ultimately, India adopted "Hindi in the Devanagari script" as the "official language" of the Union.

Hindi does not have legal standing as a "national" language, however. In fact, the Eighth Schedule to the Constitution recognizes a total of 22 official languages (including separate entries for Hindi and Urdu). English was also retained for official use; this was initially to be for 15 years, after which Hindi would be the sole official language of the Union. But after anti-Hindi demonstrations in the southern state of Tamil Nadu in the 1960s, the central government agreed to retain English indefinitely.

In most cases, the medium of instruction in state-run schools is the regional language; Hindi is a second language outside the north-central "Hindi belt." With globalization, the demand for English instruction has surged, but the promotion of Hindi throughout India remains a key goal of the Hindu nationalist movement.

## Religion

Hindus comprise 80.5 percent of India's billion-plus population, according to 2001 census figures (religious data from the 2011 census remains unpublished). Despite the mass migration at Partition, Muslims remain India's largest religious minority at 13.4 percent (followed by Christians at 2.3 percent, Sikhs at 1.9 percent, Buddhists at 0.8 percent, Jains at 0.4 percent and other religions at 0.6 percent). In fact, at 177 million, India has the third-largest Muslim population in the world, behind Indonesia and, just barely, Pakistan (Pew 2011).

Like language, religion was a subject of intense debate in framing the Constitution. The document is imbued with a secular ethos of an actively pluralist kind—recognizing that religion permeates social life, rather than defining a public arena without religion. As the cultural critic Nirad C. Chaudhuri wryly observed, "The State is secular ... but the people are not" (Jacobsohn 2003, 36).

At the same time, India's secularism is "ameliorative" (Jacobsohn 2003): it seeks to redress the socially and economically disabling effects of certain religious practices, especially caste discrimination. But significantly, while freedom of religion is placed within the Constitution's key Fundamental Rights section, other precepts pertaining to religion and social change fall under the separate Directive Principles of State Policy, which are not justiciable.

The attempt at balancing religious liberty with social reform has led to some interesting compromises and controversies. Though Article 44 of the Directive Principles stipulates, "The State shall endeavor to secure for the citizens a uniform civil code throughout the territory of India," there are in fact different personal and family laws for different religious communities. These reflect asymmetries in marriage and divorce law, property and inheritance law, and other areas. Certain aspects of the *sharia*-based Muslim Personal Law in particular stand out. Though Hindus and others are prohibited from practicing polygamy, for example, it is permitted for Muslims (though it is not common).

Muslim divorce law gave rise to one of India's most divisive Supreme Court rulings, the *Shah Bano* case. Shah Bano was a 62-year-old mother of five in 1978 when her husband divorced her by triple *talaq*—saying three times "I divorce you" before his wife and two witnesses—and refused to provide her with maintenance (alimony). In 1985, the case reached the Supreme Court, which ruled that the ex-husband must pay her a monthly maintenance. Conservative Muslim clerics resurrected a pre-Independence rallying cry, "Islam in danger," leading Rajiv Gandhi's government to fear loss of Muslim support for the INC. In 1986, the government passed the oddly named Muslim Women (Protection of Rights on Divorce) Act, which effectively nullified the Court's ruling. This in turn provoked uproar among an unlikely cross-section of "progressive Muslims, women, secularists, and Hindu chauvinists" (Hardgrave and Kochanek 2008, 212). The uniform civil code has been a rallying cry for the Hindu nationalist movement, to which we now turn.

A discussion of "political Hinduism" must begin by acknowledging the enormous diversity within "religious Hinduism," which is better understood as an amalgamated category of beliefs, rituals, and practices than as a single faith (the terms "Hindu" and "Hinduism" were coined by outsiders; they do not derive from indigenous sources). It is not only that there are differences between the religious practices of the high and low castes, or between "Sanskritized Hinduism" and traditional popular Hinduism. There is a lack of unity even within the notional Great Tradition of Hinduism, which "does not in fact contain an orthodoxy" (Jaffrelot 1996, 1–2). There is no one holy book, or even a definite canon. The Vedas, the Upanishads, the epics *Ramayana*, and *Mahabharata* (which contains the *Bhagavad Gita*, or Song of God) and still other texts inform Hindu beliefs, but none of these functions in a role analogous to that of the Torah, Bible, or Koran in their respective faiths. Many non-Hindus would know of the enormous pantheon of deities and would understand that "Hindus worship many different gods." But there are also monotheist Hindus who see these as manifesting different facets of the one Ultimate Reality, and atheist Hindus who claim Hinduism as simply a way of life.

Thus, the phenomenon of Hindu nationalism "is a challenging one for social scientists" (Jaffrelot 1996, 1). Essentially, though, it is a "modern phenomenon that has developed on the basis of strategies of ideology-building," and thus has something in common with nineteenth and early twentieth century European nationalisms (Jaffrelot 2007, 6, 4). It was a 1923 pamphlet by V.D. Savarkar, *Hindutva* (Hindu-ness), which first defined its ethos: to be Indian is to be Hindu. In this view, other indigenous religions such as Buddhism, Jainism, and Sikhism are essentially derivatives of Vedic/Hindu culture, and Christianity and especially Islam are alien allegiances.

Another of the movement's key ideologues, M.S. Golwalkar, distilled the political implications to a chilling essence in his 1938 tract *We or Our Nationhood Defined*:

> The non-Hindu people of Hindustan must either adopt Hindu culture and language, must learn and respect and hold in reverence the Hindu religion, must entertain no idea but of those of glorification of the Hindu race and culture … in a word they must cease to be foreigners, or may stay in the country, wholly subordinated to the Hindu nation, claiming nothing, deserving no privileges, far less any preferential treatment—not even citizens' rights.
>
> (Guha 2007, 13)

The Hindu nationalist movement encompasses several organizations, the most important of which is the Rashtriya Swayamsevak Sangh (RSS) or National Volunteer Organization. The movement also features political parties in the BJP and regional associates such as the Marathi chauvinist Shiv Sena (Army of Shiva) in Maharashtra.

The RSS was founded in 1925. Its basic unit is the local *shaka* (branch), in which males gather for activities such as yoga, strength exercises, games, and quasi-military training. Though the RSS also engages in extensive social service efforts, it is controversial. Critics have compared its khaki-clad ranks to historical European fascist movements. The RSS does not publish membership figures, but it claims more than 50,000 branches across India, which suggests that its volunteers may number in the millions. Many senior BJP leaders are alumni. It is at odds with the INC and the centrist establishment, which RSS acolytes deride as "pseudo-secularist" for its "pandering" to religious minorities.

The RSS was banned in 1948 following Gandhi's assassination—gunman Nathuram Godse was a former RSS member—and again during the 1975–77 Emergency. It was banned for a third time in 1992–93 after it was alleged to have played a role in the destruction of the Babri Masjid in Ayodhya, Uttar Pradesh. This mosque, built in 1527 during the rule of Babur, supposedly occupied a site previously bearing a Hindu *mandir* (temple) at the birthplace of Lord Rama, hero of the *Ramayana*. (While the historicity of Rama is unproven, the Archeological Survey of India has conducted excavations into what appear to be temple ruins.) The site was disputed as early as 1853, but it was a mid-1980s campaign by Hindu nationalists that launched the Ram Mandir campaign. BJP leader L.K. Advani made a pilgrimage to Ayodhya in 1990, riding in a Toyota truck decked out like Ram's mythical chariot.

The December 6, 1992 destruction of the mosque followed a ceremonial rally that featured speeches by BJP leaders (including Advani) and drew as many as 150,000 people. Whether the crude demolition was premeditated or an impulsive response to a charged atmosphere is debated—an official report later called it "neither spontaneous nor unplanned"—but for weeks the event sparked riots across India. Two thousand people, the majority of them Muslims, were killed. Even a decade later, the campaign to (re)build the temple continued to rally the Hindu right, and the violence in Gujarat in 2002 was directly related. In 2010, the Allahabad High Court ruled to divide the Ayodhya site between Hindu and Muslim organizations.

Still, there are limits to BJP's ability to convince four-fifths of Indians that Hindu identity should define their politics. While Hindu nationalism is a potent political force, the movement's stridency can be off-putting, even to many Hindus. Moreover, its efforts to make essential one "Hindu-ness" are limited by the crosscutting ties of region and caste.

## Caste

*Caste* in India requires some explanation. The Portuguese *casta*, from which *caste* is derived, "conflates two Indian concepts: *jati*, the endogamous group one is born into; and *varna*, the place this group occupies in the system of social stratification mandated by Hindu scripture" (Guha 2007, 8; emphasis added).

It is the fourfold *varna*s (literally "colors" in Sanskrit), that many Westerners think of as India's "caste system": these are the *Brahmins* (priests, scholars), *Kshatriyas* (warriors, rulers), *Vaishyas* (merchants, traders, artisans, agriculturalists), and *Shudras* (manual laborers, servants). References to the varnas are found in Vedic texts going back thousands of years. The first three varnas were "twice born"—eligible for ritual initiation into Vedic society—and the function of the fourth varna was to serve them. Subordinated to all four varnas were the Untouchables, those whose occupations (as scavengers, sweepers, latrine cleaners, leather tanners, and cremators) were so defiling that they were believed to embody a ritualized, permanent pollution.

In reality, this order was always somewhat of an abstraction, and this is especially true today. Jatis may have occupational origins, but their most important function is as endogamous communities, meaning that marriages are permitted only between fellow families. There are thousands of jatis across India, often very localized in nature. A traditional village may exhibit distinct spatial arrangements for its various jatis. Many rural Indians still order their lives around jati. But migration and urbanization have churned and recombined traditional identities. A perusal of the marriage proposals in any metropolitan newspaper reveals a range of attitudes and practices: though some ads may note a prospective bride or groom's "caste" (if not apparent from the family name), others offer the progressive stock phrase "caste no bar."

Non-Indians may be surprised that caste is not barred by India's Constitution. In fact, the Constitution contains features that have reinforced caste identities and, over time, encouraged political parties to mobilize votes along such lines. The Constitution lists 1,108 Scheduled Castes and 744 Scheduled Tribes, which are entitled to special reservations in government representation, public sector employment, and educational institutions. This is India's version of affirmative action. The Scheduled Castes were 15 percent of the population in the 1951 census.

In 1980, the Mandal Commission identified more than 3,700 additional castes—representing another 52 percent of the population—as Other Backward Classes (OBCs), and proposed additional reservations. Its report initially gathered dust. But in 1989, the National Front government of V.P. Singh decided to implement the recommendations, announcing 27 percent OBC reservation in government jobs. The move sparked intense opposition. Protests by university students were sometimes violent, even to the point of self-immolation by fire in dozens of instances. Hindutva-types argued that reservations detrimentally divided Hindus (those making this claim were typically high-caste citizens).

Given the subsequent surge of the Hindu right and its mobilization around the Ram Mandir issue, Indian politics since the 1990s has been seen as a kind of "Mandal/Mandir" dialectic (Padgaonkar 2005). But the electoral arithmetic of OBC mobilization has appealed to politicians from communities such as the Yadavs of Bihar and Uttar Pradesh. In some states, the proliferation of quotas has become almost absurd: in 2012 Tamil Nadu had a 69 percent combined level of reservations for SCs, STs, and OBCs in state employment and educational institutions, drawing disapproval of its policy from India's Supreme Court.

Today there is a lively debate over the future of reservations policy. There are a variety of reform proposals, from applying the quota system to private employers and institutions (many of which are opposed), to extending the policy to cover Muslims and other religious minorities ("31% Muslims Live Below Poverty Line" 2010), to discarding the emphasis on ascriptive identities altogether in favor of a more need-based approach.

### Class

If the four-fifths of Indians who are Hindu do not always form a cohesive vote bloc, what about the two-thirds who are poor?

Non-Indians may have difficulty understanding distinctions between caste and class. The two are not unrelated insofar as jati origins related to (largely pre-modern) hereditary occupations, and still today the poorest segments of Indian society are predominately the subordinate castes and tribes (Muslims too are disproportionately poor). With respect to political mobilization, the main point is that caste is a traditional identity that—along with language, region, and religion—segments people of similar socioeconomic position who might otherwise be expected to cohere around common political interests.

Unlike other agrarian Asian societies such as China and Vietnam, India did not develop a national revolutionary peasant movement prior to Independence (Mitra 2011, 54). This was not for lack of trying on the part of Indian communists, but their organization was repressed and remained weak. Slow industrialization meant a small urban working class, and trade unions grew unevenly, often connected to competing political parties; today India's largest union is connected to the BJP.

A partial exception to the rule of limited class-based mobilization is the longstanding prominence of left parties in a few states, particularly Kerala and West Bengal. The Communist Party of India (Marxist) emerged in the 1960s and led a Left Front victory in the West Bengal State Assembly election of 1977. For more than three decades, the CPI(M) became the dominant force in the state's politics.

In practice, however, the CPI(M) is as much a regional party as an ideological or class-based one. Over time it "transformed its ideological leftism into a partisan and confrontational subnationalism," espousing "an anti-center regionalist policy" (Sinha 2005, 196). The party drew support from Bengali voters of all social classes, tapping "a history of middle-class Bengali hostility to the mainstream northern and moderate Gandhi nationalist legacy" (Sinha 2005, 197).

Following India's economic liberalization in the 1990s, the CPI(M)'s supposed anti-capitalism did not prevent it from aggressively courting private investment for the state. But as its rule ossified, Mamata Banerjee and her All India Trinamool Congress essentially "out-lefted" the Left, appealing to popular discontent with the CPI(M)'s perceived embrace of "anti-poor" policies. Particularly controversial in 2007–08 was a plan by the CPI(M) state government to appropriate roughly 10,000 acres of land, largely from farmers, for a Special Economic Zone (SEZ) for development by an Indonesian industrial conglomerate. The controversy was a major factor in the CPI(M)'s 2011 defeat.

### *Formal state institutions*

This chapter's perspective places greater emphasis on tracing political development over time—and contextualizing the presence of the Indian state in the lives of India's people—than with detailed description of how the formal institutions of Indian government work (or are supposed to work). Nevertheless, a brief discussion of key institutions is in order.

The locus of power in Indian national politics is the *Lok Sabha* (House of the People), or lower house of Parliament. The party or coalition of parties controlling a majority of its 543 seats forms the government (a party without a majority may form a "minority government" with outside support from other parties, without a formal alliance). The prime minister is generally from the leading party and is usually an elected member of parliament in the Lok Sabha (though Manmohan Singh was not, being from the Rajya Sabha, or upper house). Other important cabinet ministries—such as the External Affairs, Finance and Home ministries—are usually controlled by the majority party as well, though these and other portfolios may be demanded by coalition partners.

The *Rajya Sabha* (Council of States) has 250 members, mostly elected for six-year terms by the assemblies of India's states and territories (12 are appointed positions). The Rajya Sabha must approve all non-financial legislation originating in the Lok Sabha, and though the latter is more powerful overall, the former provides continuity through changes of government and holds its own authority as a conclave of elders and experts.

India has a president, elected to a renewable five-year term by the members of both houses as well as the state assemblies. Though less powerful than the prime minister, the position is the titular head of state (like the Crown in Britain). Its occupants have been distinguished senior statespersons, often with a view toward progressive symbolism: in the past decade, both a Muslim and a woman have held the office.

Institutions at the state level parallel the national structure, though the legislatures are unicameral in most states. The powerful role of chief minister is the state-level counterpart to the Indian prime minister, while the state-level governor is an executive analogous to the national president.

One very important constitutional provision involves the president and governors, and reveals a centripetal bias in Indian federalism. President's Rule (Article 356) enables a governor to report to the president that "a situation has arisen in which the government of the State cannot be carried out in accordance with the provisions of [the] Constitution." It gives the president the power to dissolve the elected state assembly and impose central rule, subject to Parliamentary approval, for up to one year. In practice, a weak president can be manipulated by a partisan central government, and this clause originally intended for dealing with genuine threats to law and order was used for political ends in dozens of cases, with particular frequency under Indira Gandhi from 1966 to 1977 (accounting for 39 of 115 cases from 1950 to 2003). Abuse of this power bred resentment against the INC, encouraging regionalism and the formation of new parties. Recently, the Supreme Court has curtailed the abuse.

## Box 2.1: The tragedy of Indira Gandhi

Perhaps the most intriguing, controversial, and ultimately tragic figure in India's post-Independence history is Indira Gandhi, the third prime minister and the only child of Jawaharlal Nehru. No relation to Mahatma Gandhi, Indira Nehru married the journalist-politician Feroze Gandhi in 1942. Though painfully shy at first, she served as chief of staff for her widower father, gradually emerging as a power in her own right. She was elected Congress Party President in 1959; her husband died the following year.

Nehru had not intended for his daughter to succeed him, and when he died in 1964 she took a cabinet position behind the new prime minister, Lal Bahadur Shastri. But when Shastri died in 1966 a group of Congress Party bosses known as "the Syndicate"—all powerful in their own regions, but none commanding a national platform—saw an opportunity. They put forward Mrs. Gandhi as prime minister, expecting that she would allow them to wield real power. Critics derided her as *Goongi Gudiya* (mute doll).

Mrs. Gandhi inherited an economic crisis, and she undertook a surprise devaluation of the rupee in 1966 under pressure from external aid providers. Prices rose and voters punished the Congress Party in state-level elections the following year. Mrs. Gandhi then veered in a socialist and populist direction, nationalizing banks and bypassing the party machinery to appeal directly to the voting masses. "*Garibi hatao*" (abolish poverty) was the slogan of her 1971 reelection campaign. That year, she also presided over the third India-Pakistan war, which led to the independence of East Pakistan as Bangladesh. Relations with the United States were strained as India signed a Treaty of Friendship with the Soviet Union and pursued a nuclear capability.

Economic challenges persisted, and in 1974 she put down a major rail workers strike. In 1975, Mrs. Gandhi was found guilty of electoral malfeasance by a High Court in Uttar Pradesh. She refused to resign, and moved to declare a State of Emergency under Article 352 of the Constitution. The Emergency lasted until 1977. It saw the detention of thousands of political opponents, restrictions on press freedom and a coercive family planning program. Against the advice of her autocratic younger son and confidante Sanjay, she called for elections and was defeated resoundingly.

She returned to power in 1980, but soon confronted the death of Sanjay (who crashed a small airplane while illegally performing acrobatics over New Delhi). Her government was challenged by a separatist movement in Punjab, leading to a confrontation between the Indian Army and Sikh militants at the holy Golden Temple in Amritsar. Hundreds of Sikhs were killed. On October 31, 1984, Mrs. Gandhi's Sikh bodyguards took revenge by gunning her down outside the prime minister's residence. Elder son Rajiv, who was sworn in immediately as prime minister, stood by for three days while at least 3,000 Sikhs were killed in reprisal violence, before sending the army to restore order. He said, "When a big tree falls, the earth shakes" (Guha 2007, 566).

Just days after Sanjay's death in 1980, an American interviewer asked the prime minister "what one thing" she most wanted to be remembered for. "I do not want to be remembered for anything" was the bitter reply. Says biographer Katherine Frank, "It was a prophetically accurate retort. For history was not going to remember Indira Gandhi for any one thing—for a coherent strategy, ideology, policy or vision" (2002, 449). Her most dubious achievement was the organizational "decay" of the Congress Party (Manor 1981), as she centralized power and surrounded herself with sycophants who encouraged an aura of invincibility—epitomized in the slogan, "Indira is India, India is Indira."

This provision is but one reason that India's federalism is often described as having a "top-down" or unitary bias. In addition, the power to redraw state boundaries or create new states belongs to Parliament, and there have been a number of changes over the years—most extensively, a 1956 reorganization of boundaries along linguistic lines. Interestingly, the first linguistic state of Andhra Pradesh never fully cohered, due to internal economic and social divisions (see "Managing conflict," below). As of June 2014, its former subregion of Telangana is India's youngest state, bringing the total number to 29 (plus seven Union Territories).

Political decentralization in India also encompasses local government, for which the major administrative unit is the district (numbering 680 in 2014). Though reformed, local government today still bears resemblances to its Raj-era incarnation. The District Collector continues to be the most important post (the title varies in some locales). In colonial times, "For most Indian villagers the 'Collector Sahib' was in fact the government" (Hardgrave and Kochanek 2008, 130), and the same could be said in many districts across India even today. Collectors are appointed by the state government from the Indian Administrative Service (IAS), the elite "steel frame" bureaucracy descended from the Raj-era Indian Civil Service. Though the IAS is a highly competitive meritocracy and produces many outstanding officers, district officials are not all above the arbitrary use of power. State government oversight may somewhat mitigate misconduct, but it also creates the possibility of political interference from above.

There have been several waves of effort over the years, beginning in the 1880s, to decentralize democracy to representative bodies based on the traditional village council or *panchayat* (literally, "council of five"). The contemporary model, enacted in the Seventy-third Amendment Act of 1992, formalizes the panchayat system as a third tier of government. Seats are reserved for women, and in some places—especially in the South—elected panchayats have been highly effective at empowering citizens. In other cases, traditional elites have continued to exercise influence through elected proxies.

Urban government in India has received relatively little attention from political scientists, but that may be about to change. Even in megacities like Mumbai, city offices are weak relative to the state government. Delhi—being a state—is an exception, and its government has managed to enact some major initiatives in recent years, including the mandatory conversion of public transport vehicles to compressed natural gas (CNG) and the construction of a Metro rail system. As more and more Indians have moved into cities, they have become sites for increasing protest activity and political mobilization.

Though they may not attract as much global media attention as India's vast representative democracy or recent efforts at improving governance through technology, judicial institutions play important roles both in national political life and in everyday encounters between citizens and the state. The single, integrated judiciary includes several layers of subordinate courts and is topped by 24 state-level High Courts, with the Supreme Court of India, in New Delhi, at the apex (the states do not have Supreme Courts, as in the United States). Unlike in the British system, where no court may hold an act of parliament invalid, the Supreme Court may rule on the constitutionality of legislation passed by Parliament or the state legislatures. But this power of judicial review does not give the Supreme Court quite the autonomy of its American counterpart, given the detail of the Constitution itself and the emergency provisions that "severely reduce the Court's powers in the area of personal liberty" (Hardgrave and Kochanek 2008, 117).

The Supreme Court consists of the senior-most Chief Justice and, at full capacity, 30 associate justices (there were four vacancies in 2014). When it was established in 1950, the Court consisted of eight justices, but the size of the bench has expanded along with the Court's expanding caseload—and backlog. The Court divides cases among "constitution benches"— where five or more justices settle fundamental questions of law—and smaller "division benches" of two or three justices.

Justices and High Court judges are formally appointed by the president, but since 1993 a Collegium—the Chief Justice and four most senior associates—has actually determined appointees, and this system of "judges appointing judges" leaves the elected government out of the process. Even so, some see a trend toward greater politicization of the judiciary at the High Court level since the 1990s amid fragmentation of the party system, as chief ministers try to influence appointments (and this bears directly on the Supreme Court, as its appointees are drawn from High Courts).

Still, surveys show that Indians find the Supreme Court, alongside the Election Commission, the "most trustworthy" of institutions (Mitra 2011, 79). This is remarkable insofar as Indian courts, including the Supreme Court, carry an enormous backlog of unresolved cases—30 million across the entire system, with the Supreme Court alone accounting for 65,000—exhibiting the adage that "justice delayed is justice denied" (Mashru 2013). Justices hold office until mandatory retirement at 65—a constitutional provision that has become oddly incongruous with the median age of elected officials.

### A momentous election

India, 2014: Can such a big election in such a big country hold just one "big story"? Foremost among several stories was the margin of victory by the Bharatiya Janata Party (BJP): with 282 of 543 total seats, it won the first non-coalition majority victory in the Lok Sabha in a quarter-century; its partner parties in the National Democratic Alliance (NDA) brought the tally to 336. Since 1989, no general election has delivered a single-party majority. Even more, 2014 is the first time any party other than the venerable Congress (or INC) has won a majority without having to rely on coalition support. Congress itself has led a coalition, the UPA, since 2004.

The corollary of the BJP's dramatic win was the decimation of Congress. Its defeat had been widely expected, but the decisiveness of the result was still stunning, with a mere 44 seats remaining in Congress hands (down 162). Its two most visible leaders—party president Sonia Gandhi, 67, and vice president and campaign leader Rahul Gandhi, 43—both won

*Table 2.1* Top ten parties in the 16th Lok Sabha (2014 general elections)

| Party | Seats Won (543 Total) | Ideology/Base |
| --- | --- | --- |
| Bharatiya Janata Party (BJP)* | 282 | right, Hindutva/national |
| Indian National Congress (INC)** | 44 | center-left, secular/national |
| All-India Anna Dravida Munnetra Kazhagam | 37 | populist, regional/Tamil Nadu |
| All India Trinamool Congress | 34 | populist-socialist/West Bengal |
| Biju Janata Dal | 20 | center-left, populist/Odisha |
| Shiv Sena* | 18 | right, Hindutva, Marathi, nativist/ Maharashtra |
| Telugu Desam Party* | 16 | populist, regional/Andhra Pradesh |
| Telangana Rashtra Samithi | 11 | regional/AP-Telangana |
| Communist Party of India (Marxist)*** | 9 | left, regional/West Bengal, Kerala, Tripura |
| YSR Congress Party | 9 | populist, regional/Andhra Pradesh |

*National Democratic Alliance (NDA)
**United Progressive Alliance (UPA)
***Left Front

their districts in the northern state of Uttar Pradesh, the historic stronghold of their Nehru-Gandhi lineage. Sonia is the widow and Rahul the son of Rajiv Gandhi, whose mother was Indira Gandhi, whose father was Jawaharlal Nehru—India's first prime minister and political heir to Mahatma Gandhi (unrelated). But their wins may be the party's loss, for one of the main narratives of the 2014 campaign by the BJP and other challengers had been the rejection of "dynastic politics," cronyism, and corruption. (Manmohan Singh, once an esteemed former finance minister, squandered respect as prime minister as he was seen to fail in putting governance ahead of politics).

Enter the man of the year, 2014: Narendra Modi, 63. The incumbent chief minister of Gujarat, he is everything the patrician Nehru-Gandhis are not: a former tea stall worker from a "backward caste," a strident Hindu nationalist, and a bachelor whose ascetic personal life is central to his political appeal. Having no family, he boasts, inoculates him from corruptibility and ensures no dynastic designs (a late-campaign surprise of an estranged "secret wife" of almost 50 years did nothing to upset this storyline, and may have reinforced it: it was a traditional arranged marriage between two youngsters, and never consummated, he claimed).

Modi's victory had been largely a foregone conclusion since mid-2013, when he wrested leadership of the BJP from the octogenarian L.K. Advani (a holdover senior leader from the party's previous turn in power, at the head of the NDA from 1998 to 2004). Even more than his Mr. Clean image, Modi's ascendance rested on the perceived economic achievements of his state, where GDP growth has exceeded the national average every year since 2001 when he took office (that it had already done so for more than a decade, under a half-dozen governments, is less widely noted). The effect of growth on poverty reduction is hotly debated in Gujarat as in India overall, but the state's much-hyped rise conspicuously coincided with Congress's diminishing credibility at the Centre as the self-proclaimed champion of "pro-poor growth."

The biggest question about Modi is whether he will be the economy-first leader of late or, now that he has reached the top, revert to an earlier incarnation that shocked India and the world in 2002. In February–March of that year, his government stood by—in the most charitable interpretation of events—during a spasm of communal violence in Gujarat that killed nearly 1000 people, three-quarters of whom were Muslims. Critics have alleged far worse, with some holding Modi directly culpable for what amounted to a pogrom (Human Rights Watch 2002). In 2012, the Supreme Court cleared him of personal blame. Citing the 2002 violence, the United States and Britain denied visas to Modi for years, but both ended their bans as he prepared to assume power in 2014.

It was an eventful election, to say the least. It *is* possible to overstate the onetime "dominance" of the now down-and-out Congress: even at the height of its powers, in the 1950s and early 1960s, the party never actually won a majority of the popular vote. Such is the logic of first-past-the-post (or single-member-district, simple-plurality) elections: a leading party needs only to win more votes than any of its rivals, in a majority of constituencies across the country, to form a government. Likewise, even though Modi's 2014 campaign may have delivered a landslide seat share to the BJP, it yielded only 31 percent of the popular vote.

But for more than five of the almost seven decades since Independence, Congress has been the party to lead India (albeit, as noted, sharing power in a coalition government for the last decade). Congress embodied big-tent centrism: the only truly national political party in a raucously regionalized country, the central heir to the unifying consciousness of the freedom struggle, and the clearest champion of a certain Indian notion of secularism. In an 80 percent Hindu nation, an imperfect but enduring consensus has held that state policies should go some deliberate distance to assure Muslims, Sikhs, Christians, and other minorities that their rights would not be subjugated to majority rule.

Many of the "new" political actors and movements shaping India's politics today—from Hindu nationalists to mobilizers of caste and regional identities—had direct antecedents in earlier times, even in the heyday of the freedom struggle and in the first decades after Independence when the INC held a preponderant position. Thus the 2014 election may or may not herald as dramatic a break with past politics as initial impressions suggest. The answer will depend on which of two ideally complementary but potentially competing impulses prevails: majoritarian democracy on one hand, and constitutional liberalism on the other.

## Managing conflict

With respect to internal authority, it bears repeating that a unified Indian state was an unprecedented achievement when it came into being (more or less) in August 1947. But from the beginning, there were also gaps on the map. The major princely state of Jammu and Kashmir, ruled by a Hindu monarch but containing a Muslim majority, acceded neither to India nor Pakistan at Independence. Maharaja Hari Singh signed with India two months later, but only when confronted with Pashtun tribal marauders from the west (backed by Pakistan). By late October, India and Pakistan were fighting their first war. Even today, the border remains unsettled, and a Line of Control divides Indian-controlled Jammu and Kashmir from a Pakistan-controlled third of the former princely state (it was originally a ceasefire line set in 1949 under UN observation).

India has tried to govern Jammu and Kashmir, its only majority-Muslim state, with a view to delegitimizing Pakistan's claim to the territory on the basis of religion. The Constitution stipulates that Jammu and Kashmir is "an integral part" of the Union (Article 1), but it also grants it a special autonomous status (Article 370), such that India's federalism is considered asymmetric (there are also special status arrangements for several other states, mainly in the northeast). At the same time, however, the central government has imposed President's Rule (see above) on Jammu and Kashmir several times. It has interfered in state elections, and in 1987 vote-rigging gave rise to a violent Kashmiri insurgency that continues today. The Indian Army maintains a massive presence in the state, and its soldiers have been accused of committing human rights abuses, including rape, torture, and extra-judicial killings. To many Kashmiris, it is an occupying force.

Another major princely state, Hyderabad, also held out for independence when the British transferred power; had it succeeded, it would have been a large enclave in south-central India. Instead, Indian forces invaded in 1948, ending the rule of the Nizam and annexing Hyderabad. Besides the princely states, colonial powers Portugal and France still controlled maritime enclaves in India after Independence, at Goa and Pondicherry, respectively. India forcibly annexed Goa in 1961 in a small war against the Lisbon dictatorship, and France's Parliament gave up Pondicherry the following year.

India has encountered several internal challenges to its sovereign authority, with separatist movements ranging from Punjab in the northwest to Assam in the northeast. There is also the challenge of Naxalism, a revolutionary movement with roots in the Communist politics of West Bengal in the 1960s, more recently swelling into a full-blown insurgency across much of central and eastern India.

### The case of Andhra Pradesh: united by language, divided by region

Andhra Pradesh (AP) spans much of the eastern Indian coastline, and before its division in 2014, stretched deep into the inland Deccan Plateau. Undivided AP was India's fourth largest state by land area, and fifth largest by population. It now ranks eighth and tenth, respectively, after the 2014 separation of Telangana. At nearly 50 million, its truncated population equals that of South Korea. The capital, Hyderabad, is India's fourth largest city and a center of information technology (IT) and global services development; Microsoft and Google both have headquarters in its "Cyberabad" complex. Since the late 1990s, successive state governments have undertaken a range of policy reforms, and AP has experienced faster economic growth, albeit with mixed results for poverty and human development (World Bank 2013). It is a middle-income state by Indian standards.

While no single state can be considered fully representative of India, AP offers a case study in two important aspects of the national experience: both the remarkable ability of Indian institutions to channel competing interests into the political arena, as well as the limits of normal politics when some groups see themselves as so marginalized that they strike out against the state itself.

Soon after Independence, Telugu speakers—who numbered second only to Hindi speakers in India overall—demanded their own state. Nehru's government resisted, and the INC fared poorly in Telugu-speaking districts in India's first elections. In 1952, an activist named Potti Sriramulu fasted for statehood, and ultimately starved to death. Ensuing demonstrations turned violent, and the central government quickly relented. The new state, originally called Andhra State, was created in 1953 out of the Telugu-speaking regions of the former Madras presidency, where the British had ruled directly and where Tamil-speakers and Telugu-speakers had jostled for influence.

In 1956, when the broader states reorganization took place, the Telugu-speaking part of the former Hyderabad princely state—known as Telangana—was added on, and the state was renamed Andhra Pradesh. But Telangana was much poorer than coastal Andhra, and from the beginning, some foresaw conflict (Chandra, Mukherjee, and Mukherjee 2000, 303). Telangana also had a history of internal unrest: a peasant uprising in the region had been put down by the Indian Army in 1946–47.

But having consolidated the bulk of Telugu speakers into one state, Congress built a broad base of support in AP, where it held onto power even in the difficult 1967 elections. Discontent in Telangana over the distribution of resources and employment in state institutions led to demands for separate statehood in 1969, but the central government was opposed.

In the 1980s, the state's party system fragmented with the formation of the Telugu Desam Party (TDP), led by the film star N.T. Rama Rao, who advocated for Telugu "self-respect" in the face of Delhi's interference in state affairs. The TDP held power in 1983–89, and again in 1994–2004 under the technophile N. Chandrababu Naidu. During Naidu's tenure, AP experienced new economic growth, especially in the IT sector and around the capital of Hyderabad. The city is well within the Telangana region, and its sudden dynamism brought a new dimension to the conflict: though much of its development was led by coastal Andhrans, Telangana statehood advocates saw it as bolstering their case for a viable state of their own.

The TDP itself splintered when a small new party, the Telangana Rashtra Samithi (TRS) broke away. Beginning with the 2004 elections, the TRS struck opportunistic alliances first with Congress, which returned to power in that year's state election (as at the Centre), and then with the TDP, which now led the Opposition.

The TRS managed to make Telangana statehood the main issue in AP politics for the next decade. The timeworn tradition of the hunger strike, now deployed by TRS founder K. Chandrasekhar Rao, forced the Congress-led UPA government at the Centre to announce in 2009 that it would introduce legislation to create a Telangana state. But the Centre backtracked when this policy "caused a wave of protests even bigger than the one it sought to calm" ("Divide but Not Rule?" 2009). Naidu originally supported keeping AP united, but as the TDP's position slipped to third place even in the coastal region—its usual stronghold—he came out in support of Telangana.

In the run-up to the April–May 2014 general- and state-level election, the central government finally brought forward the legislation, but Congress still lost ground in the state (just as it did nationally). Naidu's TDP returned to power in the rump AP, while Rao's TRS won Telangana—officially made India's twenty-ninth state just one month after the election. AP and Telangana will share Hyderabad until 2024, at which time AP will assume a new capital—a prize for which half a dozen cities and towns are vying.

Insurgent Naxalism has affected almost half of India's states—especially Bihar, Chhattisgarh, Jharkhand, and Odisha—and almost half of undivided AP's 23 districts, with a concentration in Telangana. Though highly factionalized (Mehra 2000), it is essentially a Maoist or agrarian revolutionary movement, named after its origin in the Naxalbari village of West Bengal in the late 1960s. In recent years it has found new support among landless peasants and tribals over disputed land rights and claims of exploitation by the state. But Naxalite cadres, too, often exploit the marginalized people they claim to represent.

For about half a decade, beginning around 2002, conflict between Naxalites and state police forces killed hundreds in AP alone and several thousand in India overall. In 2003, a faction called the People's War Group attempted to blow up a car carrying Chief Minister Naidu. In 2007, Prime Minister Manmohan Singh called Naxalism "the single biggest internal security challenge ever faced by our country" ("Naxalism is Gravest Internal Threat: PM" 2006), and the central government launched a major counterinsurgency effort, employing both deadly force and increased funding for rural development.

## Economy

Even more than democracy, India's economy has become its "global calling card" (Malone 2011, 75). It did not always inspire such interest, however, and a recent growth slowdown challenges the more euphoric early-2010s projections of its potential.

The British and other Europeans came for the trade, of course, but the very system of imperialism distorted and mis-developed the Indian economy for three centuries. Self-sufficiency became a key nationalist tenet, and Indian leaders continued to pursue this goal after Independence. In the 1950s, India developed mainly in accordance with Nehru's vision for a modern industrial economy, with some concessions to the Gandhian emphasis on small industries. (Even now, Gandhian ideals live on through a policy bias that discourages small companies from expanding: labor laws make it onerous for larger firms to fire workers). Perhaps surprisingly, given that most Indians then worked in agriculture—and still did as recently as 2010, though just barely (World Bank 2014)—there was only modest investment in farm modernization until the 1960s, when the Green Revolution brought new high-yield seed varieties and other advances, raising productivity and ending dependence on foreign food aid.

The Nehruvian model was a mixed public-private economy, with state ownership and control of the so-called "commanding heights": heavy industries and strategic sectors such as steel, coal, chemicals, rail, and electricity. The Planning Commission, first chaired by Nehru himself, set Five-Year Plan targets for investment. Domestic private capital was permitted to operate in non-strategic industries, but companies had to secure state licenses for manufacturing, importing, and exporting. While the basic pattern of state-directed development was pursued by many other developing countries (Kohli 2004), India eschewed the eventual export-led strategy of other Asian states such as South Korea and Taiwan (and later mainland China). Instead, it remained committed to "import substitution": industries produced for the seductively large domestic market, and the state used high tariffs and trade barriers to stave off foreign competition.

The resulting system came to be known as the "license-permit raj." Though the rationale may have been understandable, the system was prone to rent-seeking by bureaucrats, and often stifled innovation by industry. The economy grew, but at a languid pace of under 4 percent a year, irreverently known as the "Hindu rate of growth." Factoring in population increases, it was only 1.5 percent annual GDP growth per capita.

To be sure, some Indian companies performed well under protected industrialization. Though many became sclerotic, others developed strong foundations, enabling them to become globally competitive after the economy opened up in 1991: the IT sector offers examples such as Infosys and Wipro. But despite the global attention this particular industry has received, IT and related services employ "only" about 3 million Indians directly, whose purchasing power generates another 9 million jobs indirectly, mostly in lower-paying service occupations ("Indian IT-BPM Overview" 2014). These numbers may be large in absolute terms, but they are small in a population of 1.2 billion, even if the sector does account for around 8 percent of GDP.

A distinctive feature of India's development—especially compared to other Asian economies—has been anemic manufacturing, which accounts for only 11 percent of jobs and 15 percent of GDP ("Modi's Mission" 2014). A country with as many poor and under-employed people as India could do more to promote labor-intensive industries within the formal, organized economy. As many as 90 percent of Indians work in the untidy "informal economy," often at the unproductive margins of agriculture. But structural reform is easier to proclaim as a policy goal than to achieve in practice, given the legacies of the colonial and Nehruvian eras.

Though India rebounded relatively quickly following the 2008 global financial crisis, by 2012–13 a sharp decline in the rupee led concerns that it might be entering into a new economic crisis of its own. There have been several acute economic emergencies since Independence, most notably a 1966 crisis—when India was still highly dependent on food aid, and thus subject to external pressure to devalue the rupee—and a severe currency crisis 25 years later, which prompted the 1991 reforms. India opened up to trade and foreign investment, dismantled much of the license-permit raj, privatized public enterprises, deregulated, and gave greater scope to market forces in allocating resources.

During the three decades from 1980 to 2009, annual income growth per capita increased almost threefold to an average 4.2 percent (India began to transcend the "Hindu rate of growth" even in the 1980s by virtue of piecemeal reforms, but also by government borrowing that proved unsustainable). The decade that followed the far-reaching reforms of the early 1990s saw only a slight uptick in overall GDP growth (Kohli 2006), but by 2000–09 the annual growth rate *per capita* was an average 6.1 percent, making the "oughties" India's best decade ever (Kumar and Subramanian 2011, 2).

This sweetness of recent memory makes the sting of the post-2012 downturn that much sharper. Overall GDP growth for 2014–15 fell below 5 percent, meaning that per capita growth is only about a third of the last decade's rate. A generation of Indians had become accustomed to rising incomes, and the sudden change has placed severe strains on state and society.

Poverty and deprivation remain widespread, and the notion of "two Indias" now tempers breathless declarations of an "emerging" or "rising" India (Toyama 2012). Even before the recent malaise, a World Bank report drew headlines in 2008 by finding 42 percent of Indians—more than 450 million people—living below the international poverty line of US $1.25 per day ("One Third of World's Poor in India" 2008). The Bank had estimated that by 2015—the target year for achievement of the UN Millennium Development Goals—only about 25 percent of Indians would be so poor. But this projection now looks wildly optimistic. Moreover, fully three-fourths of Indians live on less than US $2 per day. This figure points to hundreds of millions of near-poor, only "one illness away" from a ruinous personal or household financial crisis (Krishna 2010).

There is an especially visceral quality to urban poverty in India, familiar to Western audiences through recent books such as *Behind the Beautiful Forevers* (Boo 2012) and films like *Slumdog Millionaire* (Beaufoy 2009). In Mumbai, the 2011 census found nearly 78 percent of residents living in slums such as the famous Dharavi, a former fishing village where as many as one million now live inside two-thirds of a square mile. However, the most pervasive poverty is in rural India (see Text Box, "Farmer suicides and 'Bt cotton' in India"). It is even more striking to realize that many slum-dwellers have incomes above the official poverty line, and most are recent arrivals who see better prospects in the slum than in the village (Saunders 2011). But rapid, haphazard urbanization presents significant governance challenges, as the recent surge in city-based protests—against political corruption and police failures, especially—appears to bear out.

### Box 2.2: Farmer suicides and "Bt cotton" in India

A most disturbing manifestation of rural despair is the phenomenon of farmer suicides, which have occurred in large numbers in Maharashtra, Karnataka, AP, Madhya Pradesh, and Chhattisgarh. Journalist P. Sainath (2011) notes that the official country-wide counts were 17,138 in 2009 and 15,964 in 2010—bringing the total since 1995 to a quarter of a million deaths.

India's integration into global agricultural trade has pushed down the prices of many crops, even as the central and state governments have reduced subsidies to farmers in an effort to deal with strained public finances. Cash crops such as cotton have displaced subsistence agriculture, and many small farmers have taken on large debts in order to buy new seed varieties, fertilizers, and pesticides. Access to credit through formal financial institutions is limited, and local moneylenders are typically powerful persons in the village who can set very high rates of interest. Farmers may be uneducated in the use of new technologies, and the erratic monsoon rains are a constant concern for those lacking irrigation. They may be only one drought away from financial crisis—and the shame, stigma, and even personal danger that can confront them if they cannot repay a debt. Many farmers have taken their own lives by the gruesomely symbolic method of drinking pesticide—a source of their indebtedness.

Of particular controversy has been genetically modified, pest-resistant "Bt cotton" (*Bacillus thuringiensis*) such as the patented Bollgard seed sold by the multinational company Monsanto since 2002. Monsanto promoted Bt cotton as a miracle product, and by 2012 fully 90 percent of cotton growers in India had switched to the variety (Haq 2012). But several of the years during the decade of its introduction saw drought and a new surge in suicides, and Monsanto became a focal point for criticism by NGOs, who charged the company with profiting from farmers' dependency. Suicides predate Bt cotton, but a multinational corporation is an easy villain in a story with complex causes. As geneticist M.S. Swaminathan has said, "The suicides are an extreme manifestation of some deep-seated problems which are now plaguing our agriculture. They are climatic. They are economic. They are social" (Sengupta 2006). The issue has attracted attention from global media (de Sam Lazaro 2007) and research institutions (Randerson 2008). Prime Minister Manmohan Singh called the suicides a sign of "acute distress," and the central government has increased investment to promote formal credit access in rural areas.

## International relations

As with the economy, India's regional and global diplomacy recently have drawn interest, and a growing literature details the evolution of its international relations (e.g. Malone 2011; Ganguly 2010). In South Asia, India has been seen as a "reluctant hegemon"—holding a dominant regional position, but often failing to appreciate how domineering it can appear to its smaller neighbors (Mitra 2003), all of which confront significant challenges, as this book's other chapters attest.

In general, India has had more of an impact on its neighbors' internal politics than vice versa, but one important case of a boomerang effect for India concerns Sri Lanka. Early in the island's 26-year civil war between the majority Sinhalese government forces and the Liberation Tigers of Tamil Eelam (1983–2009), Indian interference took a variety of forms, sometimes contradicting itself. It began with covert support to the Tigers and other Tamil insurgents. In 1987, India airdropped food parcels into rebel strongholds while Sri Lankan forces were laying siege. But India next signed an accord with Sri Lanka to help disarm the rebels. Indian peacekeepers ended up waging war against the Tigers for three years, and were accused of gross human rights violations. In 1991, in a conspiracy involving the Tigers, a female suicide bomber killed Rajiv Gandhi while the former prime minister was in India's Tamil Nadu campaigning for a comeback.

India's most enduringly contentious relationship is with Pakistan, of course. We have seen their history of conflict over Kashmir, which led to the inconclusive war in 1947–48 and another in 1965. In the interim, a rare bright spot in relations was the signing of the Indus Waters Treaty in 1960. The 1947 partition of Punjab—which means "five rivers"—had cut off the Indus River in Pakistan from its source tributaries in India; the water-sharing agreement has held through subsequent hostilities.

In 1971, Indian military intervention in Pakistan's civil war helped East Pakistan to become Bangladesh. This third India-Pakistan war was a decisive defeat for Pakistan, left with more than 90,000 prisoners of war in India. Though the fighting did not involve Kashmir this time, the two sides agreed going forward to settle all differences—including Kashmir—bilaterally. The UN ceasefire line in Kashmir was converted into the Line of Control, and in India's view, this 1972 Shimla Agreement superseded the earlier UN framework, including its call for a plebiscite in Kashmir; Pakistan disagrees.

The India-Pakistan conflict has reignited over the last quarter-century, amid the Kashmiri insurgency, the growth of Islamist militancy in Pakistan, and the declared nuclear weapons capabilities of both sides. A year after their 1998 nuclear tests, India and Pakistan fought the limited Kargil War in a remote district of Kashmir, before a US diplomatic intervention pressured Pakistan to withdraw. Subsequent crises have flared in 2001–02, following a terrorist attack on the Indian Parliament building, and in 2008, following the terrorist attacks in Mumbai that killed 165 and injured more than 300. A Pakistan-based group called Lashkar-e-Taiba (Army of the Righteous) was a co-conspirator in the Parliament attack, and responsible for Mumbai. Analysts debate whether nuclear deterrence, third-party diplomacy or other factors have kept the two sides from going to all-out war, but the recent pattern raises the troubling prospect that non-state militants now have the power to derail India-Pakistan relations, and may even attempt to goad the two sides into confrontation (Coll 2010).

India's relationship with China also has a troubled history. Nehru initially hoped that India would enjoy cooperative relations with Mao's China, as twin lights of a new Asia rid of Western dominance. But within a decade, relations grew tense over border disputes and India's grant of asylum to the Dalai Lama following the Tibet Uprising in 1959. In 1962, China launched offensives into two disputed territories, sparking a month-long war. China prevailed easily but suddenly withdrew, making defeat all the more humiliating to India for having appealed to the United States for help at the last minute. Even now, India and China both claim a territory called Aksai Chin (for India, part of eastern Kashmir) and another territory in northeastern Arunachal Pradesh. On the heels of the war, China's nuclear test in 1964 was an impetus to India's own nuclear weapons quest.

Economic relations present a more nuanced India-China picture. China's market reforms began at the end of the 1970s, and its economic growth gave a competitive subtext to India's own liberalization in the early 1990s. Trade between the two Asian giants has grown significantly, but in a lopsided fashion: for every dollar's worth of exports to China, India imports three dollars' worth, leading to a current trade deficit of $40 billion or about 2 percent of GDP ("Friend, Enemy, Rival, Investor" 2012).

In 2009, along with Brazil and Russia, India and China began holding annual BRIC summits; South Africa joined this club of major emerging markets the following year. The BRICS summit in New Delhi in 2012 drew headlines with its proposal for a "BRICS Bank," to focus on infrastructure investment and supplement lending by the World Bank and IMF (in which the United States and Europe still wield much influence).

But in the long run, Indian and Chinese economic interests could still foment rivalry, particularly as they compete for resources from Myanmar (Burma) to the African continent. And Chinese opposition remains an obstacle to India's realization of its highest foreign policy goal: permanent membership on an expanded UN Security Council.

Finally, India's relationship with the United States has warmed considerably since the Cold War, when India and the US were prone to regard one another with suspicion despite their shared commitment to democracy. Indian foreign policy elites were wary of an ascendant America replacing Britain as a domineering Western power, while the often binary worldview of the Washington national security establishment had little use for India's policy of Non-Alignment. India was of strategic interest to both the Soviet Union and the United States, and both courted its friendship with development assistance and military aid. But in the mid-1960s, the United States lost influence, first by trying to deal evenhandedly with the second India-Pakistan war—which Pakistan had initiated—and then by trying to coerce India to alter its economic policies in exchange for food aid. US-India relations reached a nadir around the third India-Pakistan war in 1971, with India signing a Treaty of Friendship with the Soviets and President Richard Nixon sending the *USS Enterprise* into the Bay of Bengal as a warning to India while Pakistan, a US ally, bled. The United States was also critical of India's refusal to sign the Nonproliferation Treaty (NPT).

The end of the Cold War and the beginning of economic liberalization in India suggested that relations might improve, but the South Asian nuclear tests of 1998 initially set them back. A sustained engagement between US Deputy Secretary of State Strobe Talbott and Indian External Affairs Minister Jaswant Singh, originally tied to the nuclear issue, evolved into a broader strategic dialogue and set the stage for President Bill Clinton's visit to India in early 2000. It also marked a new dual-track, "de-hyphenated" US approach to its relations with India and Pakistan.

Early in the George W. Bush presidency, the 9/11 terrorist attacks led the United States back to an alliance with Pakistan, to pursue al Qaeda and its Taliban hosts in Afghanistan. But the warming trend in US-India relations continued. In 2004, the two countries announced a "strategic partnership"—though not a formal alliance—and in 2005 they came to terms over India's nuclear program with a civilian nuclear cooperation agreement. Though the deal eventually passed all the requisite hurdles (at the domestic level in both countries, and multilaterally), it was quite contentious in India, and led to the Left Front calling a no-confidence vote in the Lok Sabha in 2008 (that the Congress-led UPA survived).

The momentum in US-India relations has slowed somewhat during Barack Obama's presidency, with the main achievement so far being his pledge of US support for a permanent Indian seat on the Security Council, but with no plan for getting there.

## Opportunities and constraints

India's development has made it a different country than the Sovereign Democratic Republic of 1950, and yet the main pillars of the constitutional order are all still in place. In many ways, India has become more democratic today than it was then, particularly in the subordinate caste revolution.

Indians are a deeply religious and, at times, a deeply divided people, but they have become practiced at "working a democratic constitution," to borrow the title of Granville Austin's authoritative history (2003), and for the most part have held together though turbulent times. In this, the Indian experience may offer an example to other deeply divided societies. Still, there are tensions at the heart of India's secularism—especially between the right to religious freedom and goals of social and economic transformation.

The compromises struck between the actively pluralistic and ameliorative aspects of India's constitutional order do not satisfy all, and it would not be surprising if certain balances shift in years to come. In continually forging compromises, India defines secularism on its own terms. There are risks, as episodic experiences with extremism and violence have shown. But India's democracy has shown a surprising capacity to channel a wide range of demands into the formal political process. The Indian state has met frontal assaults to its legitimacy with a mix of accommodation and repression, and has mostly contained extremism within its borders rather than fomenting wider troubles in a troubled region.

India's greatest constraint—and greatest opportunity—in the twenty-first century is that it contains one in every three of the world's poor. It actually accounts for a higher share of global poverty today than in the 1990s, mainly because authoritarian-capitalist China has lifted more people faster. Recent economic growth has brought many Indians out of absolute poverty, but the margin for error is perilously thin for the millions of near-poor.

India's civilization is old, and so are many of its leaders. But India's bulging society is young, and so is its continuing experiment in democracy and development.

## Political chronology

| | |
|---|---|
| 1857–58: | Indian Rebellion/Sepoy Mutiny, followed by direct British rule. |
| 1885: | Indian National Congress (INC) founded. |
| 1905–06: | Partition of Bengal province; Muslim League founded. |
| 1915: | Mahatma Gandhi returns to India from South Africa. |
| 1919: | Amritsar massacre. |
| 1920–22: | Non-Cooperation Movement. |
| 1930: | Salt March. |
| 1935: | Government of India Act. |
| 1942: | Quit India campaign. |
| 1947 August 14–15: | Independence and Partition of India and Pakistan. |
| 1947–48: | First India-Pakistan War; ends with UN ceasefire Jan 1949. |
| 1950 January 26: | Constitution of India adopted. |
| 1951–52 Oct–Feb: | First general elections and concurrent state elections. |
| 1953: | Andhra State created (first linguistic state). |
| 1956–57: | States Reorganization; Telangana joins Andhra Pradesh. |
| 1962: | China-India war. |
| 1964: | Nehru dies. |
| 1966: | Indira Gandhi becomes PM. |
| 1967: | INC wins narrow majority in Lok Sabha; voted out in 8 states. |
| 1971: | Bangladesh War, followed by Indo-Pak Shimla Agreement 1972. |
| 1974: | Rail workers strike. First ("peaceful") nuclear test. |
| 1975–77: | The Emergency; elections and civil liberties suspended. |
| 1984: | Indira Gandhi assassinated; Rajiv Gandhi becomes PM. |
| 1989: | National Front wins general elections; Mandal controversy. |
| 1990–91: | Economic crisis and liberalization. Rajiv Gandhi assassinated. |
| 1992: | Babri Masjid destroyed; riots. |
| 1998: | BJP-led NDA elected. Indian and Pakistani nuclear tests. |
| 1999: | NDA wins snap election; Kargil War. |
| 2002: | Godhra train burning; Hindu-Muslim violence in Gujarat. |
| 2004: | Congress-led UPA elected, Manmohan Singh becomes PM. |
| 2008: | Indo-US Civilian Nuclear Agreement; world economic crisis. |
| 2009: | UPA reelected; Indian GDP growth recovers after crisis shock. |
| 2010: | GDP growth peaks at 10 percent. |
| 2011: | Anti-corruption campaign led by Anna Hazare; GDP growth slows. |
| 2012: | Gang rape in Delhi sparks protests to crimes against women. |
| 2013: | Aam Aadmi Party (AAP) contests its first election in Delhi on anti-corruption platform, forms government led by Arvind Kejriwal. |
| 2014: | Narendra Modi leads BJP to general election win with majority in Lok Sabha; Telangana state formed from interior Andhra Pradesh. |
| 2015: | Barack Obama attends Republic Day parade in New Delhi, first US president to do so; AAP wins absolute majority in Delhi; GDP growth surpasses 7 per cent, outpaces China. |

## Works cited

Adhikari, Anand. 2011. "Supersize Gujarat," *Business Today* (India Today Group) (January 23).

Ambedkar, B. R. (1948) 2008. *The Untouchables*. Delhi: Siddharth Books.

Austin, Granville. 2003. *Working a Democratic Constitution: A History of the Indian Experience*. New Delhi: Oxford University Press.

Beaufoy, Simon. 2009. *Slumdog Millionaire*. DVD. Directed by Danny Boyle. Twentieth Century Fox.

Bhattacharya, Sabyasachi. 2011. *Rabindranath Tagore: An Interpretation*. New Delhi: Viking/Penguin Books India.

Boo, Katherine. 2012. *Behind the Beautiful Forevers: Life, Death, and Hope in a Mumbai Undercity*. New York: Random House.

Chandra, Bipan, Mridula Mukherjee, and Aditya Mukherjee. 2000. *India After Independence: 1947–2000*. New Delhi: Penguin Books India.

Coll, Steve. 2010. "Kashmir: The Time Has Come," *New York Review of Books* (September 30).

Daruwala, Maja, G. P. Joshi, and Mandeep Tiwana. 2005. "Police Act, 1861: Why We Need to Replace It?" New Delhi: Commonwealth Human Rights Initiative.

de Sam Lazaro, Fred. 2007. "The Dying Fields," *WIDE ANGLE*, Streaming Video. Thirteen/WNET New York (August 27).

"Divide but Not Rule?" 2009. *The Economist* (December 17).

Ford, Matt. 2014. "Indian Democracy Runs on Briefcase-Sized Voting Machines." *The Atlantic* (April 15).

Frank, Katherine. 2002. *Indira: The Life of Indira Nehru Gandhi*. New York: Houghton Mifflin.

"Friend, Enemy, Rival, Investor." 2012. *The Economist* (June 30).

Ganguly, Sumit, ed. 2010. *India's Foreign Policy: Retrospect and Prospect*. New York: Oxford University Press.

Guha, Ramachandra. 2007. *India After Gandhi: The History of the World's Largest Democracy*. New York: HarperCollins.

Haq, Zia. 2012. "Ministry Blames Bt Cotton for Farmer Suicides." *Hindustan Times* (March 26).

Hardgrave, Jr., Robert L., and Stanley A. Kochanek. 2008. *India: Government and Politics in a Developing Nation*, 7th ed. Boston: Thomson Wadsworth.

Hay, Stephen, ed. 1988. *Sources of Indian Tradition*, Volume Two: *Modern India and Pakistan*, 2nd ed. New York: Columbia University Press.

Human Rights Watch. 2002. "'We Have No Orders to Save You': State Complicity in Communal Violence in Gujarat." Vol. 14, No. 3(C) (April).

"India Rape Case: 'Tsunami-sized' Call for Change." 2012. *Connect the World*. CNN (December 29).

"Indian IT-BPM Overview." 2014. NASSCOM. Accessed June 17. Retrieved from www.nasscom.in/indian-itbpo-industry

Jacobsohn, Gary Jeffrey. 2003. *The Wheel of Law: India's Secularism in Comparative Constitutional Context*. Princeton, NJ: Princeton University Press.

Jaffrelot, Christophe. 1996. *The Hindu Nationalist Movement in India*. New York: Columbia University Press.

———, ed. 2007. *Hindu Nationalism: A Reader*. Princeton: Princeton University Press.

———. 2010. "The Politics of Caste." In *Understanding Contemporary India*, 2nd ed., edited by Neil DeVotta, 249–68. Boulder, CO: Lynne Rienner.

Kohli, Atul. 1991. *Democracy and Discontent: India's Growing Crisis of Governability*. New York: Cambridge University Press.

———. 2004. *State-Directed Development: Political Power and Industrialization in the Global Periphery*. New York: Cambridge University Press.

———. 2006. "Politics of Economic Growth in India, 1980-2005, Part II: The 1990s and Beyond." *Economic and Political Weekly* (April 8).

Krishna, Anirudh. 2010. *One Illness Away: Why People Become Poor and How They Escape Poverty*. New York: Oxford University Press.

Kumar, Prabhat. 2009. "Younger India, Greying Politicians," *The Hindu Business Line* (February 6).

Kumar, Utsav, and Arvind Subramanian. 2011. "India's Growth in the 2000s: Four Facts." Working Paper Series, WP 11–17, Petersen International Institute for Economics (November).

Malone, David M. 2011. *Does the Elephant Dance?: Contemporary Indian Foreign Policy*. New York: Oxford University Press.

Manor, James J. 1981. "Party Decay and Political Crisis in India," *The Washington Quarterly* (Summer): 25–40.

Mashru, Ram. 2013. "Justice Delayed is Justice Denied: India's 30 Million Case Judicial Backlog." *The Diplomat* (December 25).

Mehra, Ajay K. 2000. "Naxalism in India: Revolution or Terror?" *Terrorism and Political Violence* 12 (2): 37–66.

Mitra, Subrata. 2003. "The Reluctant Hegemon: India's Self-Perception and the South Asian Strategic Environment," *Contemporary South Asia* 12 (3) (September): 399–417.

———. 2011. *Politics in India: Structure, Process and Policy*. New York: Routledge.

"Modi's Mission." 2014. *The Economist* (May 24).

Mustafi, Sambuddha Mitra. 2012. "Is a Youth Revolution Brewing in India?" *The New York Times* (August 27).

"Nano Wars," 2008. *The Economist* (August 28).

"Naxalism Is Gravest Internal Threat: PM," 2006. *The Times of India* (April 13). Retrieved from http://timesofindia.indiatimes.com/city/delhi/Naxalism-is-gravest-internal-threat-PM/articleshow/1489633.cms

"One Third of World's Poor in India: Survey," 2008. *The Times of India* (August 27).

Padgaonkar, Dileep. 2005. "1990: Mandal/mandir," *India Today* (December 26).

Parmar, Ram. 2012. "21 Year Old Girl Held for Facebook Post Questioning Mumbai's 'Bal Thackeray Shutdown', Get Bail" *The Times of India* (November 19).

Pew Forum on Religion & Public Life. 2011. Table: "Muslim Population by Country," *The Future of the Global Muslim Population*. Washington, DC: Pew Research Center (January).

Randerson, James. 2008. "Indian Farmer Suicides Not GM Related, Says Study," *The Guardian* (November 5).

Sainath, P. 2011. "In 16 Years, Farm Suicides Cross a Quarter Million" *The Hindu* (October 29).

Saunders, Doug. 2011. *Arrival City: How the Largest Migration in History Is Reshaping Our World*. New York: Pantheon.

Seeley, John Robert. (1883) 1922. *The Expansion of England*. Boston: Little, Brown.

Sengupta, Somini. 2006. "On India's Farms, a Plague of Suicides," *The New York Times* (September 19).

Singh, Harmeet Shah. 2012. "Arrest of 'Toilet' Cartoonist Triggers Free Speech Debate in India," CNN (September 11).

Sinha, Aseema. 2005. *The Regional Roots of Development Politics in India: A Divided Leviathan*. Bloomington: Indiana University Press.

Toyama, Kentaro. 2012. "The Two Indias: Astounding Poverty in the Backyard of Amazing Growth," *The Atlantic* (February 20).

World Bank. 2013. "IDA at Work: India: Economic Reforms Boost Andhra Pradesh." Washington, DC: International Development Association, September 2009. World Wide Web page. Accessed March 7.

———. 2014. "Employment in Agriculture (% of total employment)." Retrieved from http://data.worldbank.org/indicator/SL.AGR.EMPL.ZS. Accessed June 17.

"31% Muslims Live Below Poverty Line," 2010. *The Times of India* (March 28).

## Recommended texts

Cohen, Stephen P., and Sunil Dasgupta. 2010. *Arming Without Aiming: India's Military Modernization*. Washington, DC: The Brookings Institution Press.

Corbridge, Stuart, John Harriss, and Craig Jeffrey. 2012. *India Today: Economy, Politics and Society*. Cambridge, UK: Polity Press.

DeVotta, Neil. 2010. *Understanding Contemporary India*, 2nd ed. Boulder, CO: Lynne Rienner.

Jaffrelot, Christophe. 2011. *Religion, Caste and Politics in India*. New York: Columbia University Press.

Panagariya, Arvind. 2008. *India: The Emerging Giant*. New York: Oxford University Press.

Rudolph, Lloyd I., and Susanne Hoeber Rudolph. 2008. *Explaining Indian Democracy: A Fifty Year Perspective 1956–2006*, Vol. I–III. New York: Oxford University Press.

# 3 Pakistan

*Anas Malik*

Founded in the Partition of India in 1947, Pakistan seemed to promise different, sometimes contradictory, things to different groups. Was it an Islamic or a secular state? Was it a redistributive developmental state, or would it protect landowners from land reform? Was it to be a loose federation, or to have a strong central government? With its status (at the time) as the largest Muslim population of any country in the world, did Pakistan fulfill the theory of national identity based on Muslim religion, or did it reflect elite rivalries amid colonial withdrawal? Over two generations later, the country is heavily indebted, and has experienced civilian democratic rule as well as three long-lived military regimes. Approximately half the country's population was lost when Bangladesh was created from East Pakistan in 1971. Pakistan is nevertheless the second most populous Muslim-majority country. It is a declared nuclear power, has an enduring rivalry with India, and has violent non-state actors that have often traversed official boundaries. Pakistan remains a low-income, largely agricultural country, with high inequality, low literacy rates, and many people at or below the poverty line. Pakistani society is ethnically diverse, with historical tensions over language rights and religious sectarian identity. Fears of instability are heightened by domestic economic challenges and by Pakistan's conflicts with India, as well as its geostrategic position with respect to the United States, China, and others.

## History and political development

In the lead up to the British East India Company's advent, the Indian subcontinent had been largely under the rule of the Mughal Empire. The Mughals were a Muslim dynasty, although this identity had varying policy implications. By the mid-1700s, Mughal rule had ceased to be effective. The lack of a strong central government in the Indian subcontinent provided the British East India Company with an opportunity to expand (Raza 1997). In one narrative, the 1857 "Indian Mutiny" was partly a Muslim attempt to curtail British power in India that failed (Siddiqui 1972, 1). An Indian nationalist narrative describes this as a "War of Independence." Ultimately, Pakistan was created less from a broad, unified, and sustained struggle against colonialism, and more from powerful elites collaborating with the British against Hindu hegemony (Nasr 2001, 25). Some key popular advocates were Indian Muslims who would migrate to the new territory.

The Muslim League had advocated for the rights of Muslims in post-British India, and in the 1940 Lahore Resolution endorsed the call for a separate Muslim state, although the wording leaves some room for interpretation. Partition in 1947 was accompanied by bloody communal rioting and what later would be termed *ethnic cleansing*. The rushed British departure and inadequately transferred and apportioned political authority likely contributed to the violence that ensued (Wolpert 2006; Ganguly 1994). Casualty estimates range from hundreds of thousands to one million. Many more became refugees (one claim is that 8 million refugees entered Pakistan).

Pakistan inherited what was "Northwest India" and East Bengal due to their heavily Muslim populations; subsequently known as West and East Pakistan, the two halves were separated by hundreds of miles of Indian territory. Partition also divided the populous Punjab province. A war soon broke out over Kashmir; the ongoing rivalry between India and Pakistan and their contest over Kashmir are covered in the foreign relations section below.

A major challenge for development is building the ability to raise resources from society—particularly from taxation. A weak fiscal apparatus in Pakistan was partly a colonial legacy. Direct taxes might have caused instability and rebellion, and the British preferred to avoid them. Instead, the British prioritized stability, and made money from trade taxes and from managing credit and currency (Nasr 2001)

In the lead-up to Partition, the British colonists' revenue-raising apparatus was largely left in place in central government and financial institutions such as the Inland Revenue and Customs and Excise offices (Joshi and Little 1994). The Reserve Bank had been created in 1935 and was retained by India past independence. The British had created the Indian Civil Service for higher-level civil bureaucrats, and produced the institution and model on which the subsequent Indian Administrative Service and Civil Service of Pakistan were based. Implementation of Partition agreements on government revenue divisions were not resolved immediately but continued to be negotiated and disputed as late as 1960 (Talbot 1998).

The Pakistani state inherited not only the colonial pattern but also the intermediaries the British relied upon. This pattern of intermediaries would reappear as local "strongmen": powerful figures and entities distinct from the national government and not necessarily holding formal office, but nevertheless acting as veto-holders, gatekeepers, and enablers (Migdal 1988). National policies and electoral campaigns may succeed or fail depending in part whether strongmen acquiesce. Examples might be the landed elites in Sindh and Punjab and tribal leaders in North-West Frontier Province (NWFP; now known as KPK, or Khyber Pakhtunkhwa) and Balochistan.

The British feared the Russian threat to North-West India, and accordingly sought consent to rule through patronage. "Stability" in this area mattered more than trade and revenue (Nasr 2001). The perceived geopolitical threat from Russia was echoed in the later twentieth century: some posited that in invading Afghanistan in 1979 the Soviet Union ultimately had designs on Pakistan, and its warm-water port on the Arabian Sea.

Both India and Pakistan inherited military resources from British India, although Pakistan may have been short-changed, receiving roughly a one-third share. Defense ordnance plants were located in India (Kavic 1967). This meant that "start-up" costs of war preparation were likely to be higher in Pakistan.

Thus, common historical origin did not mean that the two states started on a level footing. India inherited more British colonial resources on the whole, and was several times larger than Pakistan in population. Nevertheless, both India and Pakistan are usually characterized as low-income countries, and have health, literacy, and educational indicators that are typical for low-income countries. Agriculture has dominated both economies, although India experienced land reform and its industrial base is proportionately larger.

State weakness at Pakistan's inception also arose because the British Raj machinery was left behind in Delhi; Pakistan's new administration "had to govern out of a hotel in Karachi without the rudiments of a national government over provinces that had no natural grid among them, and some of which were reluctant participants in the Pakistan movement"

(Nasr 2001, 26). An important question is the degree to which a strong Pakistani identity has been forged. The majority of the country's population has only known Pakistani citizenship, and indeed only the Pakistan that remained after the 1971 split. Yet there remains substantial alienation in Balochistan, and a recurrent low-level insurgency, connected to resentment over the distribution of wealth from Balochistan's natural resources. This conflict has taken a secessionist hue at times.

While Pakistan's official description refers to its federal character, the central government has often acted in a more centralized manner. The autonomy of the federating units remains a contentious issue, particularly with respect to the central government's power to dissolve provincial legislatures. This may be changing with the eighteenth amendment to the Constitution, but these guidelines have yet to be thoroughly tested in a political contest. Centre-unit tensions are often stoked by demands by provincials and subgroups for greater financial resources. An ongoing grievance from sparsely populated Balochistan is that allocated funds do not match that province's contributions from natural gas production. Defense and debt servicing burdens continue to squeeze Pakistan's budgets.

India is usually identified as a democracy, while Pakistan has undergone military rule in large periods. Although it underwent a notorious "Emergency" period under Indira Gandhi, India is generally perceived as having more viable, solid, and continuing political institutions and constitutional framework than Pakistan, due in part to the lack of a military threat to civilian rule (Harrison, Kreisberg, and Kux 1999, 3–5). Pakistan, in contrast, is not as far along in finding an effective and stable government, and has seen repeated military intervention and martial law (Harrison et al. 1999, 3–4; Siddiqa 2007). There have been shifts back and forth in executive authority from the president to the prime minister; and army chiefs have filled a quasi-presidential or presidential role at times (Raza 1997, 26–27; Rehman 2008). Martial law regimes have appeared with regularity, including Ayub Khan's rule starting in 1958, Zia Ul-Haq's regime beginning in 1977, and General Pervez Musharraf's takeover in 1999. Thus the 2013 election made history because it marked the first turnover of power from an elected civilian government that had served a full five-year term without being dismissed or displaced in a coup.

### Pakistan and Islam

"Islam" or Muslim identity was the *raison d'etre* that justified Pakistan's very existence; in seeking to mobilize public support for the soon-to-be-born state, the Muslim League used the slogan "Islam in danger." Various interested groups and parties have come up with different answers about what counts as an "Islamic" government. These include the Jamiat Ulema-e-Islam (a Deobandi pro-Pakistan ulama grouping) The well-disciplined Jamaat-e-Islami distributed literature describing its vision for the Islamic state. In 1948, a Shariat group was set up in the Pakistan Muslim League to work towards an "Islamic order" in Pakistan (Afzal 2001).

Jinnah reportedly declared that the future constitution would be based on Shariat (Afzal 2001). But Jinnah is also credited with declaring that religious practice had nothing to do with the business of state. Ill with lung disease, Jinnah died shortly after Pakistan was created. Under his lieutenant Liaquat Ali Khan, who followed as a national leader, Pakistan adopted the "Objectives Resolution," which specified both an Islamic and a democratic orientation for the country. The polity would be one "wherein the principles of democracy, freedom, equality, tolerance and social justice as enunciated by Islam shall be fully observed" and "wherein the Muslims shall be enabled to order their lives in the individual and collective spheres in accordance with the teachings and requirements of Islam as set out in the Holy Quran and the Sunnah" (National Assembly of Pakistan 2012, 1). The Objectives Resolution has since featured in Pakistan's constitutions.

---

### Box 3.1: Islam and the state

It is not that there were no answers to questions in Pakistan about how to make the country "Islamic"; rather, there were too many answers, sometimes vague and them-selves open to contested interpretations, and zealots and believers who were convinced that their interpretation was superior. Islam is not organized into a single hierarchy that defines who speaks authoritatively for the religion. Instead there are scriptural sources and diverse *ulama* (religious scholars) who seek to act as custodians of the tradition (Zaman 2002). With lithograph, print, and other transmission technologies, traditional authority has in places been supplanted by an interpretative anarchy (Bulliet 2004). Recently, new communications technologies have further augmented this process, visible in widespread satellite television channels that have religious call-in shows and feature wide debate and Internet forums.

Translating the religious lobbies into a workable prescription for an Islamic govern-ment appeared to many to be an intractable problem. The *Munir Report*, a 1954 Commission that inquired into sectarian disturbances, noted that

> "no two learned divines ... agreed" on the definition of a Muslim: "If we attempt our own definition as each learned divine has done and that definition differs from that given by all others, we unanimously go out of the fold of Islam. And if we adopt the definition given by any one of the *ulama*, we remain Muslims according to the view of that *alim* but *kafirs* according to the definition of every one else."
>
> (Jalal 2008, 270–271)

---

The inability to define who counted as a Muslim made it correspondingly difficult to define an "Islamic state," as Jalal (2008) observed. Despite these challenges, Pakistan was co-identified with Islam and Muslims in official narratives. This was a "loaded and unten-able equation," difficult to reconcile with the fact that most Muslims in post-Partition India stayed on in India rather than migrate to the homeland for Indian Muslims (Jalal 1995, 87).

Key questions about national identity and governance continue to be contested. Who is the country for? How should the country be run? Where are the external boundaries and internal jurisdictions? What powers should the central government have over the acceding units?

Regarding the "who" question, an early argument was that a homeland for the Indian subcontinent's Muslims was needed. But Muslims, although concentrated in west and east British India, were also spread throughout the region and beyond. Within Pakistan, lan-guage was not a unifying factor, and instead distinguished ethnic groups. Urdu, a courtly language developed under Mughal dynastic rule in India, was spoken by many Muslims. But there were many other languages too: Punjabi, Bengali, Balochi, Pashto, Sindhi, Seraiki, Hindko. Language became a critical issue driving ethno-nationalist sentiment in Bengali-speaking East Pakistan, and language has also been the basis for ethnic violence between Sindhis and Urdu-speaking Muhajirs in Sindh. There are inequalities in the weight given to different groups. Punjab is commonly believed to play a hegemonic role, due partly to its large population and representation in the armed forces. There are socio-economic inequalities, with the land-owning elite enjoying disproportionate privileges. The weight given to the federating units in Pakistan, and their rights and autonomy with respect to the center, remain an ongoing negotiation, as discussed below.

Sectarian agitations have sometimes included or led to violence. The Ahrar, a religious social organization, mobilizing in the 1950s against the Ahmadi community is an early example. The Ahmadis are a religious sect that claims to be Islamic, but has run into opposition from orthodox Muslims due to their beliefs regarding the finality of prophethood, a core Islamic creed. The Ahrars sought to remove Ahmadis from high office. The Ahmadis, who were previously considered "Muslim" by law, eventually found themselves declared non-Muslims. More recently, the Sipah-e-Sahaba Pakistani (Soldiers of the Prophetic Companions), founded in 1985, has been active in anti-Shia militancy, and is rivaled by its Shia counterpart, the Sipah-e-Muhammad (Soldiers of Muhammad). Violence ascribed to militant groups mobilized around sectarian identities continues to claim lives in Pakistan.

The blasphemy laws enhanced under Zia ul-Haq prescribe life imprisonment or death to those who desecrate the Quran or insult the Prophet. Although no one has been actually put to death or imprisoned for life based on this law, it nevertheless remains a stick that can be used against minorities. Alleged desecration has fueled mob violence targeting minorities, such as the seven Christians killed and many homes gutted in Gojra in August, 2009; although there are increasing efforts by Muslim religious authorities to condemn such vigilante violence, it remains a threat.

With respect to how the country was to be run—meaning the constitutional rules for governance—Pakistan has experienced instability. Pakistan's founding vision was to be a parliamentary democracy, but the process of democratic turnover has been disrupted by military coups and the dismissal of elected governments (Bashir 2008). Depending on how they are counted, Pakistan has had up to six constitutions. On attaining office, incumbent leaders repeatedly tried to deploy, suspend, or modify basic rules in ways that allowed them to consolidate their authority. Much of the history of constitutional instability in Pakistan reflects the struggle between executive and legislative authority for political supremacy. This includes the attempt to secure the executive's power to dismiss an elected government, and efforts to protect parliamentary supremacy.

The president's discretionary authority to dissolve the parliament emerged from the Government of India Act 1935 (which allowed for a continuing powerful governor-general) and the Independence Act 1947 (which created a constituent assembly to both legislate laws and frame the constitution). Jinnah introduced Section 92A into the Independence Act, which empowered him to declare governor's rule in the provinces, and the Chief Ministers of Sindh and NWFP were ousted when they clashed with Jinnah (Almeida 2008).

The Constituent Assembly, which provided legislation in early Pakistani history and worked to frame a constitution, clashed with the country's political executives. Subsequent attempts to frame and sustain a constitution (in 1956, 1962, and 1973) were ended by martial laws in 1958, 1969, and 1977, respectively.

Pakistan's first constitution established a parliamentary system and was passed nine years after its foundation. Pakistan was modeled as a federal republic with a National Assembly (elected directly by the people), Senate (with representation for each federating unit), Prime Minister, and Governor-General (later President), and an independent judiciary. Provincial assemblies would legislate on provincial subjects. This constitution did not last; before national elections were held, a military coup led by Ayub Khan in

1958 turned national government authority to the military. In a controversial move, the judiciary validated this action as a revolutionary situation in which a new constitutional setup could be accepted.

The 1962 constitution promulgated under Ayub Khan gave the president extensive legislative and executive powers and influence over the national assembly. Although the system was federal, the Provincial governor and government were basically the president's agents (Rizvi 2000). Ayub Khan's 1962 constitution, although "president-centric" with a presidential form of government, nevertheless had some restraints on the president's power to dissolve the assembly (Bashir 2008). Faced by nationwide protests over economic inequality and the outcome of the 1965 war with India, Ayub stepped down in 1969. According to Ayub's constitution, after his resignation the legislature's Speaker should have assumed the presidency. But Chief of Army Staff Yahya Khan took over, and in 1969, he abrogated the 1962 constitution. Khan's rule was comparatively brief, as national elections produced a regionally divided electorate, followed by civil war and the breakup of the country.

Under the leadership of Zulfiqar Ali Bhutto, the 1973 constitution produced a decisively parliamentary system with a very weak president, empowering the prime minister. It also had "safeguards against the PM's abuse of dissolution as a pre-emptive tactic against a vote of no-confidence or a revenge measure if the PM had already been unseated by such a successful vote" (Bashir 2008, 7). Bhutto swiftly issued emergency declarations that effectively removed these protections. The 1973 constitution also promised that the "Concurrent List," subjects on which both the federal and provincial governments legislated, would be abolished in 1983, enhancing provincial autonomy and authority. A military coup prevented this process.

Constitutional rule was suspended under Zia ul-Haq's martial law regime, which began in 1977. In 1985, Zia ul-Haq restored the 1973 constitution with controversial alterations, the most notorious being the Eighth Amendment. Article 58 Clause 2 (b) allowed the President discretion to dissolve the national assembly (and dismiss the prime minister and cabinet) "where, in his opinion, 'a situation has arisen in which the Government or the Federation cannot be carried on in accordance with the provision of the Constitution and an appeal to the electorate is necessary'" (Akhtar 1992, 258). Between 1985 and 1997, there were five elections, but no assembly finished its term, and each was dissolved by the president using Article 58 (2) (b) (Zafar 2000). The Supreme Court tended to argue that Article 58 (2) (b) provided checks and balances that could reduce the likelihood that martial law would be imposed, but parliamentarians disagreed (Zafar 2000).

In 1993, President Ghulam Ishaq Khan moved to dismiss Nawaz Sharif's government. In an unprecedented action, the Pakistan Supreme Court accepted Nawaz Sharif's appeal, and ordered his government reinstated. Revelations about political influence-peddling in the Supreme Court played a role. Former Chief of Army Staff General Aslam Baig had disclosed that he had secretly pressured the Supreme Court to not reinstate the Junejo government, which had been dismissed in 1988. These revelations of inappropriate political pressure compelled a different course in 1993 (Ziring 1997).

General Pervez Musharraf's government, which came to power in a military coup in 2000, eventually tried to civilianize its rule, while maintaining high executive power for Musharraf. This pattern of military coup leaders who seek to expand their legitimacy by holding referendums or elections while retaining key final authority generated protests. In particular, the lawyers' movement protested attempted stacking of judicial offices with Musharraf's allies. Musharraf resigned under popular pressure, and the 1973 constitution was brought back to life, with adjustments, including a repeal of the executive's authority to dismiss legislatures. Constitutional rules continue to shift for political expediency. Key questions on borders and jurisdiction remain unsettled or subject to renegotiation.

### Powerful socio-economic groups

Another key question has been who benefits from governance processes. Drawing on special connections and bribes, influence wielded by vested interests has repeatedly diverted governance away from producing public goods and towards providing private goods. Corruption and opaque informal arrangements undermine and complicate the formal rules according to which both state and market are expected to operate. Powerful groups include the military, the civil bureaucracy, great landlords disparagingly called "feudals," industrialists/business groups, religious leaders, and, possibly, new media. Pakistan has not had extensive land reform or successful agricultural taxation. Economist Ishrat Husain, a former Pakistan State Bank Governor, has described Pakistan as an "elitist state" in which the market is rigged and the state is hijacked in order to deliver most of the benefits of economic growth to this small group" (Husain 2000, xii–xiii). In contrast, successful East Asian economies have seen rapid growth, rapid poverty reduction, and more equitably distributed development benefits (Husain 2000).

Scholarly works on Pakistan's political development emphasize specific themes. To Jalal (1990), the elephant in the national policy-making room is the disproportionate national income share that has been devoted to defense and the military, a path begun from the perceived threat to survival immediately after Pakistan was founded. In Jalal (1995), the key issue is broadened to the struggle between unelected and elected institutions. To Siddiqa (2007), the overriding distributional coalition is what she has termed *milbus*, the increasingly autonomous military class that dominates the economy and polity, and has done so through business foundations, land grants, special privileges and licenses, soft loans and loan forgiveness, and other preferential treatment, in addition to the vast budgetary resources devoted to the military. To Ziring (1997) a key legacy is the "vice-regal" tradition, rule that depended on a local ruler supported by a formidable administrative and military apparatus. Malik (2011) emphasizes the political survival of incumbent leaders who have depended on narrow, elite-based coalitions, which helps explain the low provision of public goods.

## Institutions, political parties, and elections

The 2013 elections in Pakistan were a watershed, representing the first time in Pakistani history that a democratically elected government had served its full five-year term, and then seen a civilian turnover through a direct election. In spite of the threat and reality of violence from groups such as the Taliban, voter turnout was an astounding 60 percent, the highest in four decades, including millions of first-time voters. Instead of resulting in a legislature fragmented among rival parties, one party was able to procure nearly half the seats, making it possible to avoid the instability and ineffectiveness of weak coalition governments. Although some rigging and mismanagement were reported, observers described the election as relatively fair. Nawaz Sharif's PML-N party won the 2013 elections, positioning him to be prime minister for the third time; in a dramatic twist, Pervez Musharraf, the military general who deposed Sharif in a coup in 2000 and had him jailed, was now himself under arrest. Despite a history of three military coups, civil war, and insurgency, democratic processes appear alive in Pakistan.

Some impetus for Pakistan's democratic transition came from the judiciary, particularly Supreme Court Chief Justice Iftikhar Chaudhry and an allied lawyers' movement. Chaudhry had taken his oath in 2002 under Pervez Musharraf's post-coup Legal Framework Ordinance, validating the Musharraf regime, and had been named Chief Justice of the Supreme Court in 2005. In 2007, Chaudhry refused to resign despite military pressure, effectively complicating Musharraf's attempts to extend his rule. Musharraf had Chaudhry suspended and investigated for misconduct. A judicial panel then reinstated Chaudhry as chief justice. There had been previous instances of the judiciary defying the military coup leaders—such as granting bail to Prime Minister Zulfikar Ali Bhutto against the wishes of the Zia ul-Haq regime—but the judiciary had also validated military rule, famously in the judgment supporting Ayub Khan's regime. The developments of 2007 indicate an increasingly assertive, independent role for Pakistan's Supreme Court. In particular the struggle over *de facto* and *de jure*—exemplified in judicial reasoning over judicial processes when Musharraf's suspension of Chaudhry was declared illegal—highlights the broader problem of political legitimacy in a developing polity: When are executive ordinances acceptable, and when are they usurpations of rightful rule? As an arbiter of constitutionality, the judiciary has sought to assert its role in offering authoritative answers.

Since the 1973 constitution, Pakistan's legislature has been bicameral. In its form under the Eighteenth Amendment passed in 2010, the legislature includes a senate of 104 members, and a national assembly of 342 members. In the national assembly, 272 seats are directly elected through a single-member district system (each constituency elects one person among competing candidates). The remaining seats in the assembly are reserved for non-Muslim minorities and women, and assigned to the parties according to their share of the directly elected seats; for example, a party that won half the seats in the direct elections would have half the remaining seats (an indirect proportional representation system).

Constitutionally, Pakistan is a federation, and has representation in the senate from four provinces (Sindh, Balochistan, Punjab, and Khyber Pakhtunkhwa [KPK], formerly known as NWFP), the Federally Administered Tribal Areas, and the Islamabad Capital Territory. Senators are chosen by provincial assemblies and by those national assembly members representing the Federally Administered Tribal Areas and the Islamabad Capital Territory. Senators serve six-year terms.

In the senate, each province has 14 general seats, four seats reserved for women, four seats reserved for technocrats (including *ulama*, or religious scholars), and one seat for non-Muslims. FATA has eight seats and the ICT has four seats in the senate. In comparison, Punjab's share of directly elected seats in the national assembly (148, compared to 61 for Sindh, 35 for Khyber Pakhtunkhwa, 14 for Balochistan, 12 for FATA, and 2 for the ICT) reflects the demographic balance in post-1971 Pakistan, in which Punjab dominates. Thus, the senate empowers the less populous provinces.

While Pakistan may currently be described as a parliamentary democracy, a key point of contention in the past has been the degree of presidential power. Historically, the power to dissolve the legislature greatly strengthened the president's hand, allowing him to replace independent-minded legislatures with more compliant bodies. Another period of parliamentary rule in the 1990s was replaced by a military government led by General Pervez Musharraf, who reasserted presidential authority over the legislature. The Eighteenth Amendment to the constitution, passed in 2010, removed the president's ability to unilaterally dissolve the legislature. The president's role is now limited, and largely ceremonial as head of state. The president is elected for a five-year term by an electoral college composed of the provincial assemblies, the national assembly, and the senate.

According to the "responsible party government" ideal, a party declares a particular political platform, is elected amid competition, tries faithfully to implement its proclaimed governance preferences, and then is held accountable as the public evaluates the party's performance and votes in the next election. This ideal type is far from the ground realities in Pakistan, where elected governments have not usually fulfilled their full term in office, and where horse-trading and "floor-crossing" have made official platforms appear hollow. Political parties in Pakistan are typically weak entities suffering from factionalism, low party discipline, and frequent desertions. Individual party members often seek to ally with the victor to receive some spoils. Factions are brought together for opportunistic reasons, and rivalries lead to party splits. Struggles for patronage are routine, and defections plentiful, in what may be a South-Asian pattern (Sobhan 2002). Personalities rather than platforms appear to dominate parties.

Early in its history, Pakistan lacked an integrative political party that could reach across ethnic groups and geographic regions and mobilize citizens on a national agenda. The Muslim League, whose demand had originally supported Pakistan's creation, did not provide a unified and lasting force for national coherence and mobilization. Founded in 1906, the Muslim League only became a mass party in 1939; India's Congress, in contrast, started in 1885 and was transformed into a mass party in 1920 by Gandhi. The Muslim League was dominated by Jinnah and did not have effective procedures for resolving internal conflicts and aggregating diverse interests (Rizvi 2000). The Muslim League has had various groups, such as a Pir Pagaro group, referring to the powerful Sindhi Leader Pir Pagaro. The Qaiyum Muslim League was a split-off creation from the Council Muslim League, and resulted from Abdul Qaiyum Khan's rivalry with Mumtaz Daultana (Talbot 2005).

Across the five general elections to the national assembly from 1988 to 2002, the Pakistan Muslim League (PML) won 43 percent of the seats. But this is deceptive, as it arguably functioned as a unified party only in 1993 and 1997. More often, competing factions claimed the party mantle, making the PML label closer to an "ad hoc election-driven gathering of independents," taking various factional guises (known by the factional leader's initial, such as C, J, N, and Q) (Gazdar 2008, 1). The 2008 elections in Pakistan saw the Musharraf-associated PML-Q lose significant numbers to their opposition, the PML-N (referring to Nawaz Sharif's faction). One opportunistic faction was sardonically described by detractors as "Al-Faida Group" (the benefits group)—a play on "Al-Qaeda" that captures the belief that special privileges and private benefits (rather than ideology or principled stances) drive party loyalties. The 2013 elections saw a resounding victory for the PML-N, albeit one produced primarily by votes from the Punjab, where Nawaz Sharif has his support base.

The Pakistan People's Party (PPP) was the most successful vote-getter in West Pakistan in the 1970 election. Its slogan *roti kapra aur makan* (bread, clothing, and housing) and its program of nationalizing major businesses suggest that it has a leftist, socialist orientation. It demonstrated an ability to generate votes in different provinces. Despite its name and its populist rhetoric under founder Zulfiqar Ali Bhutto, the Pakistan People's Party is more a dynastic family enterprise than an organization based on transparent, institutionalized rules. Party funds are not distributed transparently. Upward mobility within the party ranks is based predominantly on the party chief's direction (interview with Ghazi Salahuddin, March 2009). The Pakistan People's Party, although dominated by the Benazir Bhutto/Asif Zardari group, has a faction associated with Murtaza Bhutto, known as the *Shaheed* (martyr) group after he was killed.

Religious parties have not been immune; for example, the Jamiat Ulema-e-Islam's powerful faction, JUI-F, is associated with Maulana Fazlur Rehman. The Jamiat Ulema-e-Pakistan,

Jamiat Ulema-e-Islam, and the Jamaat-e-Islami are established names among religious political parties. The religious groups had generally opposed the Muslim League demand for Pakistan, and therefore "needed to reestablish their credentials as loyal citizens of the state, not to mention build political bases of support among the more religious segments of the urban lower middle-classes—the commercial and trading groups in particular" (Jalal 1990, 282). The shariat lobby in the Muslim League, as well as the Deoband ulama, quickly called for an Islamic constitution. Qasim Zaman argues that the ulama have been "custodians of change"; rather than fixed, atavistic throwbacks rigidly adhering to medieval ideas, the ulama have sought to retain authority, influence, and power by posing as gatekeepers and sole authoritative interpreters in the Islamic tradition (Zaman 2002). Moreover, in an Islamic system, the ulama would have significant veto power, as they would presumably judge whether public laws were in keeping with Islam.

Founded by the well-known ideological thinker Maulana Maududi, the Jamaat-e-Islami (JI) may be a relatively "modern" party in its institutionalized internal rules, disciplined cadres, and resilience to personalized factions. Although its proclaimed agenda is "revolutionary," in practice JI tends to be an orderly, rule-bound participant in the polity. The JI has shown tactical flexibility, such as when it supported Fatima Jinnah, a female presidential candidate, against the military ruler Ayub Khan in the 1965 elections. It is a vanguardist political party with longer-term ambitions, and a disciplined corps, as well as a middle-class support base. Furthermore, the JI's "reputation for being corruption-free, its internal democracy, and the discipline and dedication of its workers set the JI apart from other parties" (Cohen 2004, 176).

Despite its reputation for superior internal discipline, the JI's success in elections has been limited at a national level. It achieved some recent success in the local and provincial elections in NWFP as a coalition partner to the religious grouping called the Muttahida Majlis-e-Amal (MMA; the Allied Action Congregation). Yet even the JI's reputation was somewhat tainted with the appearance of nepotism when its head appointed a relative to a "reserve" seat in the legislature (interview with former MMA member 2009).

Regional and ethnic tensions can be discerned from election results, although patterns are difficult to describe as alignment or realignment because there are few data points. The 1970 elections showed what observers and citizens suspected: that East Pakistan and West Pakistan had markedly different political loyalties, and no parties won significant representation across the provinces. Provinces can contain different ethnic "segments" or concentrations; a province like Balochistan contains different ethnic segments (Balochi, Pashto, and heterogeneous) and other ethnic groups, such as Seraiki, are located in both Punjab province and NWFP. While ethnically centered political parties persist, Gazdar finds that the largest ethnic segments in Pakistan (Punjabi, Sindhi, Seraiki, and Pushto) are "healthy" in that there are parties straddling ethnic boundaries and that parochial electoral outcomes within particular segments do not persist (Gazdar 2008). The PPP and the Muslim League retain a presence in these areas.

Yet there is evidence from the electoral data that Pakistan remains regionally and ethnically fragmented, as seen in electoral "waves." The Muslim League appears dominant through its position in the Punjab, reducing the party's incentives to engage in "inter-provincial accommodation"; in contrast, the PPP relies more on both Punjab and Sindh and therefore is likely to "toe a more federalist line" (Gazdar 2008, 4). PPP wins have generally drawn on a more diversified ethnic base. Muslim League victory electoral waves (1990, 1997, 2002) appear to reduce the PPP to a Sindhi party, and PPP victory waves (1988, 1993) appear to reduce the Muslim League to a Punjabi party. There is a difference, though: Gazdar notes that "a restricted PPP still retains a presence in Punjabi and Seraiki segments, whereas a restricted Muslim League virtually disappears from Sindhi-speaking segments" (Gazdar 2008, 4). Gazdar argues that victories achieved by reliance on one ethnic group and restricting others to narrow ethnic segments risks the federation's health (Gazdar 2008).

The 2013 election engaged many first-time, younger voters, and the widespread election fever contradicted the previous image of voters as apathetic. Led by Imran Khan, a national cricket hero, Pakistan Tehreek-e-Insaaf (Pakistan Movement for Justice) saw a remarkable rise, challenging the two-party rotation of PPP and PML-N. Its effort to unseat these established forces helped galvanize voters. In a dramatic accident caught on video days before the election, Imran Khan fell from a forklift at a rally, injuring his head and back, and had to be hospitalized. His rivals sent swift good wishes with Nawaz Sharif cancelling campaigning for the day following the accident. Coming amid intense competition, these affirmations of mutual respect bode well as an informal norm supporting democratic processes. Imran Khan's party did not sweep the elections as he had predicted, but nevertheless won a respectable share of seats, making it the likely candidate to be lead the opposition in the national assembly.

Nawaz Sharif's victory in the election brought him back to power for an unprecedented third term, after a 14-year break that saw him deposed in Pervez Musharraf's military coup, with much of the time spent in exile. In a remarkable reversal, Musharraf was brought into court on various charges, after having overestimated his popularity and returned to Pakistan in an attempt to run for office. To have a former chief of army staff and military ruler answering to the judicial authorities in a civilian process was unprecedented, and suggested that the rules of the political game in Pakistan were changing. Yet the judicial process was troubled: a lead prosecutor was killed, and one case was withdrawn.

Nawaz Sharif's support is centered in his home province, the numerically dominant Punjab. The election did not break the regional identifications of political parties. Sharif has a significant support base within the business community, and he promised swift action on electric power (the country has been economically hampered by frequent blackouts and brownouts) and on fiscal deficits (Pakistan's growing external debt and low 9 percent tax-to-GDP ratio). Sharif inaugurated a plan to run ten coal-fired power plants in Balochistan, using some Chinese support, and has plans for future additional "People Power Parks." The International Monetary Fund (IMF) approved a 6.7 billion dollar loan package in 2013 to help Pakistan meet its international obligations, with 540 billion dollars made available straight away. The longer-term fulfillment of the IMF deal requires painful adjustments in Pakistan that may exacerbate unemployment, and are likely to be difficult for the Sharif government to implement. The task of increasing the country's tax-paying base (about 1 percent of the population pays direct taxes) requires shifts in both bureaucratic capacity and wider culture, and a longer-term, politically unpopular effort that has typically eluded previous governments.

## Managing conflict

Choices by political leaders in Pakistan are shaped by their effort to retain their leadership position. Cynical Pakistanis believe that politicians seek *kursi*—to obtain and retain office— above all else. Yet these choices are fraught with risks, and miscalculation has frequently dethroned leaders. For instance, Ayub assumed that India would not attack and initiated the military actions that led to the 1965 war; dissatisfaction with the war fueled anti-Ayub sentiment. Yahya Khan was advised that holding free elections in 1970 would not produce a dominant party but weak groupings that he could divide and rule; instead, a dominant party emerged in East Pakistan and another sizeable party in West Pakistan, which eventually undid both Yahya Khan and the state of Pakistan. Z.A. Bhutto promoted Zia ul-Haq, the apparently compliant officer who eventually detained and then executed him. Nawaz Sharif sought to secure his position by moving against Musharraf, which precipitated Musharraf's "countercoup." In each case, bad political advice may have contributed to poor decision making. But this also speaks to uncertainty in the polity and the apparent risk-taking that political leaders are inclined towards, if only because Pakistani politics are so opaque that it is like playing chess in the dark.

### State institutions vs. government institutions

Historians Jalal (1995) and Ziring (1997) see not a simple battle between democracy and autocracy, but rather a competition between elected and unelected institutions. A related distinction is the contest between institutions of state and institutions of government; in theory the institutions of government (such as legislatures) are supposed to formulate and legislate policy while the institutions of state (such as military and civil bureaucracies) are supposed to provide professional implementation. There are principal agent problems: as the principal, the legislature's authority is eroded if the bureaucratic agents shirk their duty or defect from their expected roles. Moreover, bureaucratic institutions can engage in the ultimate subversion by capturing government institutions, dismissing them, or replacing them.

Irrespective of whether a military or civilian regime is in power, a common argument is that five "vested groups" have stalled genuine democracy in Pakistan: the military, feudals, big business, religious leaders, and bureaucracy (Iqbal 2008). Some observers believe that private media organizations are an emerging force; Pakistan Television (PTV) monopolized television news from its creation in 1964 under Ayub until Musharraf's liberalization almost four decades later (interview with former Pakistan Television administrator Hamid Rajput, July 2009). The special privileges enjoyed by these narrow segments of the population tend to persist under different regimes because these groups are seen as crucial to the political survival of incumbents (Malik 2011). The pressures of political survival mean that whatever their stated ideology, regimes and regime leaders ensure that their policies do not alienate substantial portions of these groups. This informal background factor shapes governance in Pakistan, and helps explain the failure to deliver more public goods. A key question is whether more broadly based, sustained coalitions can emerge as vital pieces of political survival strategies; if so, they may provide the basis for more public goods provision in the country.

### Ethnic divides

Pakistan has faced ethnic resentments and ethno-nationalist tensions have been manifested in demands for provincial autonomy, for new provinces, and outright independence. The most blatant example is the secession of East Pakistan following a civil and international war in 1971. Over half the country's population split away from the original polity. This outcome resulted from more than simply the huge distance separating East from West Pakistan; it had its lineage in early aspirations for provincial autonomy and the West Pakistan-based ruling establishment's effort to retain control. The country's breakup can be understood as a failure to manage this underlying conflict. East Pakistan and some other units appeared more eager to push for a confederation than a genuine federation. There were numerous grievances, including resistance to Urdu as the national language, disputes over customs revenue collections and disbursements, and a widespread belief that policies were unjust to East Pakistan.

In 1955, the "One Unit" scheme was introduced, creating an integrated "West Pakistan Province" incorporating states and provinces, partly for parity with the populous East Pakistan. There was political resistance to the scheme. In March 1957, the East Pakistan Assembly voted for a more radical autonomy in the federation; this was resisted by national leaders Iskandar Mirza and Ayub Khan, who believed that only mild autonomy could safeguard national integrity and security (Afzal 2001). In July 1957, the West Pakistan Assembly demanded that the One Unit scheme be dissolved. Resistance to the One Unit scheme grew during the 1960s anti-Ayub movement. Under Ayub's successor Yahya Khan, West Pakistan was reconstituted into Punjab, Sindh, NWFP, and Balochistan provinces on July 1, 1970 (Rizvi 2000). This difference, fed by perceptions that West Pakistan was treating East Pakistan unfairly, escalated to a severe national crisis.

East Pakistan's regional elections had brought the East Pakistan-based Awami League to power. Yahya Khan's government held national elections, the first national, universal franchise parliamentary elections in the country's history. Yahya Khan's choice was based in part on the faulty intelligence that no political party could emerge as a dominant force. However, the 1970 elections to the national assembly produced two dominant parties: the Awami League won 160 seats from the 162 allocated to East Pakistan, and the Pakistan People's Party received about half that share in West Pakistan (Rizvi 2000). Rather than a compromise or coalition government, these regionally polarized results led to the federation's dismemberment. West Pakistan did not allow the Awami League to assume the power it had won at the polls. The PPP's support was based in West Pakistan, and it was able to cultivate support with the Pakistani military and elite. A brutal military crackdown in East Pakistan took place, and a full-fledged rebellion arose, along with Indian military engagement.

Most Awami League leaders fled to India and set up a "Government of Bangladesh" in Calcutta (Sisson and Rose 1991). A total of 7 million refugees fled to India (Talbot 1998). Bangladeshi nationalist guerrillas continued raids into East Pakistan, and increasing direct Indian interventions took place (Talbot 1998). Following Pakistani and Indian attacks on each other, Indian forces reached the outskirts of Dacca (which was to become the Bangladeshi capital). India and Pakistan announced a cease-fire on December 17, 1971. Pakistan had disintegrated, with East Pakistan effectively out of the central government's control. The result was a humiliating defeat for the Pakistan army, and the creation of Bangladesh. This was a psychological blow to Pakistani nationalism, and the Muslim unity presumed in the two-nation theory.

In independent Pakistan, there are seven tribal agencies, "frontier regions" with "administrative enclaves in six settled districts and provincial tribal areas abutting on nine settled districts" (Riaz, 2008). FATA (Federally Administered Tribal Areas) and FRs (Frontier Regions) are directly under presidential authority. The president also has final authority in PATA (Provincially Administered Tribal Areas), which are under the province's governor. Governance in the tribal areas has usually been by customary law applied by chiefs, elders, and councils called *jirga*. Frontier Crimes Regulations, a colonial-era creation, provides the governance interface between the government and the tribes. The central government's authority was restricted to communications, foreign affairs, and defense. One recurrent political issue is whether FATA can be merged with the Khyber Pakhtunkhwa (KPK) province, and what role customary law would play.

The "tribal" Pukhtuns, an ethnic group predominant in the Khyber Pukhtunkhwa province (formerly North-West Frontier Province; the name change has resulted in part from Pukhtun ethno-nationalist pressures), have posed another challenge for Pakistan's consolidation as a state. Concerned about Russian influence in Afghanistan, the British had worked to retain a *modus vivendi* with the various tribes in what were then the "unsettled areas" in the northwest. Nevertheless, there were tribal agitations that had dealt serious defeats to the British (under the Faqir of Ipi in 1936). These issues did not disappear with Pakistan's creation; several tribal leaders have sought secession. Some agitating tribes from the British era such as the Wazirs and the Mahsuds remain familiar to those analyzing the recent Taliban insurgency.

The Pukhtuns were sometimes cited as candidates for irredentism, particularly as the ethnic group has been dominant in neighboring Afghanistan. Pukhtun nationalist Wali Khan famously stated that he had been a Pukhtun for 4000 years, a Muslim for 1400 years, and a Pakistani for 40 years. This neatly summarized the identities layered in the Pukhtun regions, and suggested an order of precedence. Pukhtunwali, the unwritten code that underlies Pukhtun tribal society, emphasizes protection and hospitality toward guests and revenge for all insults, embedded within self-pride and honor (Jalal 2000). Pukhtunwali has been compared to medieval chivalry (Foust and Koogler 2008). Pukhtuns have "defied external pressures more effectively than their own internal fissures," and they are reputed for their competitive spirit and emphasis on individual identity that nevertheless "coexists with a binding communitarian code, which, when it conflicts with Islamic strictures, invariably prevails" (Jalal 2000, 26).

Wali Khan's National Awami Party (NAP) was inherited from his father Ghaffar Khan's famous Red Shirt organization, a nonviolent movement that had supported the Indian National Congress and opposed British rule. The NAP was strong in four out of six settled districts in NWPF, and had little presence in the FATA or elsewhere. The Pakhtoonistan demand had little attraction for Pukhtuns who were well integrated into the military and who were integrated economically with Punjab and Karachi (Cohen 2004). A Muhajir observer from an elite civil service background traced the large Pukhtun influx into Karachi to the time when Gohar Ayub, son of national leader Ayub Khan (a Pukhtun), held power there. Pukhtuns have subsequently come to dominate the trucking and transport sector (interview of MMA member 2009). Their "docile" labor undermined unionizing activity among shipyard workers (Khan and Jacobsen 2009). The implication was that the national leadership facilitated their ethnic group's success over others. Such perceptions point to the sense that the affinity groups who are politically favored are those with whom the leader shares ethnicity.

Religious appeals can potentially cut across ethnic lines, but ethno-nationalism and ethnic tensions remain serious challenges for any Pakistani government. Since the colonial era, the unelected institutions of state—the military, especially, and to a lesser extent, the civil service—have not recruited evenly from the population. This has exacerbated Pakistan's integration problem. As the numerically dominant province in West Pakistan and the main recruiting center for the army, Punjab enjoyed special strength. Perceived Punjabi hegemony remains a source of resentment for other units in Pakistan. Traditionally, military personnel in British India were recruited largely from the Punjab and NWFP, ostensibly because they were "sons of soil" and "martial races" (a British colonial-era notion describing an ethnic grouping primordially inclined to soldiery).

Sindhis and Balochis are underrepresented in the Army, particularly at the officer level, and this has become a major grievance (Rizvi 2000). This disproportionate ethnic representation undermines the military's image as a national force. Tensions in Sindh have been fed by highly concentrated land ownership, income inequality, resentment against Punjab's dominance, and strained relations with Urdu-speaking Mohajirs settled in urban centers. Sindhi ethno-nationalism has become more apparent since the secession of Bangladesh.

Military operations against Balochi insurgents may be tainted as attempts at ethnic domination rather than an exercise in maintaining law and order. Since the early military intervention against alleged secessionism of the princely state of Kalat (now in Balochistan), the Balochi population has experienced several insurgencies against the central government of Pakistan. High poverty rates in Balochistan, combined with the sense that the province has not been adequately compensated for its gas and other natural resources, are some underlying factors. The secessionist tone of insurgent activity has escalated, and factors such as political disappearances and repeated military interventions have further stoked tensions. The dramatic missile strike that killed senior Balochi tribal leader Nawab Akbar Bugti provides one stark example from the Musharraf regime.

### Invoking Islamic symbols

Most rulers and many aspirants to political office in Pakistan have sought to use Islam to enhance their legitimacy, undermine opposition, and to increase their authority. Military ruler Ayub Khan, not usually considered an Islamist, sought to enhance his legitimacy by mobilizing support from Sufi *pirs* when confronting his Jamaat-e-Islami supported rival, Fatima Jinnah, in the 1962 election. His successor, the hard-drinking Yahya Khan, invoked God in the 1971 war. Zulfikar Ali Bhutto referred rhetorically to "Islamic" socialism and the quest for an Islamic bomb; he also outlawed gambling and drinking, and declared Ahmadis non-Muslims in an effort to obtain religious support and divide a challenger coalition.

State "Islamization" tries to make the state legitimate "Islamically." This potentially makes it harder for oppositions to rally around an Islamization platform, and may also give the government control over social resources that were previously in the control of religious figures. This was especially prominent in the regime of Zia ul-Haq, who sought to increase the role played by Shariat Court by introducing "Islamic" provisions into the legal system, and sought to direct religious *zakat* (alms) funds through a government authority. Given the constraints from traditional landed elites who prevented land reform in Pakistan, Islamization may have been an effort to find another route to enhancing state power (Nasr 2001), although the effort has not been particularly successful in enhancing the revenues the state receives (Malik 2011).

Described as a "thoroughgoing" Islamizer (Nasr 2001) and a "revolutionary Islamist" (Husain 2003), Zia ul-Haq established the Federal Shariat Court in 1980. The well-known Hudood Ordinances of February 10, 1979 proclaimed that Islamic law would be applied to the four offences subject to *hudood* (literally, boundaries): intoxication, theft, *zina* (adultery/fornication), and *qazf* (slander or false accusation). The Offence of Zina (adultery/fornication) Ordinance provoked special controversy due to its negative consequences for women's ability to prosecute rape crimes without themselves being charged with adultery. Zia ul-Haq also added two sections to the penal code prescribing life imprisonment or death for blasphemy against the Quran or the Prophet. A troubling legacy for Pakistanis has been the rise of vigilante action against alleged blasphemers—often thin cover for mob violence against weaker groups.

In the 1980s, Zia's regime benefited from substantial American military and economic aid. The shared objective was to support the Afghan resistance to the Soviet occupation. Much of the rhetoric supporting the insurgency was drawn from Islamic symbols, notably the term *jihad* (holy struggle). Drawn from the Arab world and beyond, religious militants volunteered for the fight and gained organizational support and training. The combination of American involvement and militant interest in supporting the Afghan resistance provided substantial support to Zia's regime. The flood of weapons also contributed to the violence among criminal and political groups, creating the "Kalashnikov culture" (the Kalashnikov is a popular Soviet-era gun) blamed for numerous deaths, in Karachi especially.

Among other leaders, Benazir Bhutto visited a Sufi shrine in Lahore immediately upon her arrival from exile, and under her tenure the Pakistani-supported Taliban made major territorial gains in Afghanistan. Nawaz Sharif, who headed the Islami Jamhoori Ittehad (the Islamic Democratic Alliance) and was Zia ul-Haq's protégé from the 1980s, sought Shariat rule to enhance his control. General Pervez Musharraf, who came to power in a military coup in 2000, pursued an Islamic vision that he termed "Enlightened Moderation." The post-Musharraf era has seen fractured, continuing insurgencies by religious militants, as well as sectarian violence.

## Economy

Inheriting a substantial canal irrigation system from British India, Pakistan seemed poised for significant growth in its agricultural sector. Agriculture was the primary source of the country's national income. Pakistan also became one of the early adopters of proto-liberal economic policies under the military regime of Ayub Khan, and started to post some impressive numbers in growth of its national income. However, the growth was unequal and uneven, and this fueled significant opposition to Ayub Khan's regime, particularly after the 1965 war with India damaged Ayub's legitimacy. The civil war and loss of East Pakistan had an obvious negative effect on Pakistan's Gross Domestic Product, but likely improved its per capita national income.

Pakistan was something of a development model in the early 1960s, to the point of providing a template for development planners in South Korea. Yet the situation of the two countries has clearly reversed, as South Korea has industrialized and become an exporter of heavy manufactured goods. Some in Pakistan comment that the country reversed the experience of much of the rest of the developing world: in the 1960s, while many in the global South were experimenting with redistributive, state-centric development policies, Pakistan pursued an early economic liberalism, seeking a business-friendly climate while eschewing substantial redistribution.

In the 1970s, when disillusionment with state-owned enterprises was beginning to be felt in some other developing countries, Pakistan nationalized some privately held industry, such as shipping. The reigning People's Party regime of Z.A. Bhutto's slogan *roti, kapra, aur makaan* (bread, clothes, and housing) seemed to promise a socialist wealth redistribution. However, Z.A. Bhutto's promised land reform did not materialize; although legislated, it was selective, and could be avoided through legal devices. Bhutto himself was the scion of a landholding family in Sindh province, and had landholding elites among his support coalition, making it unlikely that full land redistribution would take place. In any case, a military coup halted the official agenda.

Large-scale land reform has not been fully implemented in Pakistan, and whether the country is "feudal" remains a subject of passionate debate. The rise of a business elite, combined with the economic clout of military foundations and retired military personnel, means that landowners have less clout than previously. Yet the economy remains elitist in the special privileges and access that the well-placed enjoy. This feeds a destabilizing situation where the growing population finds itself increasingly stressed for resources and opportunities. The global rise in food prices has pushed increasing numbers of Pakistanis below the poverty line. Climate change threatens Pakistan's economy in ways that are hard to predict. The extraordinary floods the country has seen recently created enormous social and public health disruptions.

Any mention of Pakistan's economy should include the significant role of international transfers. These include the large packages of aid that Pakistan received as a US Cold War ally. Military coup leader Ayub Khan was a close American ally, and Pakistan's membership in the South East Asia Treaty Organization (SEATO) and Central Treaty Organization (CENTO) Cold War alliances generated significant aid. Most famously under the Zia military regime of the 1980s, the Soviet invasion of Afghanistan made Pakistan a frontline state in the Cold War. Zia rejected the initial American offer of aid as "peanuts"; the follow-up American offer was magnitudes greater, making Pakistan the recipient of one of the largest ever American aid commitments. There have also been international lending packages from the IMF and other lenders.

The other side of international transfers has been private remittances from overseas Pakistani workers, from the Persian Gulf region and elsewhere. These transfers are significant in supporting investment and consumption in the domestic Pakistani market, as well as philanthropic donations and initiatives. The foreign capital also makes Pakistan particularly susceptible to international shocks—regional and global economic fluctuations that affect the income of overseas Pakistanis. For example, after the events of September 11, 2001, more scrutiny on transfers, particularly those under the informal *hawala* system, squeezed money flowing from private sources into Pakistan. At the same time, political insecurity tends to generate capital flight, particularly to the Gulf region.

As an emerging market, Pakistan holds substantial promise. Pakistan enjoys a young population, with a significant number of young, educated, usually English-speaking members of the labor force. The country also enjoys a spirit of improvisation and entrepreneurship at the local level, resulting in vibrant business and social activities. Yet this energy is not harnessed to its potential. Successive national governments have had difficulties in raising taxes, contributing to a growing public debt. Along with heavy defense spending, the underinvestment of public infrastructure in public health, education, and energy continues to be a damper on the country's development prospects. The electricity provision situation is particularly lamentable—frequent blackouts and brownouts greatly affect the costs of doing business. It is not surprising that Prime Minister Nawaz Sharif, elected in 2013, made a high profile effort to improve energy provision. This is not uncontroversial—coal-fired plants generate concerns about environmental pollution, and dams for hydroelectric power create issues for downstream water users as well as ecological externalities.

## Regional/international relations

Pakistan's foreign relations have been heavily shaped by its enduring rivalry with India. A pattern of confrontation over Kashmir has emerged. Local insurgents and the Indian and

Pakistani militaries have repeatedly clashed, escalating several times into all-out war. For Pakistan, about 15 percent the size of India and with fewer inherited resources from the British, this meant a proportionately greater defense burden on its national budget. That extraordinary concern for national security has had profound consequences for Pakistan's development, particularly the oversized role the Pakistani military plays in national political and economic decision making.

Indo-Pak relations have been peppered with border clashes, wars, and brinkmanship over Kashmir, as witnessed in the 1999 Kargil crisis, a military confrontation across the "Line of Control" that divides the territory. This has led to the region being labeled the most dangerous place in the world because of the confrontation between neighboring nuclear powers. Those who believe in the deterrent effect of nuclear weapons, however, would argue that the confrontation will not escalate to full-scale war. That proposition remains controverisal, and the 1999 Kargil clashes, which happened after both states were declared nuclear powers, as well as occasional smaller-scale clashes, continue to provide disconcerting tests.

Indian apprehension had grown since the 1963 Sino-Pakistan border agreement, which saw a portion of Pakistan-controlled *Azad* (free) Kashmir given to China. As 1964 ended, Indian officials incorporated Kashmir fully into the Indian state, removing its special or undetermined status (Brines 1968). Pakistan claims this was the precipitating factor for subsequent military hostilities, as it removed the possibility of a legal resolution of the Kashmir issue and threatened to remove it from international attention (Brines 1968).

Pakistani friction with India has continued in other ways; it is routine for each side to blame the other's covert operations for terrorism. To some, it appears that when a major incident of terror (e.g. a bombing in a marketplace) takes place in one country, a comparable incident will take place in the other country shortly thereafter—as if there is a tit-for-tat in covert attacks and counterattacks. Such mutual blame testifies to the mistrust and suspicion between the security establishment of each state. Some incidents, such as the 2008 attacks by gunmen in Mumbai, have become a major sticking point, slowing a thaw in relations. Further complicating the relationship has been India's alignment with Afghanistan, given Pakistan's sometimes-troubled relationship with its western neighbor.

Narendra Modi's victory in the 2014 Indian election and his support base of militant Hindu nationalists seems to spell deterioration in Indo-Pak relations. And it seems likely that there will be some saber rattling, at least at a rhetorical level. Paradoxically, there is an opportunity for real improvement in the relationship under Modi's rule. This is due partly to his business constituency, some of whom stand to gain from improved economic relations and access to Pakistani markets. It is also due to the fact that in the political spectrum (presuming that Congress is mildly to the left, and the BJP to the right), Modi has established his reputation among the more Islamophobic Hindu rightists in such incidents as the Gujarat pogroms, and he does not have a viable national-level rival to lose them to. As a result he does not have the same worries about mobilizing a rival coalition that someone with less Hindu nationalist credentials would. This gives Modi more bargaining room for a genuine rapprochement. Finally, an important historical legacy has been previous BJP PM Vajpayee's deal with Nawaz Sharif in the 1990s that eased travel between India and Pakistan. All these possibilities are highly contingent, and may be derailed by cross-border violence, by terror attacks blamed on Pakistan, and possibly by struggle of influence in Afghanistan.

## Box 3.2:  The Durand Line and Pakistani–Afghan relations

Pakistan's tensions with Afghanistan have some origins in a border dispute. In 1893, a treaty between British India and Afghanistan had included a border drawn by British representative Sir Mortimer Durand. Known as the Durand Line, it separated the Pushtun tribes in Afghanistan from the Pushtuns in British India (Rizvi 2000). This became West Pakistan's western border and was rejected by Afghanistan's government, leading to the Afghani refusal to support Pakistan's membership in the United Nations, and to several clashes. This border is frequently in the news today as a porous region where the Pakistani military is heavily engaged. In 1993, the British treaty expired, leading some irredentists to raise questions about the border's international legitimacy.

Afghanistan had friendly relations with tribal Pukhtuns (an ethnic group that has been dominant in Afghanistan and forms a majority in Pakistan's northwestern region). At one point, Afghanistan supported an independent Pukhtunistan (a homeland for the Pukhtun ethnic group). Afghani Prime Minister Hashim Khan suggested in 1947 that the NWFP (now Khyber Pakhtunkhwa) could join Afghanistan. There were Afghani raids and military clashes with Pakistani troops. Gandhi and the Congress had promised Afghanistan a route to the sea in return for opposing Pakistan. In early 1948, an emissary from the Afghan King tried unsuccessfully to convince Jinnah to grant sovereignty to the tribal belt.

Diplomatic tensions rose in 1955 when Pakistan moved to incorporate North-West Frontier Province into the "One Unit Scheme of West Pakistan," rejecting Afghani objections as meddling in internal Pakistani affairs. Relations with Afghanistan were resumed in 1957 only to break again in 1961 before resuming again in 1963 (Rizvi 2000). The status of the Durand Line, originally an arrangement with British India and the basis for the Pakistani–Afghanistan international border, remains controversial, and is sometimes questioned publicly in Afghanistan. The porousness of the border, which served the fight against the USSR in the 1980s, poses a difficult challenge for those seeking to manage conflict in Afghanistan. More recently, Pakistan-based networks supporting Afghani insurgents have contributed to tensions with the Afghan government, amid allegations that the networks are a covert tool of Pakistani foreign policy.

Pakistan's relationship to the United States has seen close security cooperation as well as tensions. Not long after its founding, Pakistan entered into a Cold War alliance with the United States through such American-aligned security arrangements as CENTO and SEATO. Ayub Khan's military coup in 1958 forestalled the Constituent Assembly's drafted constitution and thwarted planned elections. His military regime was able to survive in part because of substantial Cold War-era aid from the United States. Yet the Pakistani security establishment perceived that in national war crises, such as the 1965 war and the 1971 war, the United States dropped its support. Pakistan acted as a secret conduit for US contacts with China, providing logistical support for the secret travel that eventually led to the opening in US-Chinese relations in the 1970s. In the 1980s, Pakistan was an American partner in supporting Afghan resistance to the Soviet Union's military presence. India was not in the American Cold War camp. This alignment may be changing with American pressure on

Pakistan to not test nuclear weapons after India's tests in 1998, concern that Pakistan's interests in Afghanistan are diverging from the US agenda, continuing drone strikes in Pakistan, and tensions over the US killing of Osama bin Laden in Pakistan. Recent years have seen a notable decline in security cooperation. Pakistan has continued relatively warm relations with China (partly driven by conflicts each country has had with India); this presents an additional twist in Pakistani-American relations.

A key question is the degree to which outside powers (originally the British and primarily the United States) remain powerful in Pakistan. With independence, the viceroy's official influence ended, but that did not mean an end to outside influence. For instance, when the Governor-General dismissed the Constituent Assembly in 1954, the Speaker tried to appeal to the Queen, showing the belief that outside power still mattered (she did not respond). It is commonly believed that American-friendly Ayub Khan's rising prominence and national leadership was enabled by the United States. Opponents who saw General Musharraf as US President Bush's lackey berated him with the derogatory label "Busharraf." A popular novel, *A Case of Exploding Mangoes*, includes a darkly comic scene in which an ambitious military general misreads the US Ambassador's comments over a football game as encouragement for a coup (Hanif 2008).

International financing plays a key role in Pakistani state resources. Aside from bilateral aid, especially military aid, IMF loans are regularly sought to relieve Pakistan's budgetary crises. Thus outside forces remain powerful in Pakistani leaders' and challengers' strategic calculus. A memorable line summarizing the "political survival" versus "ideology" dilemma came from General Pervez Musharraf to explain his policy U-turn on Afghanistan and the Taliban after the American "global war on terror" was declared. "National interest" (a key symbol in political philosophy, used to appeal and motivate people), he said, had not changed and does not change; however, "the environment" had changed. He did not mention what most observers understood—that his political survival was under serious threat unless he complied with US wishes, and that compliance would bring needed resources and outside support to the military regime.

## Opportunities and constraints

Consider an incumbent leader reviewing leadership in Pakistan's history. Being a national leader can be hazardous. Liaquat Ali Khan was assassinated. Ayub Khan abdicated when ill and pressured to do so by Yahya Khan. Zulfikar Ali Bhutto was detained and then executed. Many have expressed the belief that Zia ul-Haq, who died in a plane crash, was assassinated. Nawaz Sharif and Benazir Bhutto were both charged with crimes, and faced detention or exile; Benazir Bhutto was assassinated. Pervez Musharraf faced assassination attempts. A prominent business executive joked that Pakistan routinely "exports" its leaders, either to Allah or to outside countries (Interview, 2009). Accountability is low: Liaquat Ali Khan's assassination remains mysterious, as does Zia ul-Haq's plane crash; the Hamoodur Rehman Commission's investigation into the events leading up to Bangladesh's secession were not made public for decades, and responsible figures were not held to account; and Benazir Bhutto's assassins have not been brought to account through a transparent process. In this context, Nawaz Sharif's return to elected office, after being deposed, jailed, and exiled, is noteworthy. So is Musharraf's attempt to reenter politics in 2013; but he was barred from doing so, was placed under arrest, and his future remains unclear. Constitutional instability has reigned in Pakistan, and in that context, the military has been a powerful, organized, persistent force, emerging swiftly from secondary status beneath the civil administration (under the early civilian governments, and the government of powerful civil servant Ghulam Mohammad). Article 58 (2) (b) (a controversial constitutional power permitting the executive to dismiss the legislature and government) was quashed by the 2010 Eighteenth Amendment to the Constitution) represents one step in a difficult political evolution that seeks to both constrain the military's involvement in domestic politics while also recognizing that completely sidelining the military will produce another military coup when military interests are threatened. The military has entrenched its role in civil society through its foundations, businesses, and strategically posted retired personnel.

In Pakistan, the rules of the game are evolving. Most political actors try to rewrite the rules in their favor. The feuding over Article 58 (2) (b) captures this rather well. In practice, the military coup is clearly one selection mechanism for leadership, having launched three military rulers who have governed directly for much of Pakistan's history. Military backdoor influence is another. Judicial judgment seems to be a method also—as when both Ghulam Ishaq Khan and PM Nawaz Sharif were forced to resign, in a deal that was facilitated by the Chief of Army Staff.

Pakistan, as noted above, is threatened with secessionist attempts partly due to national governance tainted by provincial rivalries. Whether the military will successfully repress separatists is an open question. In this context, one possibility raised by analysts and observers is that Pakistan might break up into several smaller countries, such as Balochistan, Pashtunistan, Sindh, and Punjab. This remains unlikely because the military is still the dominant force-holder, and is strongly committed to a united Pakistan. Nevertheless, it is telling that Benazir Bhutto's coffin was draped not in a Pakistani flag but in a flag from her party, even though she had been PM twice. Also, the post-Benazir PPP leadership (mainly her husband, Asif Zardari, although he also named her son Bilawal as co-chair) affirmed its commitment to the Pakistani federation; this would have been unnecessary if there was no question about Pakistan's unity.

A widespread belief is that "agencies"—referring typically to Inter-Services Intelligence (ISI, military) and Intelligence Bureau (IB, civilian)—were actively involved in manipulating ethnic, sectarian, and other leaders and organizations. In 2012, the Pakistan Supreme Court found military intelligence had illegally intervened in the 1990 election. According to a former provincial assembly member, these agencies are driven by "hyper-patriots" who believe they are best able to judge the national interest, and their mission justifies law-breaking, conspiracy, and violence, often creating unintended consequences, in what might elsewhere be called "blowback" (Interview, 2009).

In civil-military relations, power continues to be skewed heavily in the military's favor. Pakistani judiciary and lawyers mobilized recently in protest against heavy-handed military interventions and its refusal to abide by Supreme Court decisions. This showed a broad wish among Pakistan's professional classes for curtailing the military's role in national politics and for the rule of law. However, the military remains a dominant player in security matters, and has obtained significant international (mainly US) support during the Cold War and later the "war on terror." Civil society in Pakistan is fragmented; rural landowners continue to be powerful members of the elite; there is a small industrialist class that has some weight; religious forces are diverse and internally divided into factions. These factors indicate that the military will continue to be the key player in the future, and that small opposition groups will likely continue their resort to political violence.

Poverty and low living standards have occupied development planners in Pakistan. Education—a key contributor to economic well-being and social mobility—has suffered, partly due to corruption and partly due to government budgets squeezed by defense and debt-servicing burdens. Public health has faced similar challenges. Perhaps the greatest constraints facing Pakistan are developmental—opportunities to advance through merit are few, as connections matter more; persistent shortfalls in providing necessary public goods render insecure the population's longer-term well-being, affecting mobility, institutions, jobs, and resilience in the face of increasing challenges related to climate change and resource scarcity. A large, marginalized, uneducated segment of the population with few prospects for success may provide a growing pool from which revolutionary groups may draw members.

The elitism that has privileged the military, powerful landowning families, civil bureaucratic staffers, wealthy business interests, and some religious groupings has kept much of Pakistan's population to the political sidelines. Uncertainty, instability, rigged elections, political horse-trading, and military-bureaucratic dominance have meant that a significant component in the population feel disenfranchised. Low historical voter turnout in Pakistan also suggests that people do not have much faith in elections. Noncompliance with taxes, and general disregard for public policy pronouncements, also suggest that a high proportion in Pakistan feel disenfranchised. Continuing unease about national integrity and the strength of Pakistan's unity as a federation recurs in ethno-nationalist postures adopted by leaders and organizations. There are also revolutionary postures taken by sectarian religious organizations, such as the Pakistani Taliban and other groups located in the tribal areas bordering Afghanistan. Alienation from the official institutional processes of government helps provide recruits for such militant entities.

Mobilizing a broad national coalition to provide sustained political backing for development is thus made more difficult. Stable turnover in office through the democratic process and the experience of repeat elections may help produce more responsible party government. The norm in Pakistan until 2008, however, has been removal of governments before their official terms are over. The path-breaking 2013 elections, hopefully, herald a shift.

## Political chronology

1940:  Lahore Resolution by Muslim League.
1947:  Pakistan created.
1948:  Jinnah dies.
1948:  Kashmir war between India and Pakistan.
1951:  Liaquat Ali Khan assassinated.
1953:  Sectarian disturbances; Ahmaddis targeted in Punjab and elsewhere.
1954:  Governor-General Ghulam Muhammad dismisses Constituent Assembly; Pakistan joins South East Asia Treaty Organization.
1955:  Pakistan joins Central Treaty Organization.
1958:  Ayub Khan's military coup.
1962:  Ayub introduces Constitution featuring Presidentialism.
1965:  India-Pakistan war.
1970:  First elections on universal franchise; E. Pakistan based Awami League gets most votes overall, while PPP gets most votes in W. Pakistan.
1971:  Civil war/Pakistan-India war; E. Pakistan secedes, becomes Bangladesh.
1973:  Z.A. Bhutto, PPP leader, heads government under a Constitution based on parliamentary democracy.
1977:  Zia ul-Haq leads a military coup, Z.A. Bhutto detained.

1979:   Z.A. Bhutto is executed, after being found guilty of murder, in a controversial judicial decision.

1979:   Soviet forces enter Afghanistan in large numbers, and Pakistan begins to supply the anti-Soviet insurgency, with support from the US.

1984:   Movement for Restoration of Democracy, anti-Zia ul-Haq coalition led by Z.A. Bhutto's daughter Benazir Bhutto, boycotts presidential referendum.

1985:   Martial law lifted.

1986:   Benazir Bhutto returns to Pakistan, leads PPP.

1988:   Zia killed in plane incident; Benazir Bhutto becomes Prime Minister following elections.

1990:   Benazir Bhutto dismissed by President Ghulam Ishaq Khan on allegations of corruption.

1991:   Nawaz Sharif in office as Prime Minister.

1993:   Nawaz Sharif and President Ghulam Ishaq Khan both resign in army-brokered deal: Benazir Bhutto re-elected under general elections; becomes Prime Minister.

1996:   President Leghari dismisses PM Benazir Bhutto on corruption charges.

1997:   General elections; Nawaz Sharif returns to office of Prime Minister.

1998:   Following Indian nuclear tests, Pakistan conducts its own nuclear tests.

2000:   General Pervez Musharraf unseats PM Sharif in a military coup; goes on to introduce "Legal Framework Order" as basic law for country.

2002:   General elections; leading politicians Nawaz Sharif and Benazir Bhutto are both in exile.

2007:   Following a Supreme Court challenge to his election as President, Musharraf dismisses Chief Justice Iftikhar Chaudhry; Supreme Court reinstates Chaudhry to office after several months. Constitutional suspension lifted; Nawaz Sharif and Benazir Bhutto return to Pakistan; Bhutto assassinated in December.

2008:   Musharraf resigns as President, threatened by possible impeachment; general elections make PPP the leading party; Yusuf Raza Gilani becomes Prime Minister and Benazir Bhutto's widower Asif Zardari becomes President.

2010:   Widespread monsoon flooding of unprecedented severity in country's history; Eighteenth Amendment to the constitution restores parliamentary supremacy.

2011:   Osama bin Laden killed by US forces in Abbottabad.

2012:   Yusuf Raza Gilani forced out of office by contempt of court charge; replaced by Raja Pervaiz Ashraf. Girls' education activist Malala Yousufzai shot by Taliban.

2013:   Musharraf returns to Pakistan to stand for elections, but is barred from politics and placed under arrest. 2013 elections make history, as one democratically elected government serves its full five-year term and is replaced by another elected government.

2014:   Nawaz Sharif continues in his third turn as prime minister. Musharraf on trial for treason. Assault on Karachi airport by Taliban-linked persons. Peace talks with Taliban collapse, and Army undertakes major operation in northwest. Malala Yousufzai wins the Nobel Peace Prize.

2015:   Deaths of American and Italian hostages in CIA drone strike highlight inaccuracy and frequent civilian casualties. Human rights activist Sabeen Mahmud killed in Karachi. China promises multi-billion investment in Pakistan as part of "Silk Road" economic corridor connecting China to the Middle East.

## Political parties

| Name | Description |
| --- | --- |
| Pakistan Muslim League (PML) | Descended from the Muslim League in British India that advocated for Pakistan in the "Pakistan Resolution" of 1940; has split into factions, such as the powerful PML-N, under former Prime Minister Nawaz Sharif, a steel industry magnate. Usually described as center-rightist in orientation, favoring business. |
| Pakistan People's Party (PPP) | Founded by Zulfikar Ali Bhutto; later led by his daughter Benazir Bhutto, and presently headed by her son Bilawal and her husband Asif Zardari. Considered to be leftist in orientation, at least in its original incarnation in the 1970s. |
| Jamaat-e-Islami (JI) | Islamic revivalist party founded by Maulana Maududi. |
| Jamiat Ulema-e-Islami (JUI) | The Assembly of Islamic Religious Scholars; a traditionalist Islamic political party with a lineage to the Deobandi sect; split into factions, notably JUI-F, associated with Fazlur Rehman. |
| Jamiat Ulema-e-Pakistan (JUP) | The Assembly of Religious Scholars of Pakistan; a traditionalist Islamic political party with a lineage to the Barelvi sect. |
| Muttahida Qaumi Movement (MQM) | United National Movement; originally Muhajir Qaumi Movement (Migrant National Movement); a party based largely in urban Sindh, particularly Karachi, that originally represented Urdu-speaking migrants from India, and has sought to appeal to other ethnic constituencies. |
| Awami National Party (ANP) | The People's National Party; a political party rooted in the Pukhtun ethnic group, and with a lineage to Ghaffar Khan, a pre-partition political organizer and Gandhi ally. |
| Balochistan National Party (BNP) | Works for Balochi interests, particularly in critiquing central government policies toward Balochistan, specifically military interventions in the province that have been associated with political killings, disappearances, and recurrent insurgency. |
| Pakistan Tehreek-e-Insaaf (PTI) | Pakistan Justice Movement; led by national cricket hero Imran Khan, this party has attempted to build support for itself for the 2013 elections, and has taken an anti-corruption stance. |

## Works cited

Afzal, M. Rafique. 2001. *Pakistan: History and Politics, 1947–1971*. Oxford: Oxford University Press.

Akhtar, Rafique. 1992. *Pakistan Year Book (1992–1993)*. Twentieth Edition. Karachi, Pakistan: East and West.

Almeida, Cyril. 2008. "The Supremacy Myth." *Dawn* (April 8): 7.

Bashir, Javed. 2008. *A tidal wave*. Book review of Osama Siddique's *The Jurisprudence of Dissolutions: Presidential Power to Dissolve Assemblies under the Pakistani Constitution and Its Discontent. Dawn Books and Authors* (June 22): 6–7.

Brines, Russell. 1968. *The Indo-Pakistani Conflict*. London: Pall Mall Press.

Bulliet, Richard. 2004. *The Case for Islamo-Christian Civilization*. New York: Columbia University Press.

Cohen, Stephen P. 2004. *The Idea of Pakistan*. Washington, DC: Brookings Institution Press.

Foust, Joshua, and Jeb Koogler. 2008. "Myth in Al-Qaeda's Home," *The Christian Science Monitor* (July 10). Downloaded on August 4, 2008 from http://news.yahoo.com/s/csm/20080710/cm_csm/ykoogler.

Ganguly, Sumit. 1994. *The Origins of War in South Asia: The Indo-Pakistani Conflicts since 1947*, 2nd ed. Boulder: Westview Press.

Gazdar, Haris. 2008. "Health of the Federation." *Dawn* (February 13).

Hanif, Mohammed. 2008. *A Case of Exploding Mangoes*. New York: Alfred Knopf.

Harrison, Selig S., Paul H. Kreisberg, and Dennis Kux. 1999. "Introduction." In *India and Pakistan: The First Fifty Years*, edited by Selig S. Harrison, Paul H. Kreisberg, and Dennis Kux. Cambridge: Cambridge University Press.

Husain, Ishrat. 2000. *Pakistan: The Economy of an Elitist State*. Oxford: Oxford University Press.

Husain, Mir Zuhair. 2003. *Global Islamic Politics*. New York: Longman.

Iqbal, Ali. 2008. "Feudals and Pirs." Book Review of *Pakistan Kay Siyasi Waderay* by Aqeel Abbas Jafri. *Dawn Books and Authors* (June 15), p. 11.

Jalal, Ayesha. 1990. *The State of Martial Rule: The Origins of Pakistan's Political Economy of Defense*. Cambridge: Cambridge University Press.

———. 1995. "Conjuring Pakistan: History as Official Imagining" *International Journal of Middle East Studies* 27 (1) (February): 73–89.

———. 2000. *Self and Sovereignty: Individual and Community in South Asian Islam since 1850*. New York: Routledge.

———. 2008. *Partisans of Allah: Jihad in South Asia*. Cambridge: Harvard University Press.

Joshi, Vijay, and I. M. D. Little. 1994. *India: Macroeconomics and Political Economy 1964–1991*. Delhi: Oxford University Press.

Kavic, Lorne J. 1967. *India's Quest for Security: Defence Policies, 1947–1965*. Berkeley: University of California Press.

Khan, Sayeed Hasan, and Kurt Jacobsen. 2008. "A New Political Party Needed." *Dawn* (September 17). Retrieved from www.dawn.com/2008/09/17/op.htm. Accessed July 2009.

Khan, Sayeed Hasan, and Kurt Jacobsen. 2009. "Political culture of Pakistan." *Dawn* (August): 7.

Malik, Anas. 2011. *Political Survival in Pakistan: Beyond Ideology*. New York: Routledge

———. 2014. "Pakistan in 2014: A Milestone in Democratic Transition." *Asian Survey* 54 (1) (January/February): 177–189

Migdal, Joel. 1988. *Strong Societies and Weak States: State-Society Relations and State Capabilities in the Third World*. Princeton, NJ: Princeton University.

Nasr, Seyyed Vali Reza. 2001. *Islamic Leviathan: Islam and the Making of State Power*. New York: Oxford University Press.

National Assembly of Pakistan. (2012). *The Constitution of the Islamic Republic of Pakistan*. (As modified up to February 28, 2012). Islamabad. Retrieved from www.na.gov.pk/uploads/documents/1333523681_951.pdf. Accessed June 20, 2015.

Raza, Rafi. 1997. "Introduction: The Genesis of Pakistan" in *Pakistan in Perspective 1947–1997*, edited by Rafi Raza. Karachi, Pakistan: Oxford University Press.

Rehman, I. A. 2008. "The Trichotomy Myth." *Dawn* (March 20): 7.

Riaz, Mohammed. 2008. "Merger of Fata with NWFP Not Easy." *Dawn* (March 25). Accessed June 20 2015, retrieved from www.dawn.com/news/1071033

Rizvi, Hasan Askari. 2000. *The Military & Politics in Pakistan, 1947–1997*. Lahore: Sang-e-Meel Publications.

Siddiqa, Ayesha. 2007. *Military, Inc.: Inside Pakistan's Military Economy*. London: Pluto Press.

Siddiqui, Kalim. 1972. *Conflict, Crisis, and War in Pakistan*. New York: Praeger.

Sisson, Richard, and Leo E. Rose. 1991. *War and Secession: Pakistan, India, and the Creation of Bangladesh*. Berkeley: University of California Press.

Sobhan, Rehman. 2002. "South Asia's Crisis of Governance: Avoiding False Solutions." In *The South Asian Challenge*, edited by Khadija Haq. Oxford: Oxford University Press.

Talbot, Ian. 1998. *Pakistan: A Modern History*. New York: St. Martin's Press.

———. 2005. *Pakistan: A Modern History*. Expanded and Updated Edition. New York: Palgrave Macmillan.

Wolpert, Stanley. 2006. *Shameful Flight: the Last Years of the British Empire in India*. New York: Oxford University Press.

Zafar, S. M. 2000. "Constitutional Developments in Pakistan, 1997–99." In *Pakistan*, edited by Craig Baxter, Charles Kennedy et al. Oxford: Oxford University Press.

Zaman, Muhammad Qasim. 2002. *The Ulama in Contemporary Islam: Custodians of Change*. Princeton: Princeton University Press.

Ziring, L. 1988. "Public Policy Dilemmas and Pakistan's Nationality Problem: The Legacy of Zia ul-Haq." *Asian Survey* 28 (8) (August).

———. 1997. *Pakistan in the Twentieth Century: a Political History*. Karachi, Oxford, New York, Delhi: Oxford University Press.

## Recommended texts

Hanif, Muhammad. 2008. *A Case of Exploding Mangoes*. Knopf.

Inskeep, Steven. 2012. *Instant City: Life and Death in Karachi*. New York: Penguin.

Jalal, Ayesha. 1985. *The Sole Spokesman: Jinnah, the Muslim League and the Demand for Pakistan*. Cambridge: Cambridge University Press.

Jalal, Ayesha. 2014. *The Struggle for Pakistan: A Muslim Homeland and Global Politics*. Harvard University Press.

Malik, Anas. 2011. *Political Survival in Pakistan: Beyond Ideology*. London, New York: Routledge.

Siddiqa, Ayesha. 2007. *Military, Inc.: Inside Pakistan's Military Economy*. London: Pluto Press.

# 4  Bangladesh

*Ali Riaz*

Bangladesh is the youngest nation-state in South Asia. It emerged as an independent country in 1971 after experiencing a genocide that cost an estimated three million lives. The nine-month long war devastated the country and saw thousands of women raped and millions displaced. The Pakistani army's defeat in December 1971 and the return from a Pakistani prison of Sheikh Mujibur Rahman, the undisputed leader of the Bengali nationalist movement, in January 1972, marked a euphoric beginning for the nation. But since then the country has seen tumultuous times, with people's democratic aspiration reflected in popular movements against military dictators and authoritarian rulers amidst massive participation in elections even as their expectations are raised and dashed in quick succession.

A long list of elements favorable to democracy can be found in Bangladesh: ethnic homogeneity, high levels of political participation, democratic aspirations, a plethora of political parties, a growing middle class, moderate rates of economic growth, a vibrant civil society, a well-written constitution, periodic elections, an elected parliament, and relatively free media. Yet democracy has remained under stress. The weakness in the rule of law and lack of accountability and transparency in government are mainly responsible for the country's democratic regression.

## History and political development

In the past 42 years Bangladesh has undergone a variety of systems of governance—from a Westminster-style parliamentary government to one-party presidential rule to a multi-party presidential system. These can be categorized as the era of populist authoritarianism (1972–75), the era of military dominated rule (1975–90), the era of representative democracy (1991–2006), the era of unsuccessful reform (2007–08), the era of democracy redux (2009–13), and the era of flawed democracy (2014–to date). The country has also invented a unique system of its own called the caretaker government (CTG).

### Era of populist authoritarianism (1972–75)

The Awami League (AL) won the general elections in Pakistan in 1970 and formed a government-in-exile (April 1971–December 1971) that assumed state power in post-independence Bangladesh. The promise of an inclusive democracy and a just society marked the beginning of the regime; and policies such as nationalization and pledges of land reforms were matched with socialist and egalitarian rhetoric that demonstrated the regime's populist agenda. Sheikh Mujibur Rahman, the head of the government, was an embodiment of the populist leader given his mesmerizing oratory, simple lifestyle, and dedication to an independent Bangladesh.

However, the failure to deliver economic success, check the deterioration of law and order, address rampant corruption, and deal with the excesses of party members decreased the regime's appeal within a very short time. In the face of growing economic and political crises, especially the growth of the opposition and the waning of ideological hegemony, the regime drifted toward coercive measures. The ruling party also utilized its overwhelming majority in parliament to manipulate the constitution. Parliament thus became a tool for legitimizing the government's coercive actions instead of being a forum for discussion and debate about the country's future direction. Manipulation of the constitution and the electoral process, the passing of repressive laws, the establishment of a paramilitary force named the Jatiya Rakkhi Bahini (JRB, the National Defense Force) with enormous power, and recourse to the military to solve law and order problems were the early and concrete indications of this shift towards authoritarianism under Mujib.

The first general election held in March 1973 was marred by intimidation of political opponents and abuse of government power to sway votes in favor of the AL. The disunity among opposition political parties and their failure to present any pragmatic alternative program to that of the AL weakened the opposition's appeal. The ruling party utilized the state-controlled mass media, including radio and television, as a virtual "party-spokesman." Yet Sheikh Mujibur Rahman enjoyed the people's confidence and was called *Bangabandhu* (Friend of Bengal).

One of the AL's major accomplishments in the early days of independence was the framing of a constitution in less than seven months. The constitution was adopted by the Constituent Assembly on November 4, 1972 and came into effect on December 16, 1972. The constitution encapsulated the four fundamental principles of the state: democracy, secularism, nationalism, and socialism. The salient features of the constitution include the introduction of a Westminster-type parliamentary system, providing the parliament with supreme authority on important issues like declaration of, or participation in, war and imposing and collecting taxes. Additionally, the constitution made provisions that appeared to guarantee the fundamental rights of the people and the separation of the judiciary from the executive. But it also contained provisions that enabled the government to act in an undemocratic fashion (Riaz 2005, 170–74).

The democratic spirit of the constitution was delivered a serious blow on September 22, 1973 when the ruling party amended the constitution and incorporated provisions relating to preventive detention and proclamation of a state of emergency. This partly allowed the government to detain anyone for an initial period of six months in order to prevent that person from engaging in any action that, in the opinion of the government, constituted a threat to public safety and the sovereignty of the state. This amendment allowed the president to issue a proclamation of emergency, make laws inconsistent with the fundamental rights enshrined in the constitution, and suspend the court's authority to enforce such fundamental rights during the period of emergency.

In late 1974, the regime officially resorted to emergency rule. The proclamation of the emergency, on December 28, 1974, essentially brought an end to parliamentary rule and the constitutional state; and the so-called Constitution Act of 1975 (Fourth Amendment) made sweeping changes, leading to one party rule with the president at the apex of the executive branch reigning supreme over the legislature and judiciary. Additionally, the amendment allowed Sheikh Mujibur Rahman to be elected to parliament as president for the next five years with an opportunity to hold office for an unlimited term. Authoritarianism was thus enshrined in the constitution, although some analysts argue that the government was compelled in this direction due to "the awesome constraints which a war-ravaged country and a political scene riddled with diverse and conflicting social groups imposed on Mujib and the Awami League government" (Jalal 1995, 85).

The era of populist authoritarianism came to an end with a high price. On the morning of August 15, 1975, Mujib, most of the members of his family, and his close associates were brutally murdered in a military coup, which led to a prolonged era of military-dominated regimes in Bangladesh.

### Era of military-dominated rule (1975–90)

The 15 years of military rule saw two strongmen—Ziaur Rahman (1975–81) and Hossain Muhammad Ershad (1982–90)—dominate the political scene of Bangladesh, but the nature and course of politics under their rule was virtually identical. These regimes faced similar crises and adopted similar policies to earn legitimacy and sustain themselves in power. While there were attempts to civilianize the regimes, and one brief interregnum (June 1981–March 1982), both regimes were characterized by repression, curtailment of democratic rights, and the manipulation of constitutional processes that brought religion into the political arena.

The brutal coup of August 15, 1975 was followed by 84 days of chaos and confusion, coups and counter coups, killings and counter-killings, and conspiracy and uprising that paved the way for the rise of Ziaur Rahman (commonly referred to as Zia) as the strongman. "Zia's success, it appears, was due mainly to the fact that, despite his pre-eminent stature in the military elite, until the decisive final stages of the power struggle—in which he was, of course, a key participant—he remained without firm ideological or personal commitments" (Peiris 1998, 51). In the meantime, the coup-makers made it clear that they did not subscribe to the secularist principles of the Mujib regime.

During this time four national leaders (Syed Nazrul Islam, Tajuddin Ahmed, Monsur Ali, and Kamruzzaman) and several army officials were murdered. The killers of Mujib (and his family and associates) were provided with indemnity through an executive order, purged bureaucrats associated with the Pakistan administration in different capacities during the 1971 war of liberation were allowed back into policy-making positions, and the organizers of the August coup were given safe passage outside the country (Lifschultz 1979; Riaz 2005).

Although Ziaur Rahman did not assume the presidency until 1977 he emerged as the de facto ruler of the country from November 7, 1975. Until 1978 the regime faced periodic rebellions within the army. These rebellions were dealt with by large-scale summary executions. For instance, at least 1,100 military personnel were executed after an abortive coup in 1977 (Makeig 1989).

In the face of violent opposition from within the military, Zia sought both political and constitutional legitimacy to his rule. To gain political legitimacy he amended the fundamental principles of the constitution and charted a new course for the country. These amendments, proclaimed through an executive order (Second Proclamation Order no. 1, April 23, 1977), included redefining the state principles, and identifying the citizens as "Bangladeshi" as opposed to Bangalee (Bengali). The most important element of these changes was Islamization of the constitution and the polity. The word "secularism," appearing in the Preamble and Article 8 as one of the four fundamental principles, was substituted with "absolute trust and faith in the Almighty Allah"; and a new clause (1A) was inserted to emphasize that "absolute trust and faith in almighty Allah" should be "the basis of all actions." Additionally, the words *Bismillah-ar-Rahman-ar-Rahim* (In the name of Allah, the Beneficent, the Merciful) were inserted above the Preamble.

Along with the process of ideological legitimation, concrete steps to gain constitutional legitimacy were initiated by the Zia regime. A referendum on his presidency in 1977 and a presidential election and the organization of a political party in 1978 were intended to provide the regime with a semblance of legitimacy. But the elections were blatantly rigged, which hardly bolstered the regime's image.

Executive orders issued between 1976 and 1979 removed the ban on forming political parties based on religious ideology and allowed individuals who had collaborated with the Pakistani army in 1971 to participate in politics. One of the key steps was the promulgation of the Political Parties Regulations (PPR) Act in July 1976, which required all political parties to register with the government and restricted their functioning (e.g. regulating scale and location of meetings). Scores of new parties emerged. The Islamists, especially those who were members of parties like the Jamaat-i-Islami (JI) prior to independence, rallied under the banner of a newly formed party, the Islamic Democratic League (IDL), which became the fountainhead of a new Islamist movement in Bangladesh.

The newly founded political party under the auspices of the government—the Bangladesh Nationalist Party (BNP)—brought together an array of anti-AL political forces ranging from radical leftists to defectors from other parties to those who opposed the war of liberation and others who had close connections with religious organizations. This combine carved out a space in the political landscape of the country and cultivated a support base within the populace, but the landslide victory of the BNP in the 1979 parliamentary election (207 out of 300 seats) was far greater than the support base could have delivered without the direct assistance of the administration. Nevertheless, the Fifth Amendment to the constitution passed by parliament in 1979 provided constitutional legitimacy to the regime and incorporated the Islamization provisions into the constitution. Zia, however, was assassinated in May 1981 in an abortive military coup.

Within 10 months the then Army Chief General Hussain Muhammad Ershad usurped power through a coup and faced a legitimacy crisis similar to that of the Zia regime of 1975. Ershad diligently tried to tread Zia's path—forming a party (1984), holding of a referendum (1985), and conducting parliamentary elections (1986, 1987) and a presidential election (1986) in quick succession. But unlike Zia he faced intense challenges from various political parties that set up two alliances—one centered on the Awami League (AL) and the other on the BNP. The Islamists, particularly the Jamaat-i-Islami (JI), distanced themselves from the military ruler in a bid to gain public acceptance and participated in the pro-democracy movement, and this despite General Ershad creating another amendment to the constitution in mid-1988 that declared Islam the state religion.

The third parliament that was elected in 1986 passed the Sixth Amendment to the constitution approving the regime's actions since its takeover, thereby rendering it a legal authority from a constitutional point of view. But public discontent continued to grow and the regime's repressive measures further alienated the ruling party. When elections, boycotted by the opposition parties (e.g. 1986, 1987), failed to garner enough public support for the ruling Jatiya Party (JP, established in 1984), the regime collapsed in December 1990 in the face of a popular upsurge.

The Zia and Ershad regimes made Islam part of the political discourse and thereby legitimated Islamists—both constitutionally and politically. Their most lasting legacy was the manner in which they undermined the secular ideal.

## *Era of representative democracy (1991–2006)*

The popular uprising in late 1990 led to debates about how to transfer power from the pseudo-military regime to popular political parties. The agreement reached led to a unique transitional arrangement whereby General Ershad handed power in December 1990 to an interim government headed by the chief justice of the Supreme Court, who presided over a council of advisors comprised of eminent citizens. The interim government oversaw the election in early 1991 and transferred power to the elected BNP government. Parliament approved this extra-constitutional measure as a one-time exception in the national interest. This marked the beginning of a new phase in Bangladeshi politics—a civilian government coming to power through a free and fair election.

The defining features of Bangladeshi politics between 1991 and 2006 include the reintroduction of the parliamentary system, holding of elections at regular intervals, institutionalization of the caretaker government, incessant squabbling between the two main political parties (AL and BNP) amidst belligerent posturing, and the rise of Islamist militancy as a serious threat to stability and democracy.

The presidential system, introduced through the Fourth Amendment to the constitution in 1975, remained effective during military rule, though many other provisions pertaining to the amendment were repealed over time. The fifth parliament elected in 1991 brought in the Twelfth Amendment to reintroduce the parliamentary system of government, which was ratified through a referendum.

Four elections were held between 1991 and 2006. Of these, three were held on time and were remarkably fair, while one was highly problematic (see the section on elections). Khaleda Zia became the first woman prime minister in the history of Bangladesh when the BNP came to power in 1991 (with the tacit support of the Jamaat-i-Islami [JI]). The honeymoon between the BNP and the JI did not last long, however. The JI later joined the AL-led opposition in 1994, organized street agitation against the BNP government and its elected representatives, and resigned from parliament in concert with all other opposition members—thus forcing the untimely demise of the fifth parliament. During this time the AL kept up demands for an amendment to the constitution to make the neutral caretaker government during an election a permanent provision.

By 1995 this demand for a caretaker government became the AL's battle cry, reflecting the suspicion that the ruling party would not hold elections peacefully, fairly, and impartially. Parliament was dissolved in November 1995 ahead of schedule amidst street agitation, and new elections were held on February 15, 1996. The election, however, was boycotted by the opposition parties and was rejected by a majority of the electorate in that only 20 percent turned out to vote. Blatantly manipulated by the state machinery, the election gave the BNP a two-third majority in parliament. This was followed by massive popular unrest and an indefinite non-cooperation movement, which led to the sixth parliament being dissolved in March 1996—but not before the legislature rammed through the Thirteenth Amendment to the constitution that set up a caretaker government (CTG) to oversee elections (Kochanek 1997).

The Thirteenth Amendment stipulated that an 11-member non-party caretaker government (CTG) headed by the chief advisor would function as an interim government for 90 days once parliament was dissolved following its five-year term. The amendment calls for the immediate past chief justice to be the head of the caretaker government (while stipulating four other options for appointing the chief advisor if the immediate past chief justice was unavailable or unwilling to take up the job). If all other options proved unworkable, the president could head the caretaker government. The caretaker government would be dissolved on the date that a new prime minister assumed office. The amendment also stipulated that during the term of the interim government the defense ministry would be under the president's control, notwithstanding his status as the titular head of state (Rashid 2006; Molla 2000). Consequently, fresh elections were held under the CTG headed by the immediate past chief justice in June 1996.

The caretaker government experienced a jolt in late May when General Abu Saleh Muhammad Nasim allegedly tried to stage a coup, a charge Nasim denied. The president dismissed General Nasim and a few other high-ranking officials without consulting the chief advisor. Uncertainty gripped the country for a couple of days, with the nation fearing the return of military rule. Despite this incident, the election was held relatively peacefully. The Awami League emerged as the largest single party in the seventh parliament, although it fell short of the majority required to form the government. The unconditional support of the Jatiya Party of General Ershad ensured the return of the AL to power after 21 years. Sheikh Hasina became the prime minister, but "just as the AL refused to accept its defeat in the 1991 elections, the BNP refused to accept defeat in 1996" (Kochanek 1997, 136).

The bitter rivalry between the AL and BNP continued throughout the five years of AL rule. This notwithstanding, the Hasina regime completed its term in 2001, becoming the first government in the history of Bangladesh to do so. Power was handed over to the CTG on July 15 and the election to the eighth parliament was held on October 1, 2001. By then, the JP had split and the party had officially withdrawn its support from the government and joined hands with the BNP and the JI to form an alliance against the ruling AL. Islami Oikya Jote (IOJ), a conglomeration of seven radical Islamist parties, also became a partner of the alliance. A center-right four-party coalition was formed in late 1998 and the alliance contested the election and secured a landslide victory with a two-thirds majority. Within a week a new cabinet that included two members from the Jamaat-i-Islami (JI) was installed. The JI openly called for the establishment of an "Islamic state" in Bangladesh. While less radical than the Islami Oikya Jote (IOJ), which expressed solidarity with the Taliban regime in Afghanistan, the inclusion of the JI in government was an ironic moment for a nation that had emerged in 1971 on the basis of secular-socialistic principles, and whose first constitution imposed an embargo on the use of religion in politics.

The most worrying development of this era was the rise of Islamist militant groups, such as the Harkat-ul-Jihad al Islami Bangladesh (HUJIB) and the Jamaat-ul-Mujahideen Bangladesh (JMB, the Assembly of Holy Warriors) in various parts of the country. Although some of these organizations were clandestinely organizing during the last days of the AL regime (1996–2001), they found a hospitable environment under the four-party rule and began to engage in violent activities. In the summer of 2004 a militant group named Jagrata Muslim Janata Bangladesh (JMJB, The Awakened Muslim Masses of Bangladesh) under the leadership of Siddiqur Rahman (alias Bangla Bhai) unleashed a reign of terror in the northwestern district of Rajshahi. Despite global media coverage, the government initially refused to acknowledge the existence of this organization but finally proscribed the JMB and the JMJB. In August 2005, 450 homemade bombs exploded all over the country in the span of one hour. These events were followed by four suicide attacks over the next several months, killing at least 30 people and wounding 150 more. The victims included judges, lawyers, policemen, and journalists. Under intense international pressure the government in October 2005 banned the HUJIB, the Pakistan-based militant organization and fountainhead of all militant groups in Bangladesh. By March 2006, seven key leaders and hundreds of members of the militant network had been arrested, and by September 2006 the death sentences of seven militant leaders were confirmed by the Supreme Court.

As the term of the BNP-led coalition government neared an end in 2006, the country gradually crept toward a political crisis. The conflict between the ruling coalition and the opposition parties under the leadership of the AL began in the summer of 2006, and centered on four major issues: the head of the caretaker government; the composition of the election commission (EC), particularly the chief election commissioner (CEC); the voters list; and the politicization of the civil administration.

The inability to agree on the composition of the caretaker government (CTG) eventually led to full-blown street battles between government and opposition supporters in October 2006 and caused chaos, with general strikes and transport blockades disrupting public life, damaging public property, and causing numerous deaths. The situation took a turn for the worse when President Iajuddin Ahmed assumed the position of head of the CTG (in addition to his responsibilities as the president) and appointed a ten-member council. While this met the letter of the constitution, it was inconsistent with the spirit of the "neutral caretaker government" and added to an already volatile situation. Hectic parleys by the diplomatic corps led by US and UK envoys persuaded the opposition to join the poll, and subsequently the Grand Alliance submitted its nomination papers. But the election commission's decision to disqualify General Ershad from becoming a candidate led to the opposition withdrawing its nominations in January 2007. The subsequent clashes between the police and opposition activists became a regular event and the economy practically ground to a halt. Despite mounting domestic unrest and international concerns, the election commission, CTG, BNP, and the JI were bent on completing the unilateral polling exercise. The government, particularly the president, also rejected a call to defer the election.

### Era of unsuccessful reform (2007–08)

It was against this backdrop of increasing violence that the international community moved to put pressure on President Iajuddin Ahmed and the CTG to back down from their controversial plan to hold elections in January. The United Nations Secretary-General Ban Ki-moon stated that the political crisis in Bangladesh had "severely jeopardized the legitimacy" of the polls, the European Commission warned that it would reassess its trade relations and cooperation with Bangladesh if the government went ahead with the election, and the UN, European Union (EU), and the Commonwealth announced that they were suspending their election observation missions with immediate effect. Additionally, the UN resident coordinator in Bangladesh stated that using the armed forces to help conduct the elections could negatively impact of the military's future participation in UN peacekeeping operations, which generates substantial revenue and foreign currency for Bangladesh. All this resulted in a state of emergency (with the support of the armed forces) being declared, Iajuddin Ahmed resigning as the chief of the CTG and the cabinet he appointed being dismissed, and elections scheduled 11 days later being cancelled (Daily Star 2007; UNDP 2010). A day after these momentous events, an 11-member military-backed technocratic interim government, headed by the former chief of the central bank, was installed.

Thus large-scale bloodshed was avoided, but the nation paid a very high price—the loss of elected governance. The new arrangement, however, received public approval notwithstanding the suppression of fundamental rights. This is because the new administration was viewed as neutral and capable of making necessary political and institutional changes for democracy to function more effectively.

The military-backed caretaker government led to fears that the country was experiencing a replay of the 1975–90 period and that the military might "not bother with such niceties and declare outright martial law" (*Economist* 2007a). On the other hand, the caretaker government's promise to institute sweeping reforms to the political system and build institutions for sustainable democracy led many to feel that the developments were "not uniformly bad" given that the army had intervened "sensibly" in a "failing democracy" (*Economist* 2007b). The interim government's campaign against corruption that saw hundreds of prominent BNP and AL political leaders arrested contributed to this sentiment.

While the interim government also pledged to reform political parties, change the political culture, and free institutions like the EC and Anti-Corruption Commission (ACC) from partisan influences, the lack of a popular mandate and resistance from entrenched political interests stymied it. It may have also operated rashly, as when it sought to force into exile the AL's Sheikh Hasina and the BNP's Khaleda Zia, which led to a backlash. Ultimately, the interregnum that lasted two years dashed the hopes of those who felt the country had an unprecedented opportunity to bring about qualitative changes to its politics.

### Era of democracy redux (2009–13)

The December 2008 election was a milestone in Bangladesh's history with the Awami League–led alliance securing a landslide victory (four-fifths of parliament seats), the BNP and its allies recording its worst ever electoral defeat, the Jatiya Party (JP) headed by General H.M. Ershad regaining its position as a key player in Bangladeshi politics, and the Islamists, particularly the Bangladesh Jamaat-i-Islami, experiencing a setback. However, the 2008 elections will be remembered for reasons beyond these results: the campaign was violence free, candidates of all parties by and large adhered to strict electoral rules, participation of the voters was higher than ever before, the election-day atmosphere was festive, and the elections were free, fair, and credible (International Republican Institute 2009; United Nations Development Programme 2010).

The regime faced a serious challenge within a month of assuming power when the paramilitary Bangladesh Rifles (BDR), responsible for patrolling the borders, mutinied. According to official sources, 74 people, including 57 military officers seconded from the army, were killed. The government showed restraint and ended the rebellion through negotiations; but it caused resentment among a section of the army.

In the following years the government (and the opposition) took steps to put democracy to the test. In May 2011 the Supreme Court annulled the Thirteenth Amendment to the constitution, which had made the CTG a permanent feature of the constitution. The court also observed that the next two elections could be held under the extant system provided the judiciary was included in the CTG. Despite civil society and prominent elements of society supporting the Supreme Court's observation, the ruling AL party disposed of the provision altogether in the Fifteenth Amendment to the constitution that was passed in June 2011. The Fifteenth Amendment also created an unprecedented option of holding parliamentary elections without dissolving the existing parliament. Doing so is inconsistent with the Westminster-style parliamentary system. This led to the BNP threatening to boycott the next election if it was superintended by a partisan political regime.

Impunity enjoyed by ruling party activists since especially 2009 has seen the law and order situation drastically deteriorate in Bangladesh. Initially it started with youth activists of the ruling party engaged in intra-party violence and extortion. The situation worsened in the following years due to increasing clashes between the activists of the BNP and the AL, and between the law-enforcing agencies and opposition activists. But the most disturbing developments in regard to the law and order situation is the increase in the number of extra-judicial killings, forced disappearances of opposition political activists, labor leaders and critics of the government, and incidents of mob justice.

The political situation took a violent turn by March 2013 after the International Criminal Tribunal (ICT), which was a Bangladeshi entity despite being branded "international," began delivering verdicts on those charged with crimes against humanity committed in 1971. A number of leaders of the Jamaat-i-Islami, which opposed the independence war and collaborated with the Pakistani army and organized a number of militia groups, were tried. The BNP and the JI describe the ICT as flawed and an instrument of political vendetta. Both lenient and harsh sentences meted out by the ICT have led to violent protests by different groups and led to numerous deaths. This was the case when Delwar Hossain Saeedi, a prominent JI leader, was sentenced to death and the party's supporters went on a rampage throughout the country attacking police stations, railways, local government offices, and minorities. This, combined with the government's coun-teractions, led to 78 people, including seven police and several children, being killed in five days.

As of late June 2015, tribunals have delivered verdicts against 20 persons in 18 cases alleging war crimes. Thirteen were sentenced to death, most of whom were JI leaders. Two JI leaders, Abdul Qader Mollah and Muhammad Kamaruzzaman, were executed in December 2013 and April 2015. While seven of those convicted have filed appeals with the apex court, two of the most senior JI leaders, former party chief Ghulam Azam and AKM Yusuf, died of natural causes while in custody in 2014.

### Box 4.1:  War crimes and justice

One of the unresolved issues of Bangladesh history is the war crimes perpetrated during the war of liberation in 1971 and how to deliver justice to the victims. During the nine-month long war of liberation in 1971, the Pakistani military committed gen-ocide, and a guerrilla war to establish an independent Bangladesh ensued. A small number of political parties, particularly the Jamaat-i-Islami (JI) and the Muslim League (ML), colluded with the Pakistani forces, and members of the JI participated in various crimes. After the war, 195 of 92,000 Pakistani prisoners of war were sus-pected of committing war crimes and Bangladesh expressed its desire to try them. However, all of them were released in April 1974 following the tripartite agreement between Bangladesh, Pakistan, and India. They were repatriated to Pakistan in return for Pakistan's recognition of Bangladesh. Pakistan promised to conduct a trial against those allegedly involved in crimes against humanity. The process to try Bangladeshis began in 1972, but was abandoned after changes in the political landscape due to the military coup in 1975. Military rulers and political parties who came to power subse-quently avoided dealing head on with the uncomfortable truth.

In 1992, Jahanara Imam, a mother of a martyr, initiated a civil society movement demanding justice and organized "war crime public trials" of a number of people. Public support for the symbolic trials was immense, while the government cracked down on the organizers. The civil society movement continued, albeit weakly. The issue gained attention in 2007 as a forum of former commanders of the liberation war started a public campaign.

The AL incorporated the demands as one of the chief objectives in its 2008 election manifesto and set up the International Crimes Tribunal (ICT) in 2010.

The JI opposed it and the BNP insisted that the tribunal was failing to meet international standards. Due to the political alliance between the JI and the BNP, many allege that the BNP is providing tacit support to the JI's demand to scrap the process. Since its establishment the international community has voiced serious concerns as to whether the accused are receiving fair trials. Many now conclude that while the public's demand for justice is sincere, the AL has manipulated the entire process for partisan and opportunistic reasons. Thus, despite these trials, the issues of war crimes and justice for them remain unresolved.

### Era of flawed democracy

As the tenure of the AL-led government approached the end of its term in October 2013, the BNP reaffirmed its decision to boycott the election unless it was held under a nonpartisan caretaker government. The AL rejected the demand. By late October the BNP launched street agitations, called for general strikes, and imposed a Dhaka blockade. International initiatives, including a UN delegation team's mission to Dhaka, failed to bring any solution to the impasse. The JP wavered between joining the election and boycotting it. The party was coerced into participating, while its leader General Ershad was practically detained at a hospital. Former PM and the leader of the BNP Khaleda Zia was put under house arrest. The JI also continued its agitation against the verdicts of the ICT, especially after Quader Mollah's life sentence was converted to death during the appeal process in September. Violence spread throughout the country when Mollah was executed on December 12, 2013; over a period of three days at least 30 people were killed. Despite all efforts by local and international mediators to have an inclusive election, the ruling party went ahead with a one-sided election on January 5, 2014. The AL won 233 seats out of 300; the JP, led by the former military ruler Ershad, took 34. Only 12 parties out of the 40 registered with the Election Commission participated in the election. There were 153 candidates elected without facing any opposition, thereby practically disenfranchising a whole segment of voters. Official sources (including the Election Commission) claimed that the turnout was 39 percent. But the local and international press reported massive rigging and very low turnout. According to the *New York Times*, the actual voter turnout was 20 percent (Barry 2014). Between November 25, 2013 (the day the election date was announced) and January 4, 2014 (the day before the election), at least 123 people were killed in politically related violence. The BNP enforced 26 days of blockades and general strikes in six installments between November 25, 2013 and January 5, 2014. On the day of the election at least 21 people were killed. Immediately afterward, a further 10 or more died in clashes and police shootings (Riaz 2014). On January 12, 2014, a new government headed by Sheikh Hasina was sworn in, with three members of the JP, which was officially declared the Parliamentary Opposition Party, included in the cabinet. General Ershad was named special envoy of the PM. The inclusion of the JP in the cabinet essentially turned the tenth parliament into one without any opposition party. This is reminiscent of the year 1975, when the Awami League introduced a one-party system.

Soon after the election, the BNP called off its agitation campaigns. Subsequently, Khaleda Zia insisted that the BNP's alliance with the BJI is tactical, not ideological. The prime minister and the ruling party had promised to continue negotiations on holding early parliamentary elections if the BNP ended its violent agitations and severed its alliance with the JI, but they reneged on this promise by saying they intended to serve a full term until 2019. Throughout 2014 the country enjoyed relative peace and stability notwithstanding opposition leaders being persecuted, with frivolous charges often filed against them. This included cases against the BNP leader Khaleda Zia.

The relative calm, however, was shattered on the eve of the first anniversary of the controversial election when the government denied the BNP-led alliance the right to hold a rally demanding a new election and confined Khaleda Zia to her party office. The BNP retaliated by launching violent general strikes and imposing a countrywide blockade. Homemade petrol bombs were freely used to target opponents and public transport, especially buses carrying passengers. Violence gripped the country for over 90 days, leading to at least 138 people killed and US $2.2 billion in economic losses. The scale and nature of the violence was unprecedented, even by Bangladeshi standards. At least 37 people were killed in the resulting crossfire and "encounters," the latter a term used by officials to describe and justify extrajudicial killings by law enforcement agencies. The government's harsh tactics partly led to at least 15,000 people, mostly opposition activists, being arrested with many being detained without any charges.

## Institutions, political parties and elections

Bangladesh has a unicameral parliamentary system. The national parliament, called Jaitya Sangsad, comprises 350 members. Of these, 300 members are elected through direct elections with 50 seats reserved for women. Women members are elected indirectly by parliamentarians. Since independence, Bangladesh has elected 10 parliaments. Three of them were elected under the presidential system of governance (1979, 1986, and 1988) and therefore had very limited powers. Two parliaments changed the system of governance after being elected. The first parliament (1973) passed the Fourth Amendment of the constitution and introduced the presidential system; the fifth parliament (1991) did the opposite. Only three parliaments had completed their tenure—the seventh (1996–2001), the eighth (2001–06), and ninth (2009–14). The sixth parliament lasted just 12 days, as it was boycotted by all parties except the ruling BNP.

Since 1991 all political parties have promised through their election manifestos to make parliament effective and be the center of all political activities, but increasingly it has become the most ineffective institution. This is in part due to the ever-increasing size of the ruling party since 1991. The behavior of the ruling party, irrespective of the party in power, has given an impression that the opposition has very little role to play in governance. Besides, the Bangladeshi political parties seem to be uncomfortable operating as part of the opposition, leading to those not in power to routinely boycott parliament.

Despite the fact that the parliament remains largely ineffective, high turnout in parliamentary elections remains a defining feature of Bangladeshi politics. For instance, more than 86 percent of voters cast their ballots in the 2008 election. The turnout was historic as it surpassed all previous records. According to the election commission, during the past three elections held in 1991, 1996, and 2001, the turnouts were 55.45 percent, 74.96 percent, and 75.59 percent, respectively. However, the one-sided election held on January 5, 2014, saw a dramatic drop; the government's claim that 40 percent of voters cast their votes is contested by independent observers who claim that the turnout was only around 20 percent.

### Political parties

Bangladesh "has a long tradition of high political participation," observed Peter Bertocci more than three decades ago (Bertocci 1982, 993). This tradition is reflected in two elements of Bangladeshi politics: the high voter turnout in elections and the existence of numerous political parties. While the former is generally considered a healthy sign of democracy and a good prospect for sustaining democratic practices, the latter is often viewed with some derision. Bertocci, for example, opined that "Bangladesh displays a bewildering array of 'political parties' and leaders" (Bertocci 1982, 993).

In 1976, as the military regime of Ziaur Rahman required registration of political parties for participation in the political process, more than 50 parties registered with the government. The number increased significantly until the late 2000s. Election commission records show that in 1991 the commission allotted symbols to 75 parties participating in the election, while the figures for 1996 and 2001 were 119 and 95, respectively (Barman, Rahman, and Siddiqui 2001, 44). In 2008 the EC required that all parties register before filing any candidates for elections and fulfill certain conditions (for example, having units in at least one-third of the country), which reduced the number of parties to 39. It is worth mentioning that there are a host of parties that did not take part in the election and therefore were not required to register with the EC. Consequently, the total number of parties in Bangladesh is much higher than these records show.

These political parties can be categorized into two groups based on their organizational strengths, efficacy, and relevance. The parties with well-developed electioneering organizations, and well-articulated and long-standing grassroots extensions, belong to the first group. By this standard, and based on the results of the last four elections, there are only a handful of political parties in Bangladesh. But in a country where money and muscle power play a pivotal role in elections, caution must be exercised in judging the relevance of parties based solely on electioneering capabilities. Their strengths may lie in their ability to articulate popular aspirations and their capacity to mobilize supporters and sympathizers at critical moments, even if they do not do well in electoral politics. Therefore, the list of this group is bound to be different from the list of parties represented in the parliament.

The second group is composed of parties with little or no support within the populace. These parties are often referred to as "name-only" political parties. They comprise a handful of leaders, a small office, and a telephone. Some cannot even boast this basic setup—their existence is limited to their own letterheads.

That the Bangladeshi political landscape was dominated by the AL until the coup of August 15, 1975 is undisputed. But a number of political parties opposed to the AL also rose to prominence. Within mainstream politics the Jatiya Samajtantrik Dal (JSD, National Socialist Party) and the National Awami Party (NAP) are worth mentioning, and among the clandestine radical parties, the Sorbohara Party (Proletariat Party) stands out. On the other hand, the Communist Party of Bangladesh (CPB) and the NAP led by Professor Muzaffar Ahmed—close allies of the ruling AL—also commanded public support. Importantly, the political spectrum was spread between the radical left and the centrists, if we may call the AL a centrist party, while the rightist elements were driven underground. But clearly two poles emerged—the AL and its opponents.

One of the significant consequences of the establishment of the Bangladesh Nationalist Party (BNP) in 1978 was that it extended the political spectrum further right. The repressive measures of the AL between 1974 and 1975 and of the military junta between 1975 and 1978 had already weakened the anti-AL parties. Thus the BNP brought some of the radical leftist and rightist elements together—united in their opposition to the AL (and its allies such as the CPB). This created the environment for a further shift to the right, and the Islamists began to emerge, first under the banner of the Islamic Democratic League (IDL) in 1976 and later through the revival of the Jamaat-i-Islami (JI) in 1979.

Throughout the late 1970s and the early 1980s, parties outside these two poles (the AL and the BNP) reorganized themselves. Left political parties, including the JSD, faced several splits and disintegrations, but these left parties also gained visibility. The parties, commonly referred to as "pro-Peking" (because of their previous support for and/or affiliation with the Chinese Communist Party), experienced bitter internal strife producing several splits and leading to the emergence of a plethora of new parties. But in a remarkable contrast to this trend, the Communist Party of Bangladesh (CPB) made major headway. In some respects this constituted the most pluralist phase of Bangladeshi politics, as no single party held an organizational monopoly.

The Jatiya Party (JP) of General Ershad entered into this overcrowded political arena in 1984. By then the opponents of the regime had formed two alliances. The JI remained outside these alliances but was in no mood to come to the aid of the JP. Thus three poles were created: a left-of-center 15-party alliance under the AL leadership, a right-of-center seven-party alliance under the leadership of the BNP, and the JI on the far right. Ideologically the JP was close to the BNP, but they were locked in a bitter battle, especially because Ershad had overthrown the BNP regime, and a number of BNP leaders suspected that he had a hand in the assassination of Ziaur Rahman. Some of the BNP stalwarts defected to the JP, but the BNP was far from ready to vacate the leadership of the right-of-center parties. In addition to the democratic aspirations of the people, the bipolar nature of Bangladeshi politics lessened the possibility of success for the JP. Faced with this situation the JP employed Islamist rhetoric to shore up support from the Islamists.

The electorate, through the 1991 election, in large measure endorsed the two-party system in Bangladesh. Almost 60 percent of popular votes were secured by these two parties. But it also brought to the fore the fact that about one-third of the electorate is yet to lend their support to either of these two parties. Both the JP and JI hoped that it would be able to capture these votes unilaterally.

Between 1991 and 1996, a major shift in the ideological and organizational position of the AL became palpable. This shift was reflected in the increased use of Islamic rhetoric and symbols and in its close relationship with the JI. The warm relationship between the AL and the JI came to light when the Awami League nominee formally sought the support of the JI in 1991 in his failed bid for the ceremonial office of president (Hashmi 1994), and then became all too obvious when MPs of both parties worked closely in the parliament leading up to their simultaneous resignation in late 1994. This move was due to their unexpected loss in the 1991 election. The party seemed to have concluded that the "liberal left" position was becoming unhelpful in electoral politics. The 1996 victory was interpreted by the AL leaders as a vindication of this position, and the party has continued to pursue the strategy since then.

The 1996 results also revealed that, "while the BNP and AL have a vote base throughout the country, the JP and JI have particular areas of strength and are less broadly represented in other areas" (Choudhury 2001, paragraph 23). The lesson for them, therefore, was to align with one of the two major parties. Consequently, the JP aligned with the AL, and the JI with the BNP. However, the JP continued to switch sides for expediency and ended up with the AL in 2008 after being part of the BNP-led alliance for some time. The 2001 election results reaffirmed that Bangladeshi politics was still dominated by two parties—80 percent of the popular vote went to the AL and BNP.

Despite differences in ideological orientation and origin, major political parties in Bangladesh share some common characteristics and ethos. The most important among these are the lack of internal democracy, concentration of power in the hands of the party chief, and heredity as the means of accession to and continuance in power. These characteristics are symptomatic of the Bangladeshi political culture rather than unique to political parties.

Lack of internal democracy in political parties has been a major issue of concern among political analysts for almost a decade. Barman et al., referring to the AL, the BNP, and the JP, maintain that "all of these parties have an internal organizational structure that is hardly democratic, and the party activities such as policy-making, decision-making, and committee structuring are centered [on] the cult of the leader" (Barman, Rahman, and Siddiqui 2001, 44). Other analysts, for example, Ahmed, concur with this contention: "none of the major parties are democratic in composition" (Ahmed 2003, 61).

Party members, even those who hold memberships in the decision-making forums, do not have the freedom to express their opinions because dissenting views are regarded as disobedience and disobedient members are typically "disciplined" without regard to the validity of their opinions (IDEA 2004). As Ahmed aptly notes, "Those who refuse to abide by the despotic decisions of the leadership risk suspension or expulsion and, in extreme cases, may lose their membership (in the parliament)" (Ahmed 2003, 72). This is not only a matter of practice but is incorporated into party constitutions. The fact is that party constitutions typically provide limitless power to the party chief to appoint any members to any committee.

The third feature of party politics—heredity as the only means of accession to power—is truer for the AL and the BNP; although this is becoming common in other parties as more family members of politicians occupy the leadership position. It is now well known that the mantle of the BNP will be carried by Tareque Zia, son of Khaleda Zia, should she be indisposed to lead the party. In the case of the AL, a significant number of central leaders are related to Sheikh Hasina and her son is considered the heir apparent.

What binds these three characteristics together is the prevalent culture of the country: patrimonialism. Bertocci (1982), Kochanek (2000), and Ahmed (2003) view this as the key element in understanding the behavior of Bangladeshi elites. In their view, the relationship between the party loyalist and the leaders is unmistakably a patron-client relationship. The patron-client relationship legitimizes hierarchy. It has led to omnipotent leaders and the absence of accountability within parties.

## Managing conflict

Despite the periodic outburst of political violence, incessant political uncertainty, and the episode of Islamist militancy in the early 2000s, Bangladesh has only once faced social conflict since independence. The exception is the ongoing ethnic conflict in the southeastern hill areas. This apparently intractable conflict can be traced back to two pre-independence actions. The first was the nineteenth century decision of the British administration to bring Bengalis into the hill tracts as plantation workers and clerks; and the second was the construction of the hydropower station on the Karnaphuli River in 1962. The dam displaced at least 100,000 people, of whom 70 percent were Chakma, and submerged 40 percent of the cultivable land in the area. Additionally, local inhabitants living in the storage reservoir area who lost their homes and farmland due to flooding were not compensated. Post 1971, this problem turned into a conflict due to the unwillingness of ruling elites to acknowledge the cultural diversity of the country.

Although Bangladeshi society is overwhelmingly homogenous, at least 14 ethnic groups, including the Chakma, Marma, Murong, Tanchangya, Bhowm, Tripura, Lushai, Khumi, Kukis, and Mizos, live in various parts of the country. The Chakma and Marma community live in the Chittagong hill tracts (CHT). The demands of these communities, especially for regional autonomy, have not been properly addressed by the Bangladeshi state; instead successive governments have confronted them with force. This has created a source of conflict that remains unresolved. The issue of autonomy emerged in 1972 when a delegation of hill people, collectively known as "jumma" (a reference to their method of cultivation), appealed to then-Prime Minister Sheikh Mujib for regional autonomy based on the Chittagong Hill Tracts Regulation of 1900, but was met with outright rejection. The constitution of 1972 did not acknowledge separate ethnic identities; it instead privileged the majority's Bengali identity. The jumma population also demanded that migration of non-hill people to the region be restricted. In 1972 they founded a political party called the Parbtaya Chottogram Jono Sanghati Samity (PCJSS, United People's Party). By 1975, the PCJSS established its military wing, called the Shanti Bahini (Peace Force).

The military regime of Ziaur Rahman (1975–81) intensified the settlement program in the hill areas and armed resistance from the jumma people ensued. In 1977 a large number of hill people took refuge in the Indian state of Tripura and the Indian government decided to provide weapons to the insurgents. The decision to support the insurgents was made because of the Indian government's dislike of the Zia regime. The Bangladesh government responded with massive military operations, intensifying the settlement program and establishing a long-term military presence in the area. These actions, in the long run, made the problem intractable. The entire region became a site of conflict between the jumma population and the military on one hand, and locals and settlers supported by the military and local administration, on the other. An attempt at a political solution in 1989 achieved only limited success.

In December 1997 the Bangladeshi government led by Sheikh Hasina, encouraged by India, signed a peace agreement with the political wing of the Shanti Bahini. The treaty offered the rebels a general amnesty in return for surrendering their arms, and on paper at least provided the tribal people greater powers of self-governance through the establishment of new elected district councils (to control the area's land management and policing) and a regional council (with the chairman supposed to enjoy the rank of a state minister). The peace agreement was strongly criticized by the opposition as a "sell-out" of the area to India and a threat to Bangladesh's sovereignty. Although more than a decade has passed and a few steps have been taken to implement various aspects of the treaty, the jumma people haven't received what they were promised. Four key problems remain to be addressed: (i) demilitarization; (ii) rehabilitation, especially of internally displaced indigenous persons; (iii) land dispute resolution; and (iv) effective devolution to autonomous regional- and district-level councils. These outstanding issues have led to intermittent violence between Bengali settlers and locals.

## Regional and International Relations

South Asia has been Bangladesh's main area of concern with regard to foreign affairs. However, the geo-strategically important location of the country provides it opportunities to play an important role in regional and international forums. In the international arena, the country has made a notable contribution to international peace keeping. Bangladesh has provided more personnel to UN peacekeeping operations than any other country in the world and received accolades for the force's professionalism. Between 1988 and 2015 the Bangladesh Army actively participated in 54 UN peacekeeping missions in 40 countries, contributing about 120,000 personnel. In 2015 a total of 9,434 security personnel were working in these missions, including a Bangladeshi contingent in the all-female UN Formed Police Unit deployed in Haiti. Over the years a total of 124 Bangladeshi peacekeepers have lost their lives while contributing to UN operations. In a similar vein, the country has played an important role in various international forums on environmental issues, including the Copenhagen Summit in 2009, Rio+20 in 2012, and the Fourth UN Conference on Least Developed Countries (LDC-IV) in 2011. In 1997 Bangladesh played a vital role in founding the Developing Eight, or D-8, a group comprising eight major Muslim states that represent 65 percent of the world's Muslim population. The goal is to further economic and political cooperation among member countries. The 1999 summit meeting was held in Dhaka. Bangladesh is also a member of the Bay of Bengal Initiative for Multi-Sectoral Technical and Economic Cooperation (Bimstec) and the Mekong-Ganga Cooperation (MGC).

At the regional level, one of the most significant contributions of the country is the initiative it took to establish the South Asian Association for Regional Cooperation (SAARC). The idea was first launched by then-President General Ziaur Rahman in 1980. The SAARC was formally created in 1985, with a Bangladeshi official as its first secretary-general. Bangladesh hosted the first, seventh, and thirteenth summit meetings of the organization.

Bangladesh's geographical location makes Indo-Bangladesh relations central to the country's foreign affairs. Geographically Bangladesh is surrounded by India—to the east, west, and north; it shares a small strip of frontier with Myanmar (Burma) on the southeastern edge and has an opening to the Indian Ocean via the Bay of Bengal. The country is located in between the Indian mainland and its insurgency-prone seven sister states in the northeast of India. India played a crucial role during the war of independence in 1971, and the Indian state of West Bengal shares common linguistic, cultural, and historical traditions with Bangladesh. However, the relationship between the two countries has not followed a smooth trajectory. While relations have never been overtly hostile, they have been marked by suspicion and ambiguity on one hand and close economic ties on the other. It is often described as a 'love-hate' relationship.

In the early years of independence, the two countries fostered a close relationship and signed a 25-year Treaty of Friendship, Cooperation, and Peace in 1972. There has always been the fear that India would use its vastly superior strength to intimidate Bangladesh, especially over economic and security matters. The relationship took a downturn after the military regime of Ziaur Rahman came to power. The Indian government's support to some AL supporters in subversive activities soon after 1975 and material support to the Chakma insurgents after 1977 (see previous section) soured the relationship. In a tit-for-tat policy the Zia regime began supporting insurgent groups (such as the United Front for Liberation of Assam [ULFA]) in India's northeast. The relationship started to improve during the final days of the Zia regime but suspicion has remained fueled by contemporaneous developments.

The close trade relationship (India is Bangladesh's second most significant import source after China, and ranks fifth among Bangladesh's export destinations) has grown over the years; but it has become lopsided, as reflected in the following fact: Bangladesh supplied a mere 0.12 percent of India's imports in fiscal year (FY) 2013, while 15.1 percent of Bangladesh's total imports came from India in the same year. Bangladesh's exports to India in recent years have grown from $97 million in FY 2005 to $305 million in FY 2010, to $512 million in FY 2011, and to $563 million in 2012–13. The growing bilateral trade deficit with India has risen from $774 million in FY 2000 to $1,933 million in FY 2005, to $2,910 million in FY 2010, and to $3,159 million in FY 2011.

However, it is not the trade disparity and the economic influence of India that serve as the prominent source of contention between these two countries, but issues of water sharing, disputes over enclaves, and migration. As Bangladesh is located downstream and shares 54 rivers with India, water sharing is closely tied to Bangladesh's existence and national security (Riaz 2011, 104–122). In 1975 India built the Farakka Dam 11 miles from its border with Bangladesh and diverted water from the Ganges to India's Hugli River to supply Calcutta. India's water diversions are blamed for environmental damage that spurred rural-urban migration within Bangladesh. In December 1996 India and Bangladesh reached a new 30-year agreement on how to divide the water in the Ganges (Padma in Bangladesh) River. Many Bangladeshis allege that the country is deprived of its agreed share (Mirza 2004).

In 2011 the Indian federal government decided to construct the Tipaimukh Hydroelectric Project near the confluence of the Barak and Tuivai rivers in the Indian state of Manipur and within 65 miles of the Bangladesh border (Jahangir 2009). If and when constructed this will reduce the water flow to Bangladesh to a historic low and adversely affect the local agriculture and fisheries sectors. India's ambitious multi-billion dollar project to connect major rivers to augment the water supply in its southern states threatens to alter ecosystems in Bangladesh (Khadka 2012). The failure on the part of India to sign an accord on sharing the Teesta River water during the Indian Prime Minister Monmohan Singh's visit to Bangladesh in 2011 has not only irked many Bangladeshis but also forced Bangladesh to defer signing the transit treaty that would allow transshipment of Indian goods through Bangladesh.

Disputes over territorial rights to pockets of land, or enclaves, along the irregular border have been a further source of tension between India and Bangladesh, and armed clashes between border troops have taken place on a number of occasions, such as one in April 2001 that led to the deaths of 16 Indian border troops and three members of the Bangladesh Rifles. Complicating matters are over 160 enclaves belonging to India and Bangladesh that are situated within the other's territory, which prevent those living in these areas from travelling about freely. The Land Boundary Agreement (LBA) that was signed in 1974 between Prime Ministers Sheikh Mujibur Rahman and Indira Gandhi was supposed to solve this problem, but the Indian parliament failed to follow its Bangladeshi counterpart and ratify it. This was finally done in May 2015.

Since the 1980s the Indian government has alleged that illegal migration from Bangladesh has substantially increased. To prevent such migration it has almost completed building an eight-feet-high barbed-wire fence along the length of its 2,500-mile frontier with Bangladesh. Bangladeshis feel as if their country is being "caged," and this has taken place at a time when the Indian Border Security Force regularly engages in killing civilians on the Indo-Bangladesh border. A New York–based human rights group, Human Rights Watch (2010), reported that almost 1,000 Bangladeshi civilians were killed by the Indian Border Security Forces (BSF) between 2000 and 2010 in violation of Indian laws and despite assurances of the Indian government to the contrary.

While the relationship with India warmed up under the Hasina regime (2008–13), concerns have been expressed by many as to whether the Indian government is exerting undue influence, especially because of its role during the 2014 election. The United States, the United Kingdom, Japan, and China, as well as multilateral organizations including the United Nations and the Commonwealth, called for an inclusive election. But India stood by the AL and echoed the regime's argument that the election was a constitutional requirement, implying that the nonparticipation of the BNP was acceptable to India. Policy makers in New Delhi were concerned that a BNP victory would be detrimental to Indian interests. India's decision to overtly support the AL put at risk the transformation of the Indo-Bangladeshi relationship into one based on state-to-state, rather than party-to-party, ties.

The relationship between the Bangladesh government and India was further cemented during Indian Prime Minister Norendra Modi's visit to the country in June 2015. In addition to finalizing the LBA, agreements and memoranda of understanding that would allow Indian investments in the energy sector in Bangladesh, Indian access to its northeastern states through Bangladesh, and entry for Indian cargo ships to Bangladeshi seaports were signed. Critics have argued that these agreements will benefit India more than Bangladesh, and that the ruling party did so in exchange for India's unqualified support on the domestic front.

The relationship with Bangladesh's other neighbor, Myanmar, is less intense; and as Myanmar moves towards democracy the relationship is warming up. Two issues have dominated the relationship in past decades, and these are the Rohingya refugees and maritime border demarcation. Facing persecution since the late 1970s, the Rohingyas, a Muslim ethnic minority group of Myanmar, have been taking refuge in Bangladesh. Two waves of Rohingya refugees crossed the border between the late 1970s and the 1990s. The total number of refugees was more than 250,000 in 1992. Although a majority was repatriated through the UNHCR, thousands have remained both legally and illegally in Bangladesh. Myanmar has refused to accept them, while international support for the refugees has dwindled. Bangladesh has repeatedly insisted that the Rohingyas must be accepted as Myanmar citizens. In the summer of 2012, after riots between Buddhist Rakhaine and Muslim Rohingya communities erupted in Myanmar and killed over 100 people, hundreds of Rohingyas tried to flee to Bangladesh. Despite pleas from the UNHCR and the United States to accept the refugees, the Bangladesh government pursued the policy of forcibly repatriating them to Myanmar. The government insisted that the international community should pressure the Myanmar government to resolve the issue at home. The second issue that has created tensions with Myanmar concerns the maritime border and the right to explore for oil and gas (the disputed region being about 50 km south of Bangladesh's Saint Martin's Island). A March 2012 verdict by the International Tribunal for the Law of the Sea, however, has brought an end to an issue that had potential for border conflict.

Since independence, Bangladesh's relations with Pakistan have fluctuated. Pakistan formally recognized Bangladesh in February 1974 and full diplomatic relations were established in 1976. Since then there have been quite a few high level visits by Pakistani leaders to Bangladesh and vice versa. For example, Pakistani Prime Minister Zulfikar Ali Bhutto visited Bangladesh in July 1974 and Pakistani President Gen. Pervez Musharraf visited Dhaka in July 2002. On the other hand, President Ziaur Rahman visited Pakistan in September 1977 and Prime Minister Khaleda Zia visited Pakistan in February 2006. However, the issue of responsibility for the events of 1971, especially an apology demanded by Bangladesh, has remained unresolved and sours feelings from time to time. President Pervez Musharraf expressed regret for the atrocities committed by Pakistani troops during the 1971 war, but in November 2012 during a visit to Dhaka, the Pakistani Minister of Foreign Affairs, Hina Rabbani Khar, rejected Bangladesh's demand for a formal apology. Consequently, Bangladeshi PM Sheikh Hasina cancelled her planned visit to Pakistan later that month. The relationship with Pakistan also soured after the execution of JI leader Quader Mollah in December 2014. The Pakistan national assembly adopted a resolution on December 16, 2013 expressing concern; Bangladesh officially condemned the resolution and asked Pakistan to refrain from such "interference" in its domestic affairs. Four days later the Pakistan government backtracked with the spokesperson for the foreign ministry saying the war crimes trial were part of Bangladesh's "internal affairs." One other unresolved issue is the non-Bengali Pakistani citizens, commonly referred to as Biharis, who opted for Pakistan after the war in 1971 but are still waiting to be repatriated to Pakistan. Soon after the war, the Pakistani government agreed to accept them and in 1991 an agreement was reached between Bangladesh and Pakistan, which provided for a phased repatriation of the Bihari refugees, but implementation has been very slow.

## Economy

The Bangladeshi economy has witnessed significant growth (see Box 4.2) in the past decades just as the country's economic structure has experienced significant changes. The share of agriculture before independence was 55 percent as opposed to 35 percent for the service sector and 10 percent for industry. By the end of the first decade after independence, however, the service sector stood equal to agriculture at 45 percent. The agriculture sector's share in the gross domestic product (GDP) has continued to slide in recent decades, accounting for just 17.5 percent in 2013, while industry's contribution has grown to 28.5 percent and the service sector amounts to almost 54 percent. The ready-made garments industry and remittances from Bangladeshis living abroad as short-term migrant workers, primarily in the Middle East, dominate the economy. The garment sector has emerged as the second-largest apparel exporter in the world, thanks to Bangladeshi entrepreneurs and 4.0 million workers, of whom 3.2 million are women. Almost 2.5 percent of the Bangladeshi population is now employed in this sector. Revenue from the garment sector was almost nonexistent in 1978–79 ($0.04 million) but a little over three decades later, in the 2014–15 fiscal year, the sector generated revenue of $25.49 billion. This dramatic success can be attributed largely to low wages and a lack of compliance with basic safety standards in garment factories. This negligence has contributed to a number of deadly accidents, including the collapse of Rana Plaza on 28 April 2013, which cost more than 1,100 lives and injured at least 2,500.

Remittances increased from $23.71 million in 1976 to $14.94 billion in 2014. In the past two decades, between 1993 and 2013, the revenue generated by remittances increased 13 fold. Bangladesh is the eighth-largest recipient of remittances in the world. Currently, 5.38 million migrant Bangladeshis, or 3.3 percent of the total population, contribute almost 11 percent of nominal GDP. The pharmaceuticals industry and shrimp exports also contribute to the growing economy. Per capita income was estimated at $2,948 in 2013 (adjusted by purchasing power parity) with a GDP of $173.8 billion in nominal terms. In 2015 the World Bank ranked Bangladesh a lower middle income country.

## Opportunities and constraints

It is no exaggeration to say that that the genesis of Bangladesh lies in the democratic aspiration of its people. The independence war in 1971 ensued only after the Pakistani elites declined to accept the will of the people expressed in the general election of 1970 and perpetrated genocide. The yearning for democracy, equality, and human dignity has remained the central element of people's aspiration since; but the past four decades of Bangladeshi politics have been tumultuous, uncertain, and often violent. Divisive and acrimonious politics have often made democracy the main casualty. If high voter turnout clearly indicates that Bangladeshis value their democracy, the plethora of political parties also highlights the country's plurality and passion for politics.

The other significant positive element of the country is the tradition of civil society associations. Nongovernmental organizations (NGOs) focusing on education, human rights, and social and political issues are active in both urban and rural areas. NGOs engaged in empowerment programs for women, marginalized groups, poverty alleviation and health care, and education have a notable record of success and have received global recognition. The Grameen Bank, for example, received the Nobel Peace Prize in 2006 for its innovative

**Box 4.2: Bangladesh Paradox**

In recent years the phrase "Bangladesh Paradox" has been used quite frequently in press and policy discourse. The literature on development argued that economic development is intrinsically connected to good governance. Some analysts also claimed that economic growth and social development cannot be achieved without a stable and transparent system of governance. But lately many have accepted that the Bangladesh experience presents a paradoxical situation. Since 1991, despite elected governments in power, the country has experienced periodic political upheaval. The country's governance is considered poor by any standard. Transparency International (TI) lists the country as among the most corrupt in the world. Additionally, the country has faced several natural calamities, including floods and cyclones. In short, the country has high population density, a limited natural-resource base, underdeveloped infrastructure, frequent natural disasters, and political uncertainty. Yet it has made significant economic progress and various social indicators have recorded positive developments.

Despite the unfavorable global economic environment, its Gross Domestic Product (GDP) has continued to grow at 5–6 percent per year since 1991. The rate of growth was 5.7 percent in 2010–11, 6.1 percent in 2011–12 and 6.7 percent in 2012–13. Impressive reductions in poverty have occurred alongside economic growth, with poverty declining from 59 percent in 1991–92 to 31.5 percent in 2010. The share of the population living below $1.25 a day fell to 43 percent in 2010 from 70 percent in 1992. This achievement has been matched by significant improvement in social indicators. According to the World Development Report 2013, between 1980 and 2012 life expectancy at birth in Bangladesh increased from 55.2 to 69.2 years and mean years of schooling from 2 to 4.8 years. The infant and child mortality rate has also declined from 87 per 1000 live births in 1994 to 39 per 1,000 in 2009. The under-5 child mortality rate dropped to 50 per 1,000 live births in 2009 from 146 per 1,000 births in 1991. Significantly, gender parity has been achieved in primary and secondary levels of education. As of 2010, the gender ratio is in favor of girls at 1.02:1 and 1.14:1 at primary and secondary levels, respectively. Free education for girls up to grade 12 has contributed to this upward enrollment trend. Primary level enrolment also reached 94.7 percent in 2010 against the Millennium Development Goals (MDG) target of 100 percent by 2015. Furthermore, the school dropout rate has also significantly decreased. It is expected that by 2015 all primary age children will be enrolled in schools.

Taking these developments into account, the Human Development Report 2013 has identified Bangladesh as one of the 18 countries that are making rapid progress in human development. The list includes China, India, Malaysia, and Vietnam. This is a major reversal in the global perception of a country that, at the time of independence in 1971, was considered a "basket case."

micro-credit lending program. All this combined with the social and economic successes the country has achieved in the past decade has led to a "Bangladesh Paradox" (see Box 4.2).

The path to economic progress, social development, political stability, and democratization is not linear, and neither is it path-dependent. It is a complex and continuing process and the factors that contribute to this process constantly change, causing new dynamics at different times under different circumstances. As such, Bangladesh will continue to be challenged and face constraints. Endemic corruption, an energy crisis, and poor infrastructure rank among the country's biggest negatives. Most importantly, the country needs a qualitative change in its political culture so there is consensus about the institutional processes for political succession. Breakdown in ensuring the rule of law, administrative politicization, and a compromised judiciary lacking independence have hindered democratic practices and will continue to do so unless they are addressed in earnest. The all-around need for accountability cannot be overstated. But achieving it takes time and requires rules and norms to get institutionalized. In short, there is much that has to change structurally if Bangladesh is to reach its potential.

## Political chronology

| | |
|---|---|
| January 10, 1972: | Sheikh Mujibur Rahman becomes Bangladesh's first President. |
| December 16, 1972: | Constitution drafted by a legislative assembly comes into effect. |
| March 7, 1973: | Bangladesh holds first general election in which Mujib's Awami League wins 294 of 300 parliament seats. Mujib becomes Prime Minister. |
| January 25, 1975: | Constitution amended to make Bangladesh a presidential system of government and one party-rule is introduced. |
| August 15, 1975: | Mujib is killed, along with most members of his family (except two daughters, Sheikh Hasina and Sheikh Rehana, who were outside the country), in a coup led by a group of young army officers. Martial law is promulgated by Khandaker Mushtaq Ahmed, a cabinet minister of Mujib's government on behalf of the officers. |
| November 3–7, 1975: | Coups and countercoups rock the nation. Four key leaders are assassinated inside the Dhaka central jail. Major General Ziaur Rahman emerges as the strongman. |
| July 1976: | Political Parties Regulations (PPR) Act comes into effect requiring all political parties to register with the government to function on a limited scale. A government proclamation removes the ban on parties with a religious agenda and several small religio-political parties emerge. |
| April 21, 1977: | Ziaur Rahman becomes President of the People's Republic of Bangladesh. |
| April 23, 1977: | Zia issues Second Proclamation Order No 1. It amends the constitution, deletes secularism as a state principle, includes "absolute trust in Almighty Allah" in the preamble, and changes the identity of citizens to "Bangladeshi." |
| May 30, 1977: | Referendum is held to confirm legitimacy of Ziaur Rahman's presidency. Official results show about 98 percent of voters say "yes." |
| June 3, 1978: | Presidential poll elects Ziaur Rahman as President. |
| September 1, 1978: | Ziaur Rahman launches Bangladesh Nationalist Party (BNP). |
| February 18, 1979: | BNP wins parliamentary elections with 207 of 300 seats. Awami League wins 39 seats. |
| May 30, 1981: | Ziaur Rahman assassinated in abortive army coup in the port city of Chittagong. His vice president Abdus Sattar succeeds him. |
| March 24, 1982: | Army Chief of Staff Lieutenant General Hossain Mohammed Ershad ousts Sattar. Military takes over. |
| January 1, 1984: | General Ershad launches Jatiya Party. |
| March 21, 1985: | Ershad wins 94 percent of vote in referendum to reaffirm his rule. |

| | |
|---|---|
| May 7, 1986: | Ershad holds parliamentary elections. His Jatiya party wins 153 of 300 seats. Awami League (AL) led by Sheikh Hasina wins 76 and the Jaamat-i-Islami (JI) 10 seats. The BNP and a group of left political parties boycott the elections. |
| October 15, 1986: | Ershad reelected president in a poll boycotted by all major political parties, including the BNP and AL. |
| December 6, 1987: | President dissolves Parliament in the face of an intense anti-government agitation. |
| March 3, 1988: | Parliamentary elections boycotted by major opposition parties held. Ershad's Jatiya Party wins 251 seats and Combined Opposition Party (COP), an alliance of lightweight parties, wins 19. |
| June 7, 1988: | Ershad amends constitution to proclaim Islam state religion. |
| December 6, 1990: | Ershad toppled in a urban popular uprising led by Begum Khaleda Zia, widow of slain President Ziaur Rahman, and Sheikh Hasina. Ershad hands over power to Chief Justice Shahabuddin Ahmed, who takes over as acting president. |
| February 27, 1991: | Parliamentary elections, billed as first free polls in Bangladesh, are held. The BNP, under Khaleda Zia, wins 146 seats, Awami League 86, Jatiya Party 35, and Jamaat-i-Islami 18. The BNP forms government with support of JI. |
| August 6, 1991: | Constitution amended to allow for a return to parliamentary system of government from presidential system. |
| February 15, 1996: | Parliamentary elections boycotted by major political parties except BNP. Opposition steps up long running campaign of strikes. |
| March 26, 1996: | Parliament passes bill proposing a non-party caretaker government to oversee all future elections. |
| March 30, 1996: | President dissolves parliament and Khaleda Zia resigns. President appoints an 11-member caretaker government headed by former chief justice of the supreme court. |
| June 12, 1996: | Parliamentary elections held under caretaker government. In free and relatively peaceful election Awami League emerges as the largest political party with BNP as the main opposition. |
| June 23, 1996: | Awami League, with the help of JP and JSD (led by A.S.M. Rob), returns to power after 21 years. Sheikh Hasina, daughter of slain President Sheikh Mujibur Rahman, becomes the PM. |
| July 15, 2001: | Hasina hands over power to non-party caretaker government, becoming the first prime minister in the country's history to complete a five-year term. |
| October 1, 2001: | Election gives two-third majority to the 4-party alliance led by BNP. The AL wins 62 seats. |
| October 10, 2001: | A 60-member cabinet of the Four-Party Coalition Government takes charges. The JI, once proscribed, became a part of the cabinet. |
| October 28, 2006: | Violent protests erupt over government's choice of a caretaker administration. President Ahmed steps in and assumes caretaker role for period leading to elections due in January 2007. |
| January 11–12, 2007: | A state of emergency is declared amid violence in the run up to the election. President Ahmed postpones the poll. Fakhruddin Ahmed heads a caretaker administration. |

| | |
|---|---|
| April 11, 2007: | Sheikh Hasina is charged with murder. Begum Khaleda Zia is under virtual house arrest. Several other politicians are held in an anti-corruption drive. |
| July–September, 2007: | Political leaders, including the two former Prime Ministers, are arrested on charges of corruption. |
| September 20, 2008: | Caretaker Government announces the date of elections. |
| December 29, 2008: | General elections held and AL-led alliance secures landslide victory. |
| January 6, 2009: | Awami League-led coalition government sworn in with Sheikh Hasina as the Prime Minister. |
| February 25–26, 2009: | Around 74 people, mainly army officers, are killed in a mutiny in Dhaka by border guards. A total of about 4,000 guards are arrested in the following months. |
| June 30, 2011: | Constitutional change scraps provision for a neutral caretaker government to oversee elections. |
| May–June, 2012: | Key figures from the main Islamist party Jamaat-i-Islami are charged with war crimes by the ICT investigating alleged collaboration with Pakistan during the 1971 independence struggle. |
| January 21, 2013: | War crimes tribunal sentences Abul Kalam Azad to death for crimes against humanity during the 1971 independence war. He was tried in absentia, as he had fled abroad. |
| February 5, 2013: | ICT sentence JI leader Abdul Quader Mollah to life term imprisonment. Youth activists outraged by leniency of the court lead nationwide protests. |
| February 28, 2013: | ICT sentence JI leader Delwar Hossain Sayeedi to death. JI activists protest nationwide. |
| November 25, 2013– January 4, 2014: | Violence spreads through the country as the BNP enforces general strikes and blockades of the capital. The government adopts a heavy-handed approach. At least 123 die in election related violence. |
| December 12, 2013: | JI leader Quader Mollah is first ever to be executed on charges of war crimes committed in 1971. |
| January 5, 2014: | The AL and its allies win parliamentary elections that are boycotted by major opposition parties. |
| January 12, 2014: | New cabinet sworn in with Sheikh Hasina as the PM. Three members of the opposition JP are inducted into the cabinet. General Ershad named special envoy of the PM. |
| January 5, 2015– April 5, 2015: | Violence grips the nation during the first anniversary of the controversial election. BNP calls for general strikes and blockades. Nearly 138 people die in bomb attacks, clashes between opposition activists and law enforcing agencies, and extrajudicial killings. |

## Political parties

| Name of the Party | Ideological Orientation |
|---|---|
| Awami League (AL) | Centrist, believes in role of government in the Economy, prefers a limited role of religion in politics, espouses liberal social values, and is a proponent of Bengali nationalism. |
| Bangladesh Nationalist Party (BNP) | Center-right, proponent of open market economy, views Islam as a central element of social and political life, espouses liberal social values, and is a proponent of Bangladeshi nationalism. |

| | |
|---|---|
| Jatiya Party (JP) | Center-right, proponent of open market economy, believes in significant role of Islam in politics, espouses liberal social values, advocates Bangladeshi nationalism. |
| Jamaat-i-Islami (JI) | Islamist, rightwing, supporter of open market economy with certain restrictions due to religious factors, espouses conservative social values, supports Muslim nationalism. |
| Communist Party of Bangladesh (CPB) | Socialist, secularist, believes in a command economy, and highly liberal on social issues. |
| Islami Oikya Jote (IOJ) | Orthodox Islamist, supports restricted market economy, espouses highly conservative social values, and promotes Bangladeshi nationalism. |
| Bangladesh Islami Andolon | Orthodox Islamist, supports restricted market economy, espouses highly conservative social values, and supports Bangladeshi nationalism. |
| Jataya Samajtantrik Dal (JSD) | Center-left, secularist, believes in role of government in economy, espouses liberal social values, and supports Bengali nationalism. |
| Socialist Party of Bangladesh | Socialist, secularist, believes in command economy, highly liberal on social issues. |

## Works cited

Ahmed, Nizam. 2003. "From Monopoly to Competition: Party Politics in the Bangladesh Parliament." *Pacific Affairs* 76 (1) (Spring): 55–77.

Barman, Dalem Ch, M. Golam Rahman, and Tasneem Siddiqui. 2001. "Democracy Report for Bangladesh," International Institute for Democracy and Electoral Assistance (IDEA), 2001, Retrieved from www.idea.int/publications/sod/upload/Bangladesh.pdf. Accessed July 3, 2005.

Barry, Ellen. 2014. "Low turnout in Bangladesh Elections Amid Boycott and Violence." *New York Times* (January 5). Retrieved from www.nytimes.com/2014/01/06/world/asia/boycott-and-violence-mar-elections-in-bangladesh.html?_r=0

Bertocci, Peter J. 1982. "Bangladesh in the Early-1980s: Praetorian Politics in an Intermediate Regime." *Asian Survey* 22 (10) (October): 988–1008.

Choudhury, Nazim Kamran. 2001. "Jatiya Sangsad Elections: Past and Future." *Daily Star* (April 13). Retrieved from http://nazimkamranchoudhury.blogspot.com/2006/06/jatiya-sangsad-elections-past-and.html

Daily Star. 2007. "Chronology of Keeping Off Polls." *Daily Star* (January 1).

*Economist.* 2007a. "No Going Back." (April 19). Retrieved from www.economist.com/node/9052421. Accessed December 1, 2008.

*Economist.* 2007b. "Not Uniformly Bad." (February 8). Retrieved from www.economist.com/node/8668962. Accessed December 1, 2008.

Hashmi, Taj ul-Islam. 1994. "Islam in Bangladesh Politics." In *Islam, Muslims and the Modern State*, edited by Hussin Mutalib and Taj ul-Islam Hashmi. New York: Martin's Press.

Human Rights Watch (HRW). 2011. *Trigger Happy: Excessive Use of Force by Indian Troops at the Bangladesh Border*. New York: Human Rights Watch.

International Institute of Democracy and Electoral Assistance and Center for Alternatives. 2004. *Bangladesh: Country Report*. Dhaka: International Institute of Democracy and Electoral Assistance and Center for Alternatives.

International Republican Institute. 2009. *Bangladesh Parliamentary Elections/Elections Observation Mission Final Report*. Washington, DC: International Republican Institute.

Jahangir, Nadim. 2009. "The Tipaimukh Dam Controversy." *Forum* 3 (7). Retrieved from www.thedailystar.net/forum/2009/july/tipaimukh.htm. Accessed March 7, 2013.

Jalal, Ayesha. 1995. *Democracy and Authoritarianism in South Asia*, Cambridge: Cambridge University Press.

Khadka, Navin Singh. 2012. "Concerns over India rivers order," *BBC News* (March 30). Retrieved from www.bbc.com/news/science-environment-17555918

Kochanek, Stanley. 1997. "Bangladesh in 1996: The 25th Year of Independence." *Asian Survey* 37 (2) (February): 136–142.

Kochanek, Stanley. 2000. "Governance, Patronage Politics and Democratic Transition in Bangladesh." *Asian Survey* 40 (3) (May–June): 530–550.

Lifschultz, Lawrence. 1979. *Bangladesh: The Unfinished Revolution*. London: Zed Books.

Makeig, Douglas C. 1989. "National Security." In *Bangladesh: A Country Study*, edited by James Heitzman and Robert L. Worden, Washington, DC: Library of Congress.

Mirza, M., and Monirul Qader, eds. 2004. *The Ganges Water Diversion: Environmental Effects and Implications*. The Netherlands: Kluwer.

Molla, Gyasuddin. 2000. "Democratic Institution Building Process in Bangladesh: South Asian Experience of a New Model of 'Care-Taker Government.'" In a Parliamentary Framework, *Heidelberg Papers in South Asian and Comparative Politics*, Working Paper No. 3, South Asia Institute. Heidelberg: University of Heidelberg.

Peiris, G. H. 1998. "Political Conflict in Bangladesh," *Ethnic Studies Report* 16 (1) (January): 1–75.

Rashid, Harun-ur. 2006. "The Caretaker Conundrum," *Daily Star* (June 28): 6.

Riaz, Ali. 2004. *God Willing: The Politics of Islamism in Bangladesh*. Lanham, MA: Rowman and Littlefield.

———. 2005. *Unfolding State: The Transformation of Bangladesh*. Ontario: DeSitter.

———. 2011. "Bangladesh." In *Climate Change and National Security: A Country level Analysis*, edited by Daniel Moran, Washington DC: Georgetown University Press.

———. 2014. "A Crisis of Democracy in Bangladesh." *Current History* 113 (762) (April): 150–156.

United Nations Development Programme. 2010. *Elections in Bangladesh: Transforming Failure into Success*. Dhaka: UNDP Bangladesh.

## Recommended texts

Ali, S. Mahmud. 2010. *Understanding Bangladesh*. New York: Columbia University Press.

Lewis, David. 2011. *Bangladesh: Politics, Economy and Civil Society*. Cambridge: Cambridge University Press.

Lifschultz, Lawrence. 1979. Bangladesh: The Unfinished Revolution. London: Zed Books.

Novak, James A. 1993. *Bangladesh: Reflections on the Water*. Bloomington: Indiana University Press.

Riaz, Ali. 2004. *God Willing: The Politics of Islamism in Bangladesh*. Lanham, MA: Rowman and Littlefield.

Riaz, Ali. 2005. *Unfolding State: The Transformation of Bangladesh*. Ontario: DeSitter.

Sisson, Richard, and Leo E. Rose. 1991. *War and Secession: Pakistan, India, and the Creation of Bangladesh*. Berkeley: University of California Press.

van Schendel, Willem. 2009. *A History of Bangladesh*. Cambridge: Cambridge University Press.

Ziring, Lawrence. 1992. *Bangladesh: from Mujib to Ershad: An Interpretive Study*. Oxford: Oxford University Press.

# 5 Sri Lanka

*Neil DeVotta*

Post-independence Sri Lanka is an excellent example of both democratic deepening and democratic regression; for the island went from a commendable democracy to one that experienced nearly 30 years of civil war and authoritarianism. In many ways Sri Lanka is experiencing the maladies of fellow South Asian states. At the same time, it also stands out for having regressed the most democratically, given how robust its institutions were around independence compared to its fellow South Asian states. A new president elected in January 2015, however, appears to herald a reversion to a more democratic climate.

Sri Lanka, like all countries in South Asia, has been enriched by a South Asian civilization that spans millennia. While the island's ancient history is disputable, the myths associated with this history and the subsequent colonial experience that lasted over 450 years have contributed immensely to its political development.

## History and political development

What one can say with certainty is that the vast majority of Sri Lankans are of Indian origin and that the country, thanks to this kinship, has been shaped by the region's beliefs and culture. Enjoying a strategic location, the country has since ancient times also benefitted from ideas and practices of seafarers—the most recent being the Portuguese, Dutch, and British, who successively colonized the island beginning in 1505. This heritage has in turn influenced the island's ethno-religious makeup.

As of 2012, the island's ethnic breakdown was as follows: Sinhalese 74.9 percent, Sri Lankan Tamil 11.2 percent, Indian Tamil 4.2 percent, and Moors (Muslim) 9.2 percent. In terms of religion, the island was 70.2 percent Buddhist, 12.6 percent Hindu, 7.4 percent Christian (with 6.1 percent being Roman Catholic), and 9.7 percent Islam. While Muslims primarily speak Tamil (with nearly all young Muslims now also speaking Sinhala), they have long used their religious identity as their ethnic identity (thereby differentiating themselves from the country's ethnic Tamils). Interethnic and intraethnic dynamics in poly-ethnic and multi-religious societies can get complicated, and this is no different in Sri Lanka. Thus while about 10 percent of Sinhalese and Tamils are Christians, one rarely encounters Sinhalese Hindus and Tamil Buddhists, although in ancient times Buddhism enjoyed a strong presence in Tamil areas (in both India and Sri Lanka).

Sri Lanka is unique in that it has access to a history book called the *Mahavamsa* (or Great Chronicle), which claims to document the country's origins beginning in 543 BCE, although scholars believe the text was first put together by Buddhist monks around the sixth century AD. While politicians and ethnic elites of recent times have manipulated the book's interpretations and thereby sowed discord among the country's ethnic groups, this text documents a chronology of especially Sinhalese kings and the special place the Buddhist religion holds within the island.

The *Mahavamsa* claims that the Sinhalese originate from the area that is now West Bengal in India and that Lord Buddha chose them to live in Sri Lanka and protect his teachings (*dhamma*). This led to notions of Sri Lanka being *sinhadipa* (island of the Sinhalese) and *dhammadipa* (island containing Buddha's teachings). The claim that the Sinhalese are the chosen people ennobled to preserve and propagate Buddhism thus forms the basis for much of the Sinhalese Buddhist nationalism evidenced in the island over especially the past 150 years. It has led to the Buddhist clergy commanding significant influence in the island's political affairs and Sinhalese Buddhist nationalists insisting on the island being a unitary state (and bitterly opposing power being devolved to minority regions).

Sri Lankan Tamils compose the second largest community in the island. Hailing from what is currently India's southern state of Tamil Nadu, they are mainly located in the island's northeast. Some Tamils argue that their ancestors first settled the island. With Sri Lanka's northernmost point being merely 22 miles from southern India, it is highly unlikely that South Indians were unfamiliar with the island until after the Sinhalese supposedly arrived. Tamils are primarily Hindus, although some converted to Christianity so that around 7 percent are currently Christian.

Their predominantly Hindu faith and cultural links saw some Tamils collaborate with South India's Hindu states (the Pandyas, Pallavas, and Cholas) starting in the fifth and sixth centuries. While such collaboration affected the fortunes of various Sinhalese kings, the resulting tensions at the time were apparently viewed within religious and regional prisms, as opposed to ethnic. That changed beginning in the early twentieth century when Sinhalese and Tamil nationalisms took hold, which led to a string of anti-Tamil policies and deadly anti-Tamil riots in 1956, 1958, 1977, and 1983, all of which combined to provoke a nearly 30-year civil war between the Sri Lankan government and the Liberation Tigers of Tamil Eelam (LTTE), the group that violently wrested leadership from Tamil moderates and sought to create a separate Tamil state until it was brutally defeated in May 2009. The July 1983 anti-Tamil violence was a veritable pogrom, and the thousands of Tamils who fled the island as refugees have since mobilized into a potent diaspora and are also at the forefront in demanding accountability for the war crimes that may have killed over 40,000 Tamils during the final stages of the ethnic conflict.

## Box 5.1:  The Liberation Tigers of Tamil Eelam

The ethnic outbidding and anti-Tamil policies successive Sri Lankan governments pursued led to marginalized Tamil youth joining numerous groups bent on creating *eelam* (a separate Tamil state) in the island's north and east. The Tamil New Tigers was one such group that was created in 1972 and rechristened itself the Liberation Tigers of Tamil Eelam in 1976. The group ambushed an army patrol in July 1983 that killed 13 soldiers and sparked anti-Tamil riots, which culminated in a gruesome civil war lasting three decades.

The LTTE was led by Vellupillai Prabhakaran, and the group exemplified discipline and commitment by practicing austerity, eschewing corruption, abstaining from sexual relations and alcohol consumption, and carrying a cyanide capsule (which many swallowed so as to avoid being captured by Sri Lanka's military). The group's reputation was burnished after it fought the Indian Peace Keeping Force—which the Indian government stationed in the island as part of an agreement with the Sri Lankan government to end the conflict—from July 1987 to March 1990 that saw around 1,200 Indian soldiers killed. The conflict remains the longest war waged by the Indian security forces. Thereafter the LTTE coopted or eliminated rival groups and claimed to be the Tamils' sole representative.

The LTTE operated more like a multinational organization, with offices, lobbyists, media, and businesses in various countries. It developed a strong presence among the Tamil diaspora and its cadres abroad often resorted to intimidation, fraud, and extortion when raising money to fight the Sri Lankan government. It had its own police force and courts in the areas it controlled, and its naval unit included nearly a dozen ships that were partly used to smuggle arms. Towards the latter stages the group also set up an air wing with a few small, slow moving planes that rattled Sri Lankans when they dropped a few rudimentary bombs.

The LTTE was notorious for its suicide bombers (Black Tigers) who killed former Indian Prime Minister Rajiv Gandhi, Sri Lankan President Ranasinghe Premadasa, and numerous politicians, military personnel, and opponents (many of whom were Tamil). It almost killed President Chandrika Kumaratunga, Army Commander Sarath Fonseka, and Defense Secretary Gotabhaya Rajapaksa. It perfected suicide jackets and is said to have influenced groups like Al Qaeda. Its suicide attacks, combined with its unlawful activities in numerous countries, bombing of civilian targets, and repression in the areas it controlled—which included taxing the civilian population and forcibly recruiting children into its ranks—led the United States and many other countries to proscribe the organization as a terrorist outfit.

Vellupillai Prabhakaran's determination to create *eelam* via military means (and hence his unwillingness to compromise), coupled with the inability of successive Sri Lankan governments to build support among the Sinhalese Buddhists to accommodate legitimate Tamil grievances, prolonged the conflict until the Rajapaksa government resorted to a no-holds-barred military operation that killed over 40,000 civilians during the final months of the war that ended in May 2009. The LTTE's split in March 2004, when its eastern wing broke away and started collaborating with the government, expedited its defeat. The alleged war crimes the Sri Lankan security forces and government officials committed when decimating the LTTE and the Rajapaksa government's intransigence when responding to the accusations have roiled Sri Lanka's relations with especially western countries that keep demanding accountability for human rights violations.

The LTTE's defeat has emboldened Sinhalese Buddhist nationalists, but Sri Lanka paid a horrendous price for its civil war. The conflict stanched development, exacerbated the "brain drain" from the country, militarized and brutalized society, helped undermine democracy, displaced over a million people, and killed over 100,000—including around 23,000 government troops and 40,000 LTTE cadre.

While the LTTE's former cadres and supporters now wage a propaganda campaign against the Sri Lankan state, Prabhakaran's death and the group's defeat has ended the quest for *eelam*. Tamils today are more marginalized than ever before, and the LTTE bears a major responsibility for this. Thus, the group was ultimately more bane than boon for Sri Lanka's long-suffering Tamils (DeVotta 2009).

While Sri Lankan Tamils have lived in the island since ancient times, a second group of Tamils, called Indian Tamils, started arriving in the country beginning around the 1830s to work as indentured laborers on British plantations. Long marginalized for their poverty and low-caste origins, many among the Indian Tamils were denied citizenship when Sri Lanka gained independence in 1948 and over half the population was relocated to India following treaties negotiated between Indian and Sri Lankan leaders (Bass 2013). The deplorable rhetoric Sinhalese leaders embraced to deny citizenship to these Tamils, most of whom were born and raised in Sri Lanka (Nayak 2014), presaged the majoritarian politicking awaiting the island's other minorities. Indian Tamils continue to work mainly on tea estates as laborers, although many belonging to the younger generation now seek employment in garment factories, shops and restaurants, and the Middle East. While they were not part of the LTTE's attempt to secede from the island, their status as Tamils who speak the Tamil language marked them for discrimination and hostility.

Muslims initially made their way to the country as traders and starting around the tenth century many from the Malabar Coast began locating along the island's littoral. Muslims opposed Tamil extremists' attempts to split the island. This exposed the community to attacks by the LTTE, with over 70,000 Muslims forcibly evicted from the Northern Province in 1990. Long considered the "good minority," Muslims have recently been vilified and attacked by Sinhalese Buddhist nationalists who have become emboldened thanks to the state's victory over the LTTE (see Box 5.3).

Sri Lanka harbors other small ethnic communities, the most prominent of which are the Burghers. This group, being Christian with ancestral links to the colonial powers, played an important role in especially the British bureaucracy. Many began emigrating following independence, and this combined with marrying into other communities is leading to the group's gradual erasure.

While today's Sinhalese Buddhist nationalists utilize notions of *sinhadipa* and *dhammadipa* to claim that Sri Lanka must be a unitary state (as opposed to a federal state or one in which power is devolved towards the provinces), the fact remains that the island was long composed of multiple kingdoms. A kingdom in the northern capital of Jaffna lasted over 400 years until the Portuguese defeated it in 1619; another surrounding the current political capital city of Kotte endured until the Portuguese took it over and then abandoned it in the late sixteenth century; and Kandy, in the central hills, held out valiantly against the British until it was forced into submission between 1815–18.

The British thus became the first entity to control the entire island, which they branded Ceylon. The Colebrooke-Cameron Reforms of 1831–32 called for the island to be administratively unified and subsequent changes were geared towards remaking the country "into a single society and space" irrespective of regional differences (Wickramasinghe 2006, 29). The British ruled Ceylon from 1798 until independence in 1948, with governors reporting directly to the Colonial Office in London—as opposed to coming under the governors-general and viceroys in British India. Had this not been the case, India would likely have claimed Sri Lanka as part of its territory when British India gained independence in August 1947, and the island's political trajectory could have turned out differently.

As part of administrative reforms, the British set up a Legislative Council in 1833 that comprised 16 members, 10 of whom the governor officially appointed. The other six members of the Council, called "unofficial members," were nominated on a communal basis, with the Europeans getting three of the six seats and the Sinhalese, Tamils, and Burghers qualifying for a seat each. In 1889, the Muslims and the Sinhalese who were part of the former kingdom of Kandy were also provided a seat each as unofficial members. This communal representation system saw the local population being heavily underrepresented, and the subsequent calls for reforms saw the Legislative Council being repeatedly enlarged in 1912, 1921, and 1924.

While a Sinhalese Buddhist revival took shape in the latter quarter of the nineteenth century in response to Christian proselytizing and was responsible for the rise of modern Sinhalese Buddhist nationalism (Malalgoda 1976), the ethnic dimension was emphasized only starting in the twentieth century. Indeed, it was class, caste, and religion that influenced politics during 1875–1925. For instance, lower-caste Sinhalese criticized the British for favoring upper-caste Sinhalese when nominating members to the Legislative Council, even as both lower and upper caste Sinhalese protested against the British nominating Christian Sinhalese to the Council. In 1910, when Europeans, Burghers, and educated locals—a group that was merely 1.8 percent of the population—were permitted to vote under a reformed electoral scheme for four additional members to the legislative Council, high-caste Sinhalese and Tamils united to elect a high-caste Tamil and defeat the lower-caste Sinhalese (Roberts 1982).

The 1915 anti-Muslim riots manifested the religious tensions during this period, which appear to have been partly based on Sinhalese business interests feeling threatened by Muslim competitors (Tambiah 1992). This was preceded by a major riot between Buddhists and Catholics in northern Colombo in 1883, which was followed by other flare-ups between Christians and Buddhists in some areas during 1907–27—presumably because Buddhists objected to Christians being too closely associated with the colonial regime (Wickramasinghe 2006). These uprisings evidence some of the tensions between communities and complaints against the British, but they in no way approximate the anti-colonial movement in British India.

Tamils in the north had especially taken to learning English as Britain consolidated its rule over Sri Lanka and Christian missionaries increased their proselytizing efforts. This helped many Tamils secure employment within the colonial apparatus, so much so that soon Tamils were highly overrepresented within the bureaucracy, military, university system, and many other prominent professions. While the arid conditions in the northeast, compared to the highly fertile areas in much of the rest of the island, induced Tamils to seek employment within the colonial structure, the British encouraged this development, as it was consistent with their penchant for dividing and ruling. The divide-and-rule system typically empowered minority communities as it made little sense for the colonial power to strengthen the majority community that was most likely to try and dethrone it. British policies—with regard to recruitment but also concerning the marginalization of Buddhism—thus contributed towards ethnic difference being emphasized.

Despite being a minority, Tamils' dominant position in the colonial setup led their elites to consider themselves a "majority" on par with the Sinhalese. Sinhalese and British elites countenanced such thinking, whereby all other groups, excluding the Tamils, were classified as minorities. But this sense of equality began to change as the country moved closer to becoming more democratic, and this too contributed to Sinhalese-Tamil tensions.

Initially English-educated and westernized Sinhalese and Tamil elites came together to seek greater representation, and they formed the Ceylon Reform League in 1916, which became the Ceylon National Congress (CNC) in 1919. These elites, however, sought the vote only for their own class, and it was the transplanted British liberals who clamored for greater elective representation. However, both groups' collective efforts led to the Donoughmore Constitution in 1931.

The Donoughmore Constitution was notable for introducing two major reforms. First, it created an executive committee system, whereby members sat on committees overseeing the business conducted by the legislature and executive. This meant that seven committees located within the State Council, with the chairman of each executive committee holding a ministerial position and all the chairmen together forming the Board of Ministers, ran the government. The chairmen acted as independents and policy got made within a clannish culture that encouraged a degree of consensus and discouraged political parties.

The second major reform the Donoughmore Constitution introduced was to discard communal electorates and permit universal franchise. In the 1920s only about 4 percent of the island's population qualified to vote; by 1931 all adults could vote. Sri Lanka thus not only became the first non-white country that was part of the British Empire to enjoy universal suffrage, but this radical development took place 17 years before independence and only three years after Britain allowed its women the right to vote! It is instructive that universal franchise was instituted against the opposition of most CNC members, who preferred to only extend the franchise to those who were educated and owned property (Tambiah 1992).

The one-person-one-vote principle, however, favored the majority community, and this inevitably saw politics during the Donoughmore era (1931–47) being dominated by ethnic considerations (Russell 1982). For instance, during this period Tamil elites, seeking parity of status, called for a 50-50 formula (or balanced representation between the Sinhalese and minorities), which would have given the Sinhalese, who were around 70 percent of the population at this time, only 50 percent representation. Such demands and the accompanying debates heightened communal feelings and created the space for especially Sinhalese Buddhist nationalists to influence politics in the years ahead.

Yet notwithstanding the fundamentally exploitative nature of colonialism and simmering ethnic tensions between especially Sinhalese and Tamils, Sri Lanka had much going for it as it approached independence. The British had managed relations with most local stakeholders relatively well, developed some significant infrastructure (roads, bridges, and railways), and helped create fairly well-governed institutions. Consequently, the island ranked relatively high on various socio-economic indices, especially when compared to other Asian and African states undergoing decolonization, and many believed that it was likely to be the post-colonial state with "the best chance of making a successful transition to modern statehood" (Wriggins 1961, 316). Most importantly, Sinhalese and Tamil elites agreed to the new Soulbury Constitution the British designed in 1946 and the terms under which power was transferred, so that Sri Lanka's transition from colonialism to independence was a tepid affair that contrasted starkly with the pre-independence mobilization and ruckus in neighboring India. Indeed, the change was so seamless that people in rural areas hardly realized a major political transformation had taken place.

## Institutions, political parties, and elections

While the Soulbury Commission that drafted the Soulbury Constitution disregarded the Tamils' demand for 50-50 parity of representation between the Sinhalese and minorities, it sought to make allowances to shore up minority representation. For instance, recognizing that minorities mostly lived in less populated areas, the commissioners recommended that a parliamentary seat be allocated for every 75,000 persons and 1,000 square miles. The Commission also permitted six nominated members and five multimember constituencies, with voters in the latter allowed as many votes as there were candidates and permitted to cast all their votes for a single candidate if they so desired. Furthermore, the Soulbury Constitution allowed for a Delimitation Commission for redistricting purposes. Yet the island's demography was such that even this sort of tinkering failed to prevent the Sinhalese being an absolute majority in 73 constituencies and controlling "75 out of 95 elected seats" (Weerawardana 1960, 87).

The Soulbury Constitution also failed to codify stringent minority guarantees, and instead merely required the government to treat all ethno-religious communities fairly. Opportunistic politicians were to soon take advantage of this lack of constitutionally guaranteed minority rights and propel Sri Lanka toward ethnic turmoil (see the section titled Managing Conflict). The subsequent ethnocentric politics that the Sri Lanka Freedom Party (SLFP) and United National Party (UNP) adopted shaped in no small way how Sri Lanka's institutions have become compromised.

For instance, in 1972 the government led by the SLFP's Sirimavo Bandaranaike created a new constitution that gave Buddhism "foremost status," thereby relegating Hinduism, Islam, and Christianity to second-class status. The constitution also branded the island a "unitary" state, thereby disregarding demands by moderate Tamil politicians for a federal arrangement that would have allowed Tamil areas a degree of autonomy.

In the 1977 elections the UNP trounced the SLFP so as to command a five-sixth super majority in parliament, which meant the party could pass whatever legislation it wanted. The UNP's leader, J.R. Jayewardene, used this majority to introduce the 1978 constitution, which saw a mixed electoral system with a powerful president who is both head of state and head of government. The president is elected for a six-year term but can call for early elections after completing four years. President Mahinda Rajapaksa, who was first elected president in November 2005, called elections nearly two years early in January 2010 to capitalize on the government's victory over the LTTE; and he did likewise when seeking a third term in January 2015, but lost to Maithripala Sirisena.

The president picks the prime minister and cabinet and presides over cabinet meetings. Under the Westminster system, prime ministers operated as the executive; but under the presidential system that Jayewardene set up, the prime minister is merely a figurehead, leading his first prime minister, Ranasinghe Premadasa, to bemoan that he was nothing more than a peon.

Up until April 2015 the president was able to suspend parliament one year after the previous election and prorogue parliament for a two-month period, a stratagem the country's fourth president, Chandrika Kumaratunga, resorted to in 2000 when dealing with a hostile parliament. While parliament may impeach the president, this is structurally hard to do given the president's ability to sack members of parliament and pick Supreme Court justices (who tend to be partial towards their patron). This was evident when parliament sought to impeach Jeyawardene's successor, Ranasinghe Premadasa, but failed.

Prior to the 1978 constitution, Sri Lankans resorted to the first-past-the-post electoral system to elect members of parliament. This meant that whoever won the highest number of votes in a district, be it a majority or plurality, ended up being the victor. The 1978 constitution introduced a proportional-representation-cum-preferential voting system, whereby voters select a party and also list three candidates in order of preference from the chosen party. The number of candidates a party acquires from the 22 electoral districts is based on the percentage of votes polled in the respective district; and the candidates who qualify for a seat in parliament are those who obtain the most preferential votes in their districts. Thus, for example, if the votes the UNP obtained in a district qualified it to send five members to parliament from that district, the five UNP candidates who obtained the most preference votes in the district would be the ones elected. The system also rewards the party that garners the most votes in a district with a bonus seat.

The unicameral legislature Jayewardene's constitution set up has 225 members. Of these, 196 are elected through the 22 multimember electoral districts, while 29 are reserved for National List (NL) members. A party's national vote determines how many NL members it qualifies to have, and this allows a party to nominate prominent supporters and skilled and qualified citizens to parliament. Most NL appointees, however, have been as opportunistic as elected parliamentarians and have abandoned their party when in opposition to cross over to government ranks in exchange for cabinet portfolios.

Jayewardene's constitution was designed to ensure the UNP stayed perpetually dominant (Oberst 1984). He bragged that the only thing he could not do under the new constitution was change a man into a woman and vice versa. In this spirit, he amended the constitution 16 times between 1978 and 1988, often in a partisan and whimsical fashion, and ruled in an autocratic manner. In 1980 he vindictively stripped SLFP leader Mrs. Sirimavo Bandaranaike of her civic rights for seven years (in retaliation for her previous extension of SLFP rule by two years until 1977) and expelled her from parliament, thereby ensuring that his most effective opponent could not challenge him for reelection in 1982. He then refused to hold scheduled parliamentary elections that would most certainly have led to a loss of seats for the UNP and instead held a severely compromised referendum in December 1982 that extended the party's five-sixth majority for another term. He even forced all UNP ministers to turn in signed but undated resignation letters, which ensured that they followed his dictates. His attitude toward the democratic process was best captured when he boasted: "We are contesting the election to win and at a time most favorable to us. We intend ... to demolish and completely destroy the opposition politically. After that I say to you, roll up the electoral map of Sri Lanka. You will not need it for another ten years" (Samarakone 1984, 86).

Jayewardene used his power to dominate and assault those who crossed him. For instance, he used hoodlums belonging to the UNP's labor union to suppress strikes, beat protestors, harass journalists and Supreme Court justices, and attack political opponents. These forces were also used to foment anti-Tamil riots in 1977 and 1983, with dire consequences for the island. Ranasinghe Premadasa, Dingiribanda Wijetunga, Chandrika Kumaratunga, Mahinda Rajapaksa, and Maithripala Sirisena have succeeded Jayewardene as president. Except for the lackluster but dignified Dingiribanda Wijetunga, who served a short term, and Maithripala Sirisena, who has mounted a strong campaign to abolish the executive presidency, the others have used executive powers to operate in even more ham-handed ways than Jayewardene, leading to the separation of powers being diminished. The separation of powers that promote transparency, accountability, and rule of law was most crippled under Mahinda Rajapaksa, whose authoritarian tendencies saw state institutions deliberately weakened and power concentrated within the so-called Rajapaksa "First Family."

### The Rajapaksa "First Family" and the tilt toward authoritarianism

Mahinda Rajapaksa, besides being president, was also the minister for defense, finance, highways, planning, and ports and aviation. These combined portfolios placed 78 government institutions directly under his control. While charming and politically savvy, the president brooked little dissent. This led to a supine cabinet of ministers who dared not cross Rajapaksa lest they lost their positions and perks. And it led to a president bent on authoritarianism. This was partly evident by the way in which Rajapaksa targeted retired army commander Sarath Fonseka, who was responsible for the military strategy to defeat the LTTE, but thereafter challenged Rajapaksa in the 2010 presidential election: he was forcibly dragged away from his office, court-martialed for improper military procurements, divested of his civil rights and military honors, and sentenced to jail for three years. Rajapaksa's authoritarian proclivities were especially evident when he forced through the Eighteenth Amendment to the constitution, which was incorporated in September 2010. The amendment abolished the Seventeenth Amendment and terminated the two-term limit for presidents.

Sri Lanka's parliament passed the Seventeenth Amendment unanimously in 2001; and while it failed to achieve full enforcement, the amendment mandated the creation of a Constitutional Council with sole powers to appoint and dismiss commissioners overseeing elections, public service, police, finance, human rights, and bribery and corruption. The Constitutional Council was further empowered to appoint the chief justice and other justices on the Supreme Court, president and judges of the Court of Appeal, members of the Judicial Services Commission (excepting its chairman), attorney general, inspector general of police, auditor general, parliamentary commissioner for administration (or ombudsman), and secretary general of parliament. This was a belated attempt to halt political interference and promote independent, impartial, and professional operations among and within these institutions.

The Eighteenth Amendment did away with the Constitutional Council and empowered the president to appoint personnel to lead the institutions under its purview. The president merely had to take into consideration the "observations" of the prime minister, speaker, and leader of the opposition when doing so. The Eighteenth Amendment also permitted the president to contest more than two terms, which President Rajapaksa utilized to run for a third term in January 2015. The president engineered crossovers from the opposition to ensure he commanded the requisite two-thirds majority to pass the amendment, and by some accounts some of these politicians were paid over half-a-million dollars to abandon the parties under whose banner they got elected. The amendment promotes democratic regression by making a powerful executive branch even more powerful.

Under President Rajapaksa, his younger brother, Basil, was the Minister of Economic Development, which included the Board of Investment and the Tourist Promotion Bureau. Another brother, Gotabhaya, was the country's Defense Secretary, who played a leading role in defeating the LTTE. In addition to superintending the armed forces, police, and coast guard, Gotabhaya Rajapaksa also oversaw immigration and emigration, the Land Reclamation and Development Corporation, and the Urban Development Authority. Gotabhaya was often referred to as Sri Lanka's most powerful man. He refused to demobilize the military and instead used it to supposedly develop the island, which catapulted the military into hitherto civilian business spheres. It is Gotabhaya Rajapaksa who instituted the policy of not tolerating criticism against the military, and he was most responsible for militarizing Sri Lanka, going so far as to get university entrants to undergo disciplinary training in army camps and putting over 4,000 school principals through a military training program and thereafter granting them military titles. Gotabhaya was widely feared and journalists resisted reporting on him negatively. Many in the opposition, media, and diplomatic corps considered him responsible for the paramilitary outfits that used white vans to disappear critics of the government. Sri Lanka's former army commander has claimed that it was Gotabhaya Rajapaksa who ordered surrendering LTTE cadres carrying white flags be shot.

A third brother, Chamal, was made Speaker of Parliament, which allowed him to block any attempt to impeach the president. Thanks to the crossovers Mahinda Rajapaksa engineered, the SLFP-led United People's Freedom Alliance (UPFA) coalition enjoyed a two-thirds parliamentary majority that allowed it to amend the constitution at any time. Indeed, his government had 62 members who had crossed over from the UNP alone. This, combined with the all-powerful executive, led parliamentarians within the UPFA to be

## Box 5.2:  Militarization

Sri Lanka's military has failed to demobilize despite the civil war having ended in May 2009. The Rajapaksa government claimed it would be unfair to summarily release military personnel—who sacrificed much to defeat the LTTE and are widely considered war heroes—especially when they have few alternate employment options. Maithripala Sirisena, when campaigning against Rajapaksa, also promised not to demobilize the military despite the institution eating up around 20% percent of the country's budget. Former military personnel have joined criminal gangs and resorted to destabilizing activities (often in alliance with politicians), and this makes demobilization without guaranteed alternative employment dangerous. Besides, firing poor soldiers is politically unwise, since they are bound to vote against politicians seen to undermine their livelihood.

But such a large number of military personnel cannot be left idling, and President Rajapaksa's Ministry of Defense put these soldiers to work by claiming that they were necessary to develop the country. As a result, the military was—is—fully engaged in businesses that were traditionally part of the civilian domain. Military personnel have built roads and bridges, farmed and sold vegetables, overseen a canal boat service, conducted whale and dolphin watching tours, run hotels and guesthouses, refurbished schools and government buildings, superintended cricket stadiums, and operated travel offices. Soldiers have hung street lanterns during Buddhist religious festivals and cleaned drains whenever malaria or dengue was rife. They even supposedly supervised workers collecting garbage. And Rakna Arakshaka Lanka Ltd., a firm operating under the Ministry of Defense, was responsible for security at the airport, Port's Authority, universities, and all state institutions. The military also operated tea shops and barber salons along the A-9 highway leading north. The military need not worry about standard overhead costs and, consequently, represented unfair economic competition to entrepreneurs.

During Rajapaksa rule, military dictates superseded civil administration in the north, with the governor who is appointed by the president disregarding the TNA-led provincial council. Surveillance was common across the island, but was most acute in the north where people in villages were recruited to monitor and report on neighbors' activities, with many rehabilitated LTTE cadre dragooned into doing so. Personnel from the Criminal Investigation Department (CID) visited northern Tamil villages regularly and people had to inform the military of all family, community, associational, and political gatherings since such meetings got interpreted as insurgencies in the making. New military camps amidst the confiscation of civilian properties in the north smacked of Sinhalese Buddhist colonization of traditionally Tamil areas and contributed to a sense that the Rajapaksa government was determined to dominate and subjugate an already downtrodden ethnic group.

Sri Lanka's military never had it this good: its increased role in the country's postwar development and support for it, among especially Sinhalese, have made military service pretty satisfying for most personnel. And the Rajapaksas also cultivated an image of being pro-military and contributed to a climate where the military was beyond reproach—so much so that flagging military malpractices automatically led to one being branded a traitor. A military that is being treated well is one that is unlikely to turn against the ruling elite, and the Rajapaksas were banking on this. However, Sri Lanka's army commander (and Inspector General of Police) refused to go along with the Rajapaksas when they sought to extend their rule by annulling the January 2015 election results and imposing a state of emergency. One major challenge now facing the new government is how to downsize the military without victimizing its personnel and demoralizing the institution.

pliant and disengaged, which in turn allowed the Speaker to get his brother's executive preferences easily rubber stamped and further vitiated the separation of powers between the executive and legislature.

Chamal's son, Shashindra, was the Chief Minister of Uva Province (one of the island's nine provinces), and the president's eldest son, Namal, was—is—a member of parliament—as are two of the president's cousins. Nearly 130 Rajapaksa relatives were provided prominent government postings. The 28-year-old Namal was being groomed to eventually succeed the president, and he controlled the *Tarunayata Hetak* (A Tomorrow for the Youth) and *Nil Balakaya* (Blue Brigade) youth groups. Many members in these groups were provided employment abroad while some others were given state employment. Many among them were responsible for violence against opposition candidates during elections.

The Rajapaksa brothers controlled between 60 to 70 percent of the country's budget through their portfolios. Mahinda Rajapaksa's father and uncle were prominent politicians in the country's south but the family's gains during Rajapaksa's presidency was due mainly to nepotism. Their stunning ascendance and widespread involvement in government affairs marginalized and upset members of the SLFP old guard, which was what led to Maithripala Sirisena, the longstanding SLFP General Secretary, and other SLFP leaders, including former President Chandrika Kumaratunga, to form a common opposition that defeated President Rajapaksa in the 2015 presidential elections.

Already-compromised institutions were further weakened under the Rajapaksa government thanks to diktats that undermined legitimate institutional actors. For instance, decisions made by bureaucratic heads and ministers were summarily overturned, thereby confusing and compromising ministers. This contributed to ministers and their powerful secretaries at times abdicating their responsibilities, although overlapping ministerial portfolios also assisted in this outcome. There was less transparency, with officials often relaying decisions by phone as opposed to in writing. Even government circulars, which ought to be part of the public domain, were hard to locate, and oftentimes government agents (especially in the Northern Province) were forced to act on requests without access to the circulars. At the cabinet level, memos and minutes failed to get distributed, so that cabinet ministers themselves were often unsure what they may have agreed to in past meetings. In short, most major decisions were based on directives by the president and his brothers, with the bureaucracy becoming playthings of the First Family.

Mediocre parliamentarians, who merely seek power and spoils and are disinterested in governance, abdicated their legislative responsibilities and helped Rajapaksa and his family monopolize power. Weak and divided oppositions also helped the executive branch grow more powerful. The decline in standards and professionalism that undermined state institutions further allowed the presidency to hold sway vis-à-vis entities that in the past provided a check against excessive and extra-constitutional executive power. But in the case of

President Rajapaksa, an insidious patronage system (sometimes tied to intimidation) and a secretive operating culture within the executive branch also eroded checks and balances.

The separation of powers was further weakened by Sri Lanka's politicized, corrupt, and pliant judiciary. The Rajapaksa administration's malpractices intensified the judiciary's deinstitutionalization, leading to conformity and subservience to the executive branch taking precedence over independence, impartiality, and the rule of law. This led to instances of "telephone justice," whereby those working within the executive branch called and influenced judges' decisions, with the pliant judges provided perks ranging from travelling abroad, having their spouses appointed to head government establishments, and being promised sinecures after retirement.

The judiciary's weakened position and the government's authoritarian nature was especially highlighted when the country's first ever female chief justice was impeached in January 2013. President Rajapaksa appointed Shirani Bandaranayake chief justice in May 2011; and she, like her predecessors and fellow justices, initially contributed to court rulings that strengthened the executive presidency. Yet when Chief Justice Bandaranayake ruled that the government's desire to create a *Divinegume* (Improving Lives) Department—which amalgamated the operations of three extant entities under the Minister of Economic Development and presidential sibling Basil Rajapaksa and provided him with an additional $600 million (under the guise of development) to expand the First Family's patronage system—violated aspects of the constitution, the president set up a Parliamentary Select Committee (PSC) composed of politicians from the ruling coalition that found her guilty of financial and official misconduct, leading to her impeachment. This was done despite the Supreme Court ruling that the PSC had no right to investigate a senior judge and the Appeals Court ordering parliament to abandon the impeachment process. Civil society organizations, clergy members, foreign governments, and various international bodies likewise objected strenuously. President Rajapaksa disregarded their entreaties and summarily signed the order removing the chief justice, even as pro-government goons brandishing poles gathered outside her official residence to make sure she relinquished her post. A message was thus sent to those in the island's lower courts (magistrate's courts, district courts, high court, and court of appeal): if the chief justice could be treated in such a humiliating fashion, so could everyone else. In the lead-up to this, parliamentarians among the governing coalition affirmed their willingness to throw out the chief justice by signing a blank sheet of paper devoid of the impeachment motion. Parliamentarians who are part of a governing party are expected to support that party's policies within the legislature, but this action highlighted the degree to which parliament has abdicated its role as a potential counter to executive overreach and the manner in which it affects other institutions that are supposed to afford checks and balances befitting a democracy.

The nepotism and massive corruption associated with the Rajapaksas saw over 40 parties and organizations support the common opposition candidate Maithripala Sirisena in the 2015 presidential election. President Rajapaksa sought to impose emergency rule and annul the election results when it became clear that Maithripala Sirisena had defeated him. (The final result was Sirisena 51.28 percent; Rajapaksa 47.58 percent, with 81.5 percent voter turnout.) He retreated after the attorney general, solicitor general, army commander, and chief of police refused to support him in this. Sri Lanka underwent a failed coup in 1962 (Horowitz 1980); the island's military has otherwise subordinated itself to elected leaders. Rajapaksa's failed attempt to illegally perpetuate his rule strengthens civilian leadership over the military and bolsters Sri Lanka's democratic credentials, even as it provides the country an opportunity to abandon corruption, nepotism, and malgovernance. Indeed, President Sirisena—who was general secretary of the SLFP and the minister of health in the Rajapaksa cabinet when he left the UPFA coalition to become the common opposition candidate—promised to put an end to the presidential system and steer the country towards good government. While his election heralds a move away from authoritarianism, only time will tell if he can help Sri Lanka regain good governance.

### Political parties

The first political parties in Sri Lanka were leftist. The Trotskyist Lanka Sama Samaja Party (LSSP; Lanka Equal Society Party) was formed in 1935, and the pro-Moscow Communist Party (CP) was formed in 1943. While neither endeared themselves to a mainly conservative and anti-communist electorate, the two parties were at the forefront in organizing workers and laborers in the period leading up to independence. Indeed, one reason that Indian Tamils were so easily disenfranchised was because mainstream politicians (and their western allies) feared that these estate laborers were bound to become a natural constituency for the leftists.

The conservative United National Party was not created until April 1946, less than two years before Sri Lanka gained independence. The UNP has been labeled the "Uncle-Nephew Party," given that four of the party's six leaders have been related to its founder (and Sri Lanka's first prime minister) D.S. Senanayake: Dudley Senanayake took over from his father D.S., and Dudley's cousin, Sir John Kotelawala, succeeded him; J.R. Jayewardene was closely related to D.S. Senanayake, and the UNP's present leader, Ranil Wickremasinghe, is Jayewardene's nephew. The UNP draws strong support among minorities during presidential elections (since minorities usually vote for ethnic parties during parliamentary, provincial, and local elections). The party, however, fared poorly under Wickremasinghe, who, despite losing a string of elections and serious infighting, held on to the leadership position. The UNP-led United National Front won only 60 seats in the April 2010 parliamentary elections. Crossovers and fissures within the party allowed the Rajapaksa family to monopolize power amidst corruption and mismanagement. Wickremasinghe's inability to get a majority of Sri Lankans to vote for him as president is the reason the UNP supported candidates from other parties to contest the 2010 and 2015 presidential elections (see below). Maithripala Sirisena's presidential victory, however, saw Ranil Wickremasinghe becoming the country's prime minister.

The UNP's archrival is the Sri Lanka Freedom Party, which was created in September 1951, after its founder, S.W.R.D. Bandaranaike, left the UNP on realizing that Prime Minister D.S. Senanayake was grooming his son, Dudley, to take over the party's leadership. The SLFP has consistently appealed to Sinhalese Buddhists and drawn support mainly from rural areas. The party long operated as a dynasty, with three family members—Mr. and Mrs. Bandaranaike and their daughter, Chandrika Kumaratunga—serving as the country's leaders for over 26 years. Many believed that Mahinda Rajapaksa's rise and the family's dynastic ambitions had ended the Bandaranaike political dominance. But Chandrika Kumaratunga's role in creating the common opposition that led to Maithripala Sirisena defeating Rajapaksa suggests that the Bandaranaike family may continue to chart the SLFP's future.

The Janatha Vimukthi Peramuna (JVP; People's Liberation Front) is another party that has played an important role in Sri Lanka's politics. Originally composed of disgruntled Sinhalese Marxist students, the group was formed in the mid-1960s and mounted an insurrection in 1971 that nearly toppled the Sirimavo Bandaranaike government. The insurrection was violently suppressed, and thousands of JVP cadres were killed and imprisoned.

The group entered mainstream politics in the late 1970s after the UNP, headed by J.R. Jayewardene, released the imprisoned cadres. The UNP believed the JVP, given its

Sinhalese Buddhist composition and appeal in rural areas, would undercut the SLFP when campaigning for votes. The JVP, however, was unfairly banned following the July 1983 anti-Tamil pogrom when the same UNP government, in order to shield its own party members, implicated the JVP for the rioting. The group went underground and unleashed a second insurrection during 1987–89, by which time it had morphed into a rabid nationalist party. It killed thousands in an attempt to undermine the government. When the new UNP government headed by Ranasinghe Premadasa retaliated, it too murdered thousands of JVP cadres and sympathizers. Those killed included all in the JVP's politburo except one, who fled to London but eventually returned to head the party.

The JVP reentered the political mainstream in 1994 and allied with the SLFP-led governing coalition for a while. It clamored for a military (as opposed to political) solution to the ethnic conflict and insisted on the island maintaining its unitary political structure. It supported Mahinda Rajapaksa becoming president after Rajapaksa promised not to consider federalism as an alternative. The JVP, however, split in April 2008. The new faction, called the Jathika Nidahas Peramuna (National Freedom Front), soon thereafter joined the Rajapaksa government.

The split, plus President Rajapaksa successfully positioning himself as the defender of Sinhalese Buddhists, weakened the JVP's appeal. Yet, the party's leaders are among the very few in today's Sri Lankan parliament who raise serious issues about the government's affairs, and in that sense the JVP provides a valuable service to what is otherwise an impotent political opposition. In the January 2015 presidential election, the JVP supported the common opposition candidate Maithripala Sirisena and its grass roots organizers played no small role in contributing to Rajapaksa's ouster.

While Buddhist monks have long exerted influence on Sri Lanka's main political parties, in recent years monks have contested elections and entered parliament. One such party is the Jathika Hela Urumaya (JHU; National Sinhalese Heritage Party), which is mainly centered on the Buddhist clergy. Its formation caused Buddhists to debate whether the *vinaya* (monastic law code) permitted monks to participate directly in politics and how doing so may tarnish the clergy's image (DeVotta and Stone 2008). The party stunned most observers by winning nine seats in the April 2004 elections, although it won just three seats in the April 2010 elections. The JHU was part of the SLFP-led UPFA alliance. In 2012, two JHU monks broke away and formed the Bodu Bala Sena (BBS; Buddhist Power Force), which has resorted to racist agitprop with state connivance against Christians and especially Muslims. While the BBS supported President Rajapaksa during the 2015 presidential election, the JHU left the UPFA to support the common opposition candidate Maithripala Sirisena.

### Box 5.3:  Bodu Bala Sena

Extremist ethno-nationalist forces thrive by successfully portraying an opponent as threatening the nation; and the LTTE, given its attempt to sunder Sri Lanka, fit this bill perfectly for Sinhalese Buddhist nationalists. With the LTTE militarily defeated in May 2009, these nationalists have taken to targeting Christians and especially Muslims. While some protestant church houses have been attacked episodically over the past decade, it is Sri Lanka's Muslims who have recently experienced the most violence at the hands of such extremists. And leading this anti-Muslim charge is a group called the Bodu Bala Sena (BBS; Buddhist Power Force).

The BBS was organized by two radical monks around July 2012 claiming the Sri Lankan state was not doing enough to protect Buddhist rights and that it was necessary for a militant Buddhist movement to ensure the majority community's rightful privileges. Ethno-nationalists are often obsessed over population figures and fertility rates; and with Sri Lanka's Muslims having a slightly higher fertility rate, the BBS has called on Sinhalese to abstain from birth control methods (because, they claim, such methods hinder Sinhalese Buddhist procreation even as Muslims are allowed to take multiple wives) and encourages Sinhalese families to have five to six children so as to ensure the Sinhalese race grows and Buddhism thrives.

The BBS taps into heightened global Islamophobia, the irrational scare-mongering targeting Muslims and/or Islam, when vilifying Muslims and hence its demand for a ban on *halal* (permissible under Islam) products, women wearing the *niqab* (the veil some Muslim women use to cover the face), mosques being built using funds from the Middle East, and Sri Lankan women seeking employment in the Middle East.

The BBS claims that Muslims are mainly responsible for pushing narcotics in Sri Lanka (even though all concerned know that it is mainly politicians who control the illicit drug business). It has put up posters and sent text messages asking people not to shop at Muslim stores. In some instances Muslim shop owners were sent notices demanding that they vacate the premises. Demands have been made to ban the slaughter and sale of beef, a profession Muslims usually engage in. And mobs led by monks have attacked mosques and Muslim-owned businesses. BBS leaders have claimed that Muslim-owned businesses comprise predatory Muslim men who sexually target Sinhalese women and try to convert them; force Buddhist employees to work on Buddhist holidays (which are typically national holidays) and thus prevent them going to the temple; lock Buddhist workers inside their work places without air-conditioning or lighting when the Muslim owners attend the mosque on Fridays; sell undergarments with Buddha's image on them; and also market a unique female underwear that causes Sinhalese women to become sterile.

The anti-Muslim rhetoric and attacks are eerily similar to what the extremist 969 Movement has been perpetrating in Burma-Myanmar. Indeed, that group's leader, Ashin Wirathu, and the BBS monks have maintained close contact and say they want to work together to protect Buddhism across the world.

Many believe that the BBS operated with the connivance of the Rajapaksas, who besides being Sinhalese Buddhist nationalists also resent Muslims for not voting for Mahinda Rajapaksa. Many Sinhalese businesspersons also support the group since they would prefer to see their Muslim business competitors eliminated or weakened. With many Muslims owning businesses and with two-thirds of Muslims living in districts that have a Sinhalese majority, the Muslim community is highly vulnerable should anti-Muslim violence erupt.

The belief that the Rajapaksas tacitly supported the BBS attacks on Muslims pushed the community to vote overwhelmingly for Maithripala Sirisena. President Sirisena appears committed towards ensuring ethno-religious harmony. But it is only a matter of time before Sinhalese Buddhist nationalists bent on manipulating ethno-religious sentiments for political gain target Muslims once more.

Within a few years after independence Tamil elites also formed their own parties, which sought to challenge the UNP and SLFP even as they competed with each other. The Ceylon Tamil Congress (CTC) and Federal Party (FP) were the most prominent in the three decades following independence. These moderate parties became marginalized as they achieved little by engaging with Sinhalese politicians. Some Tamil militant groups that were strongly anti-LTTE and disbanded ended up creating political parties and competing in elections, and the Eelam People's Democratic Party (EPDP) in the Northern Province and Tamileela Makkal Viduthalaip Pulikal (TMVP; Tamileela People's Liberation Tigers) in the Eastern Province stand out in this regard. The TMVP was organized after the eastern and northern wings of the LTTE split in March 2004, which turned out to be a big reason for the LTTE's eventual defeat. Both the TMVP and EPDP were part of the UPFA even as their cadres often operated as state-sponsored paramilitaries.

Currently the Tamil National Alliance (TNA), which comprises four Tamil parties and was considered an LTTE proxy during the civil war, is the largest Tamil party. The TNA enjoys fairly strong support among Tamils abroad, and the Rajapaksa government claimed the TNA operates as a proxy for this Tamil diaspora that continues to aspire to a separate Tamil state in Sri Lanka. Tamils currently command little influence within Sri Lanka; yet the TNA has become the most vocal in highlighting Tamils' legitimate grievances.

Notwithstanding the attempts by the Rajapaksa government and other Tamil parties to discredit it for its links with the LTTE, Tamils in the north especially have continued to vote for the TNA. The first ever Northern Provincial Council elections held in October 2013 saw the TNA win over 78 percent of votes and capture 30 (out of 38) seats. The UPFA won just seven seats and suffered its first ever provincial council elections defeat under President Rajapaksa. The Rajapaksas, however, did not allow the TNA to govern as per the wishes of the predominantly Tamil population in the Northern Province. Under Mahinda Rajapaksa, the governor of the Northern Province was a former military commander who, like the government, used the LTTE bogey to prevent the TNA from running the province. One of President Sirisena's first acts was to replace the former military commander with a seasoned diplomat who is likely to respect provincial council governance as per the Thirteenth Amendment to the constitution.

The Thirteenth Amendment devolves some powers to the provinces and was passed in 1987 (with Indian input) to specifically accommodate Tamil grievances in the northern and eastern provinces. The militarization of the Northern Province, and the creation of more military camps, contributed to a culture where military preferences outranked those of civilian authorities. Militarization and the Rajapaksa government's unwillingness to allow the Northern Provincial Council even a modicum of self-governance, which is enjoyed by other provincial councils, were primary reasons for the TNA also supporting the common opposition candidate during the 2015 presidential election. The Sirisena government has asked the military to vacate camps not necessary to maintaining security and return hitherto occupied lands to their rightful owners. It is also trying to meet legitimate Tamil demands through the Thirteenth Amendment, which would satisfy many Tamils and the international community. The new government apparently wants to compromise with the TNA and Tamils, and this is a welcome change from the ethnocentric Rajapaksas who were determined to keep the Tamil minority down.

The Indian Tamils have long been mainly represented by the Ceylon Workers Congress, and their leaders have usually allied with the ruling party. During the 2015 presidential election, the CWC leadership supported President Rajapaksa, even though the vast majority of Indian Tamils voted for Maithripala Sirisena.

Sri Lanka's Muslims used to vote for the UNP and SLFP, but many switched to voting for the Sri Lanka Muslim Congress (SLMC) after the party began contesting elections in 1989. The SLMC originated in the Eastern Province but gradually spread its influence to the south. With the UNP and SLFP oftentimes depending on coalitions to govern, the SLMC and other ethnic parties can sometimes wield influence disproportionate to their small parliamentary representations. The SLMC split after its founder, M.H.M. Ashraff, died in a helicopter crash in September 2000. The new faction, and other Muslim parties, have weakened the SLMC's clout. The SLMC has allied with both the UNP and SLFP at various points, and it operated as part of the UPFA coalition until just before the 2015 presidential election when it too joined the common opposition against President Rajapaksa. While rural Muslims in especially the Eastern Province have different preferences from those in urban areas like Colombo, most Muslims, like most minorities, usually vote for the UNP candidate during presidential elections. In 2015 they voted en masse for the common opposition candidate and against President Rajapaksa given the government's tacit support for the BBS.

There were 53 registered political parties in Sri Lanka as of January 2008. That number had climbed to over 60 by January 2015. If one included unregistered parties, the number exceeds 80. With few having a fair chance of winning a single seat in parliament, most have apparently been organized to try and make money by selling radio and television time allotted them. For example, 52 parties/coalitions contested the April 2004 parliamentary elections, yet only seven won at least a single seat. In the April 2010 parliamentary elections, 23 parties obtained at least one seat.

A sense of *noblesse oblige* once influenced Sri Lankan politicians, who forfeited personal fortunes to run for office. Now, however, candidates contest elections mainly to secure personal gain through kickbacks on contracts and sundry bribes. This has certainly affected the quality of candidates standing for election. Furthermore, the quest for acquiring wealth, prestige, and power via politics has undermined party loyalty as opposition politicians eagerly cross over to the governing party provided they are afforded ministerial portfolios. Some have done so four and five times.

One irony in Sri Lankan politics is how voters are more loyal to parties than are the party candidates. For instance, soon after Mahinda Rajapaksa became president, 11 UNP parliamentarians (including some senior party members) crossed over to the government, claiming they wanted to ensure good governance. All were provided ministerial portfolios. Ultimately, nearly 50 parliamentarians (including over two dozen UNP members) elected through the April 2004 parliamentary elections left their parties to join the government or operate independently. During President Rajapaksa's second term, the number of cabinet ministers, senior ministers, deputy ministers, and project ministers totaled 110 at one point, which is in sharp contrast to the island's first cabinet that had just 14 members. This meant that nearly 50 percent of parliament and 70 percent of UPFA parliamentarians held some sort of portfolio, which made meaningless the separation of powers that is supposed to exist between the executive and legislative branches. The 2015 presidential elections saw some individuals cross over to the Rajapaksa camp, but most of the crossovers this time went from government ranks to the common opposition candidate citing corruption, nepotism, erosion in the rule of law, and the Rajapaksa tendency towards authoritarianism.

Violence and deadly weapons are part and parcel of Sri Lankan politics, and there are three main reasons for their proliferation. The civil war forced the government to recruit Sinhalese home guards from villages bordering LTTE-controlled areas, and the arms they were provided have been used to settle personal and political scores. When the second JVP insurgency targeted politicians through 1987–89, the UNP distributed nearly

15,000 weapons among political parties. Very few of these were returned; politicians and their supporters now use them to perpetuate violence. Finally, the civil war saw over 60,000 military personnel desert the military. Many absconded with their arms and ammunition and some now work for politicians as bodyguards and storm troopers.

Elections won by corrupt practices are almost never overturned in Sri Lanka, which discourages free and fair polls. Furthermore, preferential voting forces politicians to compete against party colleagues in their districts, adding intraparty violence to the existing interparty violence. Many unions are linked to political parties and their members often resort to violence during elections. Some student unions in the universities are affiliated with political parties, with the JVP's Inter-University Student Federation especially known for its politically influenced "gangsterism" on campuses. The upshot is that parties and their candidates increasingly rely on violence to influence politics and win elections. Thanks mainly to an assertive elections commissioner, the 2015 presidential election saw less violence than recent past elections. The elections commissioner and his colleagues also acted proactively to minimize rigging, and their efforts played a significant role in ensuring President Rajapaksa's defeat (especially given that the Rajapaksas did try to steal the election).

Sri Lanka saw a commendable turnover of power between the UNP and SLFP in 1956, March and July 1960, 1965, 1970, and 1977. But power between parties and their coalitions have changed hands just twice (in 1994 when the SLFP under Chandrika Kumaratunga came to power and in 2015 when Maithripala Sirisena defeated Mahinda Rajapaksa) since the 1978 constitution and presidential system were introduced. The island's presidential system is considered the biggest reason for Sri Lanka's democratic regression, and Chandrika Kumaratunga, who was president from 1994–2005, and Mahinda Rajapaksa both promised to get rid of the executive presidency. Neither did after becoming president, and Rajapaksa went out of his way to arrogate more power to the presidency by passing the Eighteenth Amendment (see above). A major promise made by those associated with the common opposition candidate Maithripala Sirisena was to change the 1978 constitution, or at least amend it, so presidential power ceases to be unaccountable. The extent to which they succeed will influence the separation of powers and the quality of Sri Lanka's democracy.

## Managing conflict

Class divisions, political rivalries, and ethno-nationalism have combined to unleash violent conflict in post-independence Sri Lanka. The JVP rebellions in 1971 and 1987–89 highlighted class-based disparities, although the party has also manipulated Sinhalese Buddhist nationalism whenever this was convenient. Political rivalries, both interparty and intraparty as described above, also lead to conflict especially during elections. The most intense conflict Sri Lanka has experienced has been along ethno-nationalist (mainly Sinhalese versus Tamil) and ethno-religious lines. The latter has led to Sinhalese Buddhist nationalists occasionally attacking Christian evangelicals especially, claiming they resort to unethical conversions, although the most troubling recent ethno-religious violence has been by these same Buddhists nationalists who have resorted to Islamophobia and targeted the island's Muslims (see Box 5.3).

Sinhalese and Tamil ethno-nationalism and the resultant civil war are what is mainly responsible for the democratic regression Sri Lanka has experienced since independence in 1948. This section briefly discusses the events that led to the civil war and the island's failure to mitigate ethno-nationalist tensions between its two main communities.

The most revolutionary post-independence event in Sri Lanka took place in 1956, when the SLFP's S.W.R.D. Bandaranaike and his coalition championed a "Sinhala-only" policy to win parliamentary elections. English had continued to operate as the national language even after independence, despite only around 10 percent of the population speaking it fluently. Initially the SLFP, UNP, Tamil elites within the UNP, and Tamil parties supported English being replaced by both Sinhala and Tamil as national languages. But when a grassroots movement began clamoring for Sinhala only, Bandaranaike recognized that he could use the issue to capture the premiership. When the UNP, led by the abrasive and hyper-westernized Sir John Kotelawala, belatedly recognized that the party could not win the election by championing linguistic parity, it too embraced a Sinhala-only policy. The UNP and SLFP thereafter resorted to "ethnic outbidding," trying to outdo each other on who best could promote Sinhalese preferences—often at the minorities' expense (DeVotta 2004). Bandaranaike handily won the contest, but the Sinhala Only Act of 1956 led to Tamil protests and the first ever anti-Tamil riots, which were followed by more severe Sinhalese-Tamil riots in 1958.

In 1949, the prominent Tamil politician S.J.V. Chelvanayakam and others left the Tamil Congress (TC) and formed the Federal Party (FP) because of concerns over government-sanctioned Sinhalese colonization of historically Tamil areas and disagreement concerning the entry of the TC leader, G.G. Ponnambalam, into the UNP Cabinet. As its name indicates, the FP mainly clamored for a federal structure, but Sinhalese nationalists opposed federalism, claiming it would be the first step toward separatism. The FP won ten seats in the April 1956 elections to become the largest Tamil party. This, combined with Tamil protests over the Sinhala Only Act, led S.W.R.D. Bandaranaike to meet with Chelvanayakam to try and accommodate Tamil grievances. The result was the July 1957 Bandaranaike-Chelvanayakam (B-C) Pact, under which the FP agreed to drop its demand for linguistic parity and the government agreed to permit the use of Tamil for all administrative purposes in the northeast and to create regional councils to deal with education, agriculture, and Sinhalese colonization of Tamil areas. The B-C Pact provided Tamil leaders a way out of their demands for devolution, but it was vilified by Sinhalese Buddhist nationalists and the UNP. Under pressure, Bandaranaike abrogated the pact in April 1958.

The FP provided support in parliament to Dudley Senanayake's UNP government during March 1965 and May 1970. The two parties had agreed to the Senanayake-Chelvanayakam Pact of 1965, under which the UNP promised to recognize the Northern and Eastern Provinces as Tamil-speaking, amend the previous government's Language of the Court's Act of 1961 so that both Sinhala and Tamil could be used in the courts system, and provide Tamils-first preference when colonizing Tamil areas while placing district governments under national authority. The SLFP failed to honor the agreement. Thus for the second time a Sri Lankan government discarded an agreement reached with Tamils and provided a fillip to the budding separatist tendencies among disenchanted Tamil youth.

The Sinhala-only movement was not merely about defending language and culture; it also had to do with socio-economic realities and perceived opportunities. Sinhalese were goaded into thinking that Sinhala only would radically transform their fortunes. This did not happen and it led to disenchantment with Bandaranaike. The prime minister's attempts to belatedly accommodate the Tamil language also upset Sinhalese Buddhist extremists, and in September 1959 a Buddhist monk assassinated him.

Bandaranaike's wife, Sirimavo, soon thereafter took over the SLFP and became the first ever elected woman head of state in the world, in July 1960. Her two governments (July 1960–March 1965 and May 1970–July 1977) claimed it was furthering the revolution her husband had begun, but the numerous anti-Tamil policies it embraced further marginalized the Tamils. The Dudley Senanayake–led UNP government that ruled in-between failed to alleviate Tamil grievances; although neither did it aggravate them.

Mrs. Bandaranaike's policies blatantly promoted Sinhalese dominance and Tamil subordination. For instance, Tamil civil servants were forced to learn Sinhala to be promoted; Sinhalese civil servants were stationed in Tamil areas and Tamils forced to interact with them in Sinhala; Sinhala only was instituted into the courts system, including in the predominantly Tamil northeast region that Tamils consider part of their historic homeland; Tamils' areas were provided little development assistance despite foreign aid earmarked for these regions; publications promoting Tamil culture from nearby Tamil Nadu state in India were banned; Tamil students were required to score higher than their Sinhalese peers to enter university; a quota system was developed to ensure that rural Sinhalese students got into the university more easily; and Sinhalese from the south were transplanted to the northeast to promote Sinhalese colonization and alter the region's demographics. While these discriminatory policies radicalized Tamil youth, Mrs. Bandaranaike's programs pertaining to education were also influenced by the JVP's 1971 insurrection. But promoting Sinhalese (and especially Sinhalese Buddhists) merely because they were Sinhalese and Buddhists drastically altered the standard operating procedures of state institutions and forced Tamil youth to rebel against the state.

Constitutional change and devolution are related issues with which Sri Lanka has grappled especially since the mid-1990s. Presidents typically eschew relinquishing presidential powers whenever constitutional engineering is contemplated. The devolution debate, on the other hand, has ranged between perpetuating the unitary state and introducing a federal structure, with further debates on whether devolution should only be extended to the northeast or all nine provinces, and if the latter, whether devolution ought to be symmetrical or asymmetrical (meaning whether all provinces enjoy the exact same powers or if some enjoy more powers than others).

Chandrika Kumaratunga's People's Alliance (PA) government released a draft constitution in October 1997 that sought to do away with the executive presidency and devolve power to the regions. The attempt failed. In July 2000, the PA and UNP agreed to a watered down version of the 1997 draft of the constitution only to have the UNP back off amidst stiff opposition from Buddhist clergy and Sinhalese nationalist forces. The possibility that the Northern and Eastern Provinces may not remain merged caused Tamil parties also to oppose the parliamentary bill to amend the constitution. Kumaratunga's insistence that she should be allowed to complete her presidential term irrespective of when the new constitution took effect did not help matters.

Chandrika Kumaratunga's malpractices notwithstanding, she promoted a federal solution to the ethnic conflict and even castigated those Sinhalese opposing devolution as "racists." Mahinda Rajapaksa's government, however, contemptuously abandoned any discourse on federalism. This suited the nationalist mindset of the Rajapaksa regime, and with the LTTE now vanquished there is little, except perhaps Indian and international pressure, to force any Sri Lankan government to consider meaningful devolution to especially the north and east.

Sri Lanka has nine provinces and 25 districts. In July 1981, J.R. Jayewardene and the UNP discarded the existing village and town councils and instituted a District Development Council (DDC) scheme, hoping to satisfy Tamil demands for broad devolution. Rather than promoting autonomy, the DDCs reiterated the state's predilection for centralization. The DDCs that operated between 1981 and 1987 are thought to have played a minor role facilitating economic development, but these and subsequent local/regional institutions hardly satisfied Tamil demands for autonomy.

Most Tamils consider the Northern and Eastern Provinces to be their homeland, and it is here that the LTTE sought to create the state of Eelam. The Indo-Lanka Peace Accord of

1987 recognized the historical presence of the Tamils in the northeast and merged the two provinces as part of the Thirteenth Amendment to the constitution. That same year, the Supreme Court upheld the Thirteenth Amendment. Sri Lanka thus consisted of eight provinces between 1987 and 2006, when a different Supreme Court ruled that the merger was invalid. The decision was hailed by Sinhalese nationalists who view the merger and any devolution as precursors to the island's dismemberment.

Provincial Council elections were first held in 1987 throughout the island and have since been conducted with regularity outside the northeast; but the state's embedded paternalistic and centripetal tendencies have prevented the sharing of power between the central government and the regions. Currently, the provincial councils are white elephants beloved by party leaders desperate to accommodate loyal supporters within the government echelon. Thus, today national party leaders, not provincial leaders, mostly choose provincial councilors; and the country currently has nearly 5,000 representatives of the people at local, provincial, and national levels. A further irony is that a system that was primarily passed off as one to ensure some Tamil autonomy was not instituted in the Northern Province until September 2013.

Currently there are 18 municipal councils, 42 urban councils, and 270 *pradeshiya sabhas* (local councils incorporating several old village councils) overseeing local public health, beautification, voter registration lists, and postal services. Unsurprisingly, some units function more efficiently than others. Overall, however, the lack of funding, widespread corruption, ambitious provincial councilors, and overbearing parliamentarians combine to undermine the responsibilities and effectiveness of these units. Such malgovernance has vitiated the role local government could otherwise play in managing tensions between the center and regions, and especially between the center and the predominantly minority northeast.

## Economy

During the post-Second World War period, many western European countries adopted socialist policies. This influenced newly independent states like Sri Lanka. Consequently, while the UNP traditionally embraced pro-western and pro-market policies so as to be considered right-of-center and the SLFP preferred a left-of-center platform that embraced state centrism, both resorted to populist, socialist practices until 1977.

Mrs. Bandaranaike's second government (1970–77) was economically radical in that it pursued central planning and autarky (or a policy of economic independence by discouraging imports). This led to the most basic goods becoming scarce and rationed. The government also nationalized mostly foreign-owned plantations and corporations, insurance companies, and banks. Its failed economic policies were mainly responsible for its massive defeat in the 1977 election.

The J.R. Jayewardene government that came to power that year collaborated with the World Bank, IMF, and western governments to introduce structural adjustment reforms—which led to deregulating financial markets, lower tariffs and increased imports, significant privatization, curtailing the state-employed workforce, dismantling food subsidies, and tax-free policies that encouraged foreign investment. Sri Lanka thus embraced open-market reforms 14 years before India. Thanks also to significant aid from friendly western countries, the Jayewardene government oversaw a relatively high degree of development, even as it created a class of nouveau riche that contributed to economic disparity and disgruntlement. Jayewardene's UNP successor Ranasinghe Premadasa and the SLFP's Chandrika Kumaratunga and Mahinda Rajapaksa continued with open-market policies even as they instituted various programs to accommodate society's poorer segments. President Rajapaksa especially avoided privatizing money-losing state corporations and used them to provide employment for supporters and to secure transactions that generated kickbacks. His regime even took over private enterprises that had been leased state lands and set up state-owned businesses. The state-centric economic model was amplified by the military's increased involvement in the business sphere.

Until 1977, Sri Lanka depended mainly on an agriculture-based economy, with tea, rubber, and coconut responsible for much of its foreign earnings. Since then increased tourism, garment manufacturing, and remittances from those working in the Middle East and elsewhere—numbering nearly two million—have also contributed immensely to the country's economy. But much of the island's gross domestic product is generated within the Western Province, which includes the commercial capital Colombo.

Patronage dictates how most governments in the developing world especially operate but the patronage system the Rajapaksas resorted to was blatantly partisan and ethnocentric. Those not supporting the president were disregarded despite being qualified, while cronies and family members were favored irrespective of their qualifications; and while the government sought to improve somewhat the livelihoods of those inhabiting predominantly Sinhalese Buddhist rural areas in the South, it acted less enthusiastically in predominantly minority areas, especially the Northern Province, given that minority voters tend not to vote for the SLFP, especially during presidential elections. The big exception was infrastructure development, which led to roads and bridges built at a rapid pace throughout the island. The Rajapaksa government considered infrastructure development to be directly connected to economic development (as well as a panacea for minority grievances). Yet many considered the Rajapaksa government's development priorities to be misplaced. This is because much of the infrastructure was built using non-concessionary loans from China while neglecting important sectors like health and education. Furthermore, many projects appear to have been pursued for political as opposed to sound economic reasons—and to extract rents, with the government resorting to a debt rollover strategy by borrowing to pay off outstanding loans.

China became Sri Lanka's largest investor during the Rajapaksa regime by using mainly state-owned banks to provide the country loans at relatively high interest rates while often stipulating that Chinese contractors (and sometimes workers) should carry out the projects funded. Such agreements came at the expense of employment opportunities for Sri Lankans. The terms associated with most Chinese loans were often unpublicized, and this allowed government officials to pocket a percentage of the loan. Thus much of the infrastructure development that took place under the Rajapaksa government saw Chinese banks, contractors, and workers—together with certain Sri Lankan politicians—benefit, with little immediate gains trickling down to Sri Lankans who must ultimately pay back all loans. The Maithripala Sirisena government has promised to scrap some grandiose China-backed projects in the works and evaluate transactions between Sri Lanka and China during the Rajapaksa years.

An International Monetary Fund team that visited the country in September 2013 gave it a mixed rating, while noting that the island was maintaining a fairly strong financial system. According to the Department of Census and Statistics, Sri Lanka's economy grew 7.3 percent in 2013. While well below the 8 percent that the government claims, this is still impressive and currently marks Sri Lanka as one of the fastest growing economies in Asia.

The Rajapaksas realized that economic failure was bound to delegitimize the regime the most and they were bent on preserving the island's economic growth. The problem was that the high growth benefitted few while rising cost of living contributed to conspicuous economic disparities. The government imposed 17 direct and indirect taxes on the populace, with nearly 80 percent of revenue generated via indirect taxation. Stagnant revenue amidst high expenditure thanks to infrastructure projects, loss-making state corporations, and a bloated public sector—which has gone from 600,000 employees in 2005 to 1.4 million today—are the major reasons for the country's balance of payments problems.

Sri Lanka is now considered a middle-income country and has solid potential to develop a much more vibrant economy, but misguided investments, widespread corruption, and widening economic disparities among the population that were aggravated under Mahinda Rajapaksa's government pose stiff challenges for the new regime led by President Sirisena. The new government too is determined to maintain economic growth while cutting back on wasteful spending and corruption, and the IMF and some western governments appear eager to collaborate with it (partly to counter Chinese influence in the island). Their success in working together will not only have an impact on the island's economy but also condition its international relations.

## Regional and international relations

As noted above, the UNP has traditionally been pro-western while the SLFP, up to Mrs. Bandaranaike's rule especially, claimed to practice a nonaligned foreign policy that was nevertheless overly sympathetic towards states that were critical of the west. The UNP's J.R. Jayewardene tilted Sri Lanka's relations towards the United States and west at a time when India was suspicious of American designs, and this caused the island to pay a heavy price. The SLFP's Mahinda Rajapaksa, on the other hand, sought to tilt relations in favor of China, which may be one reason for his defeat in 2015 (given claims that Indian intelligence helped the opposition consolidate its ranks and topple Rajapaksa).

India remains South Asia's major power by virtue of its size, economy, and geopolitical positioning and it is important for Sri Lanka to take Indian security considerations into account when pursuing its foreign affairs. J.R. Jayewardene was inherently pro-western but he acted more so because he needed western assistance to develop the country and successfully carry out structural adjustment reforms. This, in the early 1980s, clashed with the so-called Indira Doctrine, which argued that South Asian states should not pursue foreign policies that could undermine India's preferences and regional dominance. Jayewardene disregarded this and allowed the United States to send a nuclear-powered aircraft carrier to the Colombo harbor and (among other things) also allowed the United States to build a powerful Voice of America (VOA) station. India and the United States enjoy strong ties today but their relations were quite prickly during the Cold War and India was convinced that the VOA station was partly meant to eavesdrop on Indian communications. Jayewardene and India's Indira Gandhi also disliked each other and all this combined led to India secretly arming and training Tamil rebels so as to destabilize Sri Lanka. India did not intend for the rebels to succeed in creating a separate state, as that would have inspired separatist groups within India itself. But she did not foresee the way in which a group like the LTTE would use such training to grow into one of the most formidable separatist and terrorist forces. India did send a peacekeeping force to Sri Lanka in 1987 to try and halt the conflict but that force ended up waging war against the LTTE, which also used a suicide bomber to assassinate former Indian Prime Minister Rajiv Gandhi. Sri Lanka's civil war would most certainly not have evolved as it did and lasted so long if India (initially) and the Sri Lankan Tamil diaspora (subsequently) had not internationalized it. Thus regional and international actors have influenced the island's politics, just as the country's ethnic affairs have affected especially India (given the large Tamil population in the southern Indian state of Tamil Nadu).

The Rajapaksa government's poor human rights record saw India and western governments refuse to sell it heavy weapons to prosecute the war against the LTTE, even though they had all banned the group as a terrorist organization and eagerly sought its demise. This allowed states like China to supply Sri Lanka's military with weapons. The manner in which the final stages of the war was prosecuted without differentiating between LTTE cadres and civilians, leading to at least 40,000 innocent people being killed and other atrocities, forced western countries led by the United States and the United Nations to call for a credible domestic investigation or international investigation into war crimes. The Rajapaksas' stiff refusal to do so led to bilious relations between the United States especially and Sri Lanka, which only pushed the country further into the arms of China. While India too has put pressure on Sri Lanka, it has emphasized reconciliation with the Tamils more than accountability for alleged war crimes. China conveniently claims that it does not interfere in the domestic affairs of states and has used this position to counter western criticism of Sri Lanka and support the island in international forums. It has also loaned the country nearly $5 billion, which has caused many within and without Sri Lanka to wonder if the Chinese are hoping to use Sri Lanka as part of a grand security strategy.

This is because besides roads and railway lines, China has used its loans to build a port in Hambantota (in the south of the island) that provides the country strategic depth in the Indian Ocean (as part of its attempt to create what has been called a "string of pearls" or naval bases stretching from the South China Sea to the Persian Gulf). The Rajapaksas and China's leaders claim the port in Hambantota is nothing more than a commercial enterprise, but with over 70 percent of China's oil imports moving through the sea lanes south of Hambantota, it is clear that this is a commercial enterprise that can also provide the Chinese navy with rest and recuperation facilities. Furthermore, the Chinese are expanding the port in Colombo, the busiest in South Asia, and a Chinese submarine and war ship going there in late 2014 riled India and convinced many that the Chinese influence in Sri Lanka was likely moving from a trade realm to a military/security realm.

India sought to counter Chinese influence by sending radar operators and field medical units to Sri Lanka during the latter stages of the civil war. It also trains Sri Lankan officers every year without cost. Furthermore, the Indian government provides Sri Lanka significant aid and long-term loans, and it maintains oil deposit farms in Trincomalee, a strategic port in the northeast. It helped rebuild the railway line to the northern capital of Jaffna that was destroyed during the war. In addition, India hopes to construct roads, set up educational and training institutes, create an undersea power transmission line, and expand trade between the two countries.

The way the Mahinda Rajapaksa government played China against India (and the international community) to prosecute the civil war and avoid reconciliation and accountability with the Tamil minority suggests that Sri Lanka could be an important cog as India, China, and the United States jostle for dominance in the region. In that sense, Sri Lanka's future democratic status will condition its relations with all three states: a liberal democratic Sri Lanka that especially accommodates minority concerns will more easily be able to develop closer ties with India and the United States, just as the authoritarian Sri Lanka under the Rajapaksas sought to capitalize on the victory over the LTTE to subjugate minorities, repress free speech, and subvert free and fair elections (with inspiration and help from China and other authoritarian states).

Most of Sri Lanka's exports head to the United States and Europe. Most of its tourists come from India and Europe. Its better-heeled citizens crave to travel, settle, and educate their children in western countries. While the country's links with China go back in time, it has been nourished by South Asian civilization. Thus historically and culturally, economically and geopolitically, Sri Lanka is more integrated with India and the west than it is with other states. And until the country took an authoritarian turn and adopted an anti-western attitude under the Rajapaksas, it was not beholden to China.

While many Sri Lankans harbor a love-hate relationship towards India (due to India's civilizational influence and interference in the civil war, respectively), the country remains one of the most important international actors vis-à-vis Sri Lanka, if not the most important. Most countries, including those in the west, take India's considerations seriously when dealing with states in South Asia, and India's position on Sri Lanka thus influences the degree to which western states especially engage the island and hold it responsible for human rights violations. Indian pressure was crucial in getting the Rajapaksa government to hold the Northern Provincial Council elections, and could be so again in nudging Sri Lanka towards meaningful reconciliation and accountability. Sri Lanka's new government has signaled that it will work with India to accommodate legitimate minority grievances and follow a balanced foreign policy. Its proclivities were clear when the Indian ambassador to Sri Lanka met Rajapaksa's successor the day he took the oath of office, while the Chinese ambassador had to wait six days to secure a meeting. The Indians and western governments are likewise doubling up efforts to help stabilize the island politically and economically. All this suggests that Sri Lanka, provided it maintains a semblance of domestic political stability, is likely to follow a practical foreign policy going forward.

## Opportunities and constraints

From a political standpoint, Sri Lanka is a strong, centralized state, and the military's success over the LTTE has centralized it even more. This is to the liking of Sinhalese Buddhist nationalists. The war against the LTTE led to triumphalism among Sinhalese Buddhist supremacists who subscribe to a Sinhalese Buddhist nationalist ideology that claims Sri Lanka is the designated sanctuary for Buddhism, the Sinhalese Buddhists are its chosen guardians, minorities live in the island thanks to Sinhalese Buddhist sufferance, the country cannot deviate from its unitary state structure, and those who challenge all this are traitors or part of an international conspiracy to tarnish, pillage, and destroy the Sinhalese Buddhists and Sri Lanka (DeVotta 2007). Consolidating democracy in Sri Lanka would require its leaders to turn away from such ethnocentrism. While this was not going to happen under the Rajapaksa government, there is now hope that the new regime led by President Maithripala Sirisena and his team will pursue policies that promote a liberal democratic dispensation.

Liberal democracy entails a press that operates freely, an independent judiciary not beholden to politicians, a security force that is not above the law, stringent policies and institutions that prevent and prosecute corruption among government officials, equal treatment for all ethnic groups (with or without devolved powers to Tamils), and a strong civil society that protects human rights, socializes people regarding liberal democracy, and promotes dispassionate governance. This is a tall order for any country. It is especially so for one that was engulfed in a nearly 30-year civil war and spent the past decade under a government that was increasingly authoritarian. But democracy is not alien to Sri Lankans, who have exercised their franchise since 1931. For instance, voter turnout in the January 2015 presidential election was 81.5 percent, the highest in the country's history. This, together with the defeat of the Rajapaksa regime, provides the new government a golden opportunity to reinstitute liberal democracy and good governance.

The new government also has the opportunity to reset relations with India and the west and practice a more balanced foreign policy. It appears determined to do so and is likely to benefit in terms of aid, grants, investments, and trade. It will encounter pressure to continue to develop the country's infrastructure and do so minus the massive graft that was common in the Rajapaksa era. Only time will tell if the government is up to the task.

While the post-war years especially saw high economic growth, this benefitted very few people, which is one big reason the Rajapaksa government was defeated. The new government must craft policies that maintain high growth while minimizing the disparity between the haves and have-nots. The redistribution of wealth is difficult and controversial. Yet the inability to do so sufficiently over the past five decades partly contributed to two insurrections (by the JVP) and an ethnic conflict. Thus ensuring a more balanced and fair overall economy is vital if Sri Lanka is to move away from its post-independence violent history.

The new government will also need to pursue genuine reconciliation with the Tamil minority but do so in a way that minimizes vociferous opposition by Sinhalese Buddhist nationalists. Accomplishing this will pacify Tamils and satisfy India and the government's western partners. But this means that the Tamils will need to compromise and not make demands that the government is unable to deliver on (such as federalism). Similarly, a domestic credible investigation into the crimes committed towards the latter stages of the conflict will likely ward off demands for an international investigation, which the vast majority of Sinhalese are against. Doing this in a manner that ensures a modicum of justice will be one of the biggest challenges facing the island moving forward.

Sri Lanka's democratic prospects were bound to be bleak had Mahinda Rajapaksa been reelected for a third term. His defeat in 2015 stems democratic erosion. The degree to which Sri Lanka's various parties will be able to cohere and revive democratic institutions will determine whether the island can regain the democratic promise that got squandered due to ethnocentrism, ethnic conflict, and authoritarianism.

## Political parties

| | |
|---|---|
| **United National Party** | Created in 1946 and has played a leading role in the country's post-independence history. Considered pro-market and -western and usually garnered more support from the country's minorities. Was severely weakened during President Rajapaksa's rule but joined Maithripala Sirisena in defeating Rajapaksa. |
| **Sri Lanka Freedom Party** | The UNP's archrival that was formed in 1951 by S.W.R.D. Bandaranaike and operated as a political dynasty until Mahinda Rajapaksa became president. Has traditionally appealed to the country's rural Buddhists and used to be more socialist. SLFP leaders have ruled the country continuously since 1994, with President Sirisena being the third consecutive president. |
| **Tamil National Alliance** | A four-party coalition representing Tamils that was vilified as the LTTE's proxy during the civil war. It supported President Sirisena's candidacy against Mahinda Rajapaksa and is currently the Tamils' main representative. |
| **Janatha Vimukthi Peramuna** | Was responsible for two insurrections that sought to topple the country's governments in 1971 and 1987–89. Helped Mahinda Rajapaksa come to power in 2005 but supported his opponent in the 2010 and 2015 presidential elections. |

**Jathika Hela Urumaya**     Formed in 2004 and is centered on some Buddhist clergy. Played an important role in propping up President Sirisena's candidacy and helping to defeat Mahinda Rajapaksa.

**Communist Party of**     Formed in 1943 and played a significant role in Sri Lanka's left
**Sri Lanka**     movement. Was part of the SLFP-led United People's Front Alliance. Presently garners little support.

## Political chronology

| | |
|---|---|
| Fifth century BCE: | As per Sinhalese mytho-history, Indo-Aryan migrants settle the island and the Sinhalese become dominant community. |
| 1505: | Portuguese begin colonizing the island. |
| 1658: | Dutch replace Portuguese. |
| 1796: | British replace Dutch. |
| 1815: | Britain conquers Kingdom of Kandy and administratively unifies the island sometime thereafter. |
| 1931: | Britain introduces universal suffrage. |
| 1948: | Ceylon granted full independence and the UNP comes to power. |
| 1949: | Indian Tamils denied citizenship. |
| 1956: | The SLFP under S.W.R.D. Bandaranaike comes to power by promising to institute Sinhala only as the national language; first ever anti-Tamil riots take place. |
| 1958: | Another series of anti-Tamil riots take place. |
| 1959: | Bandaranaike is assassinated by a disgruntled monk. |
| 1960: | Bandaranaike's widow Sirimavo leads SLFP to power and begins instituting policies that upset Tamils. |
| 1965: | UNP returns to power. |
| 1970: | Sirimavo Bandaranaike and SLFP returns to power; resorts to state-centric policies and extends policies that marginalize minority Tamils. |
| 1971: | JVP attempts to overthrow government and the insurrection is violently put down. |
| 1972: | Government introduces new constitution; makes Buddhist the island's foremost religion; and changes country's name from Ceylon to Sri Lanka. |
| 1976: | The Tamil New Tigers, formed in 1972, is rechristened Liberation Tigers of Tamil Eelam. |
| 1977: | The UNP under J.R. Jayewardene wins a supermajority in parliament and starts to open up country's economy. |
| 1978: | J.R. Jayewardene introduces a new constitution and a presidential system of government. |
| 1983: | The LTTE kills 13 soldiers, which sparks an anti-Tamil pogrom that leads to civil war. |
| 1987: | India and Sri Lanka sign an agreement that leads to deployment of Indian Peace Keeping Force. |
| 1988: | JVP opposition to Indo-Lanka Agreement leads to a second insurrection even as IPKF ends up fighting LTTE. |
| 1990: | IPKF leaves Sri Lanka (making the war with the LTTE India's longest). |
| 1991: | LTTE suicide bomber assassinates former Indian Prime Minister Rajiv Gandhi. |
| 1993: | LTTE suicide bomber assassinates President Ranasinghe Premadasa. |

| | |
|---|---|
| 1994: | Chandrika Kumaratunga becomes president (and the third in the Bandaranaike family to lead the country). |
| 1995–2001: | Civil war continues. |
| 2001: | UNP led coalition comes to power while Kumaratunga remains as president. |
| 2002: | Government and LTTE agree to a ceasefire backed by Norwegians. |
| 2004: | LTTE splits when its eastern wing breaks away; the tsunami on December 26 kills over 35,000 Sri Lankans. |
| 2005: | Mahinda Rajapaksa becomes president. |
| 2006: | War with LTTE intensifies despite government claiming that the cease-fire continues to be in place. |
| 2009: | LTTE militarily defeated. |
| 2010: | President Rajapaksa calls for early elections and is reelected president for second time; Rajapaksa forces through Eighteenth Amendment, which further strengthens the presidency and allows him to run for more than two terms. |
| 2011–12: | International pressure against Rajapaksa government seeking account-ability for human rights violations especially during latter stages of the war escalate. |
| 2013: | Sri Lanka's first female Chief Justice of the Supreme Court is impeached in controversial fashion for obstructing Rajapaksa legislation. |
| 2013: | Government allows elections for the Northern Provincial Council, which TNA wins handily. |
| 2015: | Mahinda Rajapaksa is defeated in presidential election and his fellow SLFP challenger Maithripala Sirisena becomes Sri Lanka's sixth president. Notwithstanding attempts by some within the SLFP to weaken President Sirisena and bring back Mahinda Rajapaksa as prime minister, the government in April passes the Nineteenth Amendment to the constitution, which reduces the presidential term to five years, bars a person from serving more than two terms as president, and introduces a Constitutional Council with powers to set up independent commissions that the Eighteenth Amendment nullified. |
| June 2015: | Parliament was dissolved and new elections scheduled in mid-August. |

## Works cited

Bass, Daniel. 2013. *Everyday Ethnicity in Sri Lanka: Up-Country Tamil Identity Politics*. London: Routledge.

DeVotta, Neil. 2004. *Blowback: Linguistic Nationalism, Institutional Decay, and Ethnic Conflict in Sri Lanka*. Stanford: Stanford University Press.

———. 2007. *Sinhalese Buddhist Nationalist Ideology: Implications for Politics and Conflict Resolution in Sri Lanka*. Policy Studies 40. Washington, DC: East-West Center.

DeVotta, Neil. 2009. "The Liberation Tigers of Tamil Eelam and the Lost Quest for Separatism." *Asian Survey* 49 (6) (November/December): 1021–51.

DeVotta, Neil, and Jason Stone. 2008. "Jathika Hela Urumaya and Ethno-Religious Politics in Sri Lanka." *Pacific Affairs* 81 (1) (April): 31–51.

Edrisinha, Rohan, and Naganathan Selvakkumaran. 2000. "The Constitutional Evolution of Ceylon/ Sri Lanka 1948-98." In *Sri Lanka's Development Since Independence: Socio-Economic Perspectives and Analyses*, edited by W. D. Lakshman and Allan Tisdell, 95–112. Huntington, NY: Nova Science.

Horowitz, Donald L. 1980. *Coup Theories and Officers' Motives: Sri Lanka in Comparative Perspective*. Princeton, NJ: Princeton University Press.

Malalgoda, Kitsiri. 1976. *Buddhism in Sinhalese Society 1750–1900: A Study of Religious Revival and Change*. Berkeley: University of California Press.

Nayak, Sharada. 2014. *The Raj Agent in Ceylon 1936–1940*. New Delhi: Educational Resources Center Trust.

Oberst, Robert. 1984. "Proportional Representation and Electoral System Change in Sri Lanka." In *Sri Lanka in Change and Crisis*, edited by James Manor, 118–33. London: Croom Helm.

Roberts, Michael. 1982. *Caste Conflict and Elite Formation: The Rise of a Karava Elite in Sri Lanka, 1500-1931*. Cambridge: Cambridge University Press.

Russell, Jane. 1982. *Communal Politics Under the Donoughmore Constitution, 1931–47. Ceylon Historical Journal 26*. Dehiwala: Tisara Prakasakayo.

Samarakone, Priya. 1984. "The Conduct of the Referendum." In *Sri Lanka in Change and Crisis*, edited by James Manor, 84–117. London: Croom Helm.

Tambiah, Stanley Jeyaraja. 1992. *Buddhism Betrayed?: Religion, Politics, and Violence in Sri Lanka*. Chicago: University of Chicago Press.

Weerakoon, Bradman. 2004. *Rendering Unto Caesar: A Fascinating Story of One Man's Tenure Under Nine Prime Ministers and Presidents of Sri Lanka*. Colombo, Sri Lanka: Vijitha Yapa.

Weerawardana, I. D. S. 1960. *Ceylon General Election 1956*. Colombo, Sri Lanka: M. D. Sunasena.

Wickramasinghe, Nira. 2006. *Sri Lanka in the Modern Age: A History of Contested Identities*. London: Hurst and Company.

Wriggins, Howard W. 1961. "Impediments to Unity in New Nations: The Case of Ceylon." *American Political Science Review*, Vol. 55, no. 2 (June): 313–20.

## Recommended texts

De Silva, Chandra Richard. 1997. *Sri Lanka: A History*, 2nd Revised Edition. New Delhi: Vikas.

De Silva, K. M. 1981. *A History of Sri Lanka*. Delhi: Oxford University Press.

McGilvray, Dennis B. 2008. *Crucible of Conflict: Tamil and Muslim Society on the East Coast of Sri Lanka*. Durham, NC: Duke University Press.

Seneviratne, H. L. 1999. *The Work of Kings: The New Buddhism in Sri Lanka*. Chicago: University of Chicago Press.

Uyangoda, Jayadeva, and Neloufer de Mel, eds. 2012. *Reframing Democracy: Perspectives on the Cultures of Inclusion and Exclusion in Contemporary Sri Lanka*. Colombo, Sri Lanka: Social Scientists' Association.

Wilson, A. Jeyaratnam. 2000. *Sri Lankan Tamil Nationalism: Its Origins and Development in the 19th and 20th Centuries*. Vancouver: University of British Columbia Press.

# 6 Nepal

*Prakash Adhikari and Mahendra Lawoti*

Nepal is a landlocked country, occupying an area of 147,181 square kilometers. It is roughly the size of Tennessee. The country is the home of Mount Everest and birthplace of Lord Buddha. Nepal has a population of 26.5 million with more than 55 percent of the people living below two dollars a day. There are 125 different castes and ethnic groups speaking 123 different languages and practicing 10 different religions in the country.[1] Between 1996 and 2006 Nepal also witnessed a bloody Maoist civil war that killed over 13,000 individuals. Additionally, the country is surrounded by India and China, two economic and demographic giants competing with each other on both the economic and security fronts. All this plays into Nepal's struggle to consolidate a democratic political system even as the country seeks to create a working constitution. What has been the cause of the failure of democracy in Nepal? What are the future prospects for the emergence of a democratic state?

## Historical and political development

The modern history of Nepal begins with Prithvi Narayan Shah who conquered various principalities into a single administrative unit during the latter part of the eighteenth century. Shah was originally the ruler of Gokha Kingdom, which is now a district in west Nepal. Prithvi Narayan Shah died in 1775 but his descendants continued with the conquest, expanding the Gorkha Kingdom to the Tista River (now in India) in the east and Kumaon and Garhwal in the west (also in India).

The Gorkha expedition was halted when the East India Company fought the kingdom from 1814 to 1816. The Anglo-Nepali war ended with Nepal conceding defeat and signing the 1816 Sugauli Treaty. As per the terms of the treaty, Nepal ceded Kumaon, Garhwal, Sikkim, and some parts in the southern plains to the British, agreed to host a British residency in Kathmandu and provide Gorkha soldiers for the British army (Thapa and Sijapati 2004; Thapa 2005; Whelpton 2005). After the death of Prithvi Narayan Shah, Nepal was ruled for the next 70 years by several young, weak, and inapt kings. Family and factional feuds among the Shah Rulers and top administrators paved the way for the seizure of power by the Kunwars in 1846.

In 1846 the Kunwars captured power from the Shah Kings following a bloody royal court massacre popularly called the Kot Massacre. Over 30 royal officials were killed in the coup orchestrated by Jung Bahadur Kunwar. After seizing power from the Shahs, the Kunwars rebranded themselves the Ranas, thereby raising their social status with that of the Shahs. In 1856 Jung Bahadur Rana forced King Surendra Shah to issue a royal decree that reduced the monarchy to a figurehead. The royal decree also sought to ensure the position of prime minister stayed within the Rana family. The Rana family thereafter ruled Nepal for the next 104 years until a popular mass movement forced its abolition in 1950.

Once Jung Bahadur Rana captured power his regime pursued an aggressive policy to prevent mass revolts or challenges from other prominent families. This led to many nobles, including members of the royal family, fleeing to India and elsewhere to avoid persecution. Within Nepal the Ranas in turn pursued a policy of "backwardness and ignorance by discouraging the spread of education or travel abroad" (Joshi and Rose 1966, 37). Although Nepal was not formally colonized, the Ranas pursued a policy of appeasing the British government in India. During the Sepoy Mutiny of 1857, when Indian soldiers rose up against the East India Company, the Ranas supplied the British with Nepali troops who helped brutally put down the rebellion. The Ranas also allowed the British to recruit soldiers during the first and second world wars, and the British showed their appreciation by formally recognizing Nepal as an independent state in 1923.

The anti-British movement in India inspired the anti-Rana movement in Nepal. Although the Ranas actively promoted an autocratic regime in Nepal, Nepali political leaders (both within the country and in India) revolted against the Ranas and established The Nepal Praja Parishad in Kathmandu in 1936 seeking to overthrow the Rana regime. In 1947 a group of Nepali exiles in Banaras, India formed the Nepali National Congress (NNC) party. And when the British departed India in 1947 the time was right for the pro-democratic parties to launch a decisive move against the Ranas.

In 1950, the Nepali Congress (NC) party, which was formed by merging the Nepali National Congress and Nepal Democratic Congress, launched an armed rebellion to oust the Ranas. India in response brokered a compromise between the Ranas, King Tribhuvan, and Nepali Congress in early 1951. Under the terms of the compromise, the king's powers were restored and an interim government was formed jointly by the Ranas and Nepali Congress. The interim government was supposed to hold an election for a Constituent Assembly (CA) that in turn would write a new democratic constitution for Nepal. The Rana-Congress interim government took office in February 1951 and issued an Interim Constitution two months later. This was Nepal's very first experiment with democracy. Under the Interim Constitution, the role of the king was reduced to that of a constitutional monarch.

The coalition government, however, fractured within months, and this led the palace to intervene. Subsequent governments did not last long. In December 1957, King Mahendra called for parliamentary elections as opposed to a constituent assembly, thereby violating the terms of the tripartite agreement brokered by New Delhi. The King declared that "he would grant a Constitution to the people" (Joshi and Rose 1966, 281). On February 12, 1959, King Mahendra issued a new constitution prepared by a special constitution drafting committee he had established in 1958.

The first general elections were held on February 18, 1959 and led to the Nepali Congress forming a majority government in the new parliament. The Nepali Congress government headed by popular Nepali leader Bishweshwar Prasad (B.P.) Koirala introduced several reforms including discontinuing a tax-free landholding system. However, King Mahendra had his own ambitions. In December 1960, King Mahendra dissolved parliament, thus ending Nepal's first experiment with democracy. Leaders of the main political parties were jailed and others escaped to India and began preparing for a revolt against the king. In 1962 the king proclaimed a new constitution for Nepal and introduced a party-less dictatorship called the *Panchayat* system, a system of guided democracy, which prevailed until 1990.

A historic people's movement in 1990, led by an alliance of the Nepali Congress and moderate communist parties and partly inspired by the pro-democracy movement in Eastern

Europe, restored multiparty democracy. An interim government was formed in April with Krishna Prasad (K.P.) Bhattarai of the Nepali Congress party as prime minister. Its main responsibility was to draft a constitution and conduct an election for a new parliament. During this time the radical left-leaning parties presented two main demands—that the people, not the king, be made the source of sovereign authority and that elections first be held for a constituent assembly, which would draft a constitution. However, the Nepali Congress party was not keen on listening to the demands of the radical left. Instead, the party agreed to maintain a constitutional monarchy. A new constitution, drawn by the Constitutional Recommendation Commission, was promulgated in November 1990. The preamble to the constitution recognized the Nepali people as the "source of sovereign authority" but the demand for elections to a constituent assembly was dismissed.

In the May 1991 parliamentary elections that were held under the new constitution, the Nepali Congress emerged victorious and Girija Prasad (G.P.) Koirala became prime minister. But factionalism within the Nepali Congress led to Koirala dissolving parliament in July 1994. Mid-term elections held in November 1994 saw no party acquiring a majority, resulting in a hung parliament and a minority government that lasted nine months. Thus, Nepal had its first coalition government and a third prime minister in 1995—five years after returning to democracy. This was followed by a series of coalition governments and a new cabinet every year or so, causing Nepali politics to become highly unstable and government institutions becoming venues for corruption and nepotism. Indeed, every successive government appeared to be only concerned with amassing public property. Little was done to consolidate institutional democracy, and the population understandably began to sense that the new democratic government was little different from the historically autocratic regimes.

The political confusion proved to be an opportunity for anti-democratic forces in the country. Capitalizing on the grievances of the masses and lack of democratic culture within the pro-democratic parties, the Communist Party of Nepal-Maoists (CPN-M), launched an armed rebellion in 1996. Amidst this political tumult Nepal experienced a bizarre tragedy in 2001 that put the country at the center of world attention when King Birendra and his family were killed in a royal massacre (see Box 6.1).

---

**Box 6.1: The royal massacre**

The beginning of the end of Nepal's royal family took place on the night of June 1, 2001, when an intoxicated Crown Prince Dipendra fatally shot his father (King Birendra), mother (Queen Aishwarya), brother, sister, uncle, and a number of other royal family members and thereafter shot himself. Dipendra succumbed to his self-inflicted gun wound three days later, but not before being declared king while in hospital. Thereafter, King Birendra's brother Gyanendra Bir Bikram Shah was proclaimed king. The investigation commission that King Gyanendra authorized found that Crown Prince Dipendra was under the influence of alcohol and drugs when he went about the palace massacre. Gyanendra's authoritarian proclivities, partly due to the ongoing Maoist uprising and instability in the country, led to him being an unpopular monarch. His reign ended in May 2008, and with it Nepal's monarchy, when the Constituent Assembly proclaimed the country a republic.

King Birendra was a liberal king and his family continues to be adored by many Nepalese. Most people at that time did not believe that Crown Prince Dipendra was mainly responsible for the massacre. Instead, many believed that the killings were arranged by Gyanendra Shah and/or his son Paras Shah. While Paras was at the party and escaped unhurt, Gyanendra was on a visit to the town of Pokhara on the fateful night. These facts further fueled people's suspicions. Prior to the royal massacre, Paras Shah had been implicated in numerous unpopular incidents, including the death of a popular singer in a hit and run accident. Such actions had led to enraged commoners in Kathmandu demanding amendments to the provision of royal immunity under the 1990 constitution.

As the Maoist rebellion kept on growing and expanding, the government began to recognize it as a political problem, and the two sides declared a ceasefire in July 2001 and pursued talks. However, the Maoist unilaterally broke the ceasefire in November 2001 and attacked a military installment for the first time. Seeking to thwart the Maoists, Sher Bahadur Deuba declared a state of emergency in November 2001 and mobilized the Royal Nepalese Army (RNA) to fight the insurgency. In May 2002, the king dissolved parliament on the recommendation of the prime minister and thereafter also postponed elections for an indefinite period, handpicking in the process prime ministers and cabinet ministers of his choice. In February 2005, the king imposed a state of emergency and assumed full control of the state. The dysfunctional post-1990 political chaos thus paved the way for a return to autocracy.

King Gyanendra's authoritarian turn brought major political parties and the Maoists together. This culminated in what came to be known as "People's Movement II," when in April 2006 millions of Nepalese gathered in the streets of Kathmandu and forced King Gyanendra out of power and to reinstate the House of Representatives, dissolved in 2002. A Comprehensive Peace Accord (CPA), signed between the CPN-M and the government formed by the alliance of seven political parties, ended the decade long Maoist rebellion in November 2006. Elections to the constituent assembly were finally conducted in April 2008 and the CPN-M emerged as the largest party in the assembly. In May 2008 the first sitting of the assembly declared Nepal a republic, thus ending 240 years of monarchical rule.

Nepal has largely been an exclusionary state where the male Thakuris and Bahuns (hill Brahmins) have occupied influential positions under both autocratic and democratic regimes. Dalits (the "lowest" caste according to Hindu tradition), indigenous nationalities, Madhesi, and Muslims as well as women have been largely excluded from various influential spheres. This was attained by promoting the nation-state based on Nepali aka Khaskura, a Hindu monarchy practicing a form of Hinduism more specific to the hills and rooted in an "upper" caste hill Hindu male culture (Lawoti 2005).

This led to various groups being discriminated against. For instance, the promotion of Nepali language discriminated against indigenous nationalities, Madhesi, and Muslims. All discriminated against the Dalits even as indigenous nationalities considered "middle" caste were also treated as "lower" caste by the ruling group. The hill Hindu monarchy promoted "upper" caste hill Hindu culture that discriminated against other religions like Buddhism, Muslim, and Kiratis. Nationalism based on hill culture and values discriminated against the Madhesi and Muslims. Madhesi who shared language and culture with North Indians were often suspected of being disloyal to the Nepali state and as a result many were deprived of citizenship certificates, without which one could not seek public employment and purchase property. Indeed, all except the dominant "upper" hill caste faced socio-cultural discrimination in at least one realm. The discrimination led to their marginalization and exclusion in social, economic, and political spheres. Collectively the marginalized groups form more than a two-third majority but they are divided along caste, ethnic, linguistic, and religious lines, and this prevents a combined effort to fight against discrimination, exclusion, and inequality. The political reforms initiated after 2006 have begun to promote inclusion of these marginalized groups, but the dominant group with its entrenched power keeps resisting major changes.

## Institutions, political parties, and elections

The history of political parties in Nepal can be tied to the anti-Rana movement during the 1930s and 1940s. The parties evolved as movement organizations and successfully established democracy in the country. However, soon after democracy was established in 1950 the parties started disintegrating due to a lack of discipline within party organizations. The failure to consolidate democracy led to renewed autocracy in 1960. But 30 years later political parties came together to form an alliance to restore democracy. Once in power the parties unfortunately reverted to their old habits, which allowed King Gyanendra to reassert himself as an absolute monarch in 2005. This and the threat of a communist revolution forced the parties to form an alliance to restore democracy from 2002 onward.

Nepal's political parties can be grouped under different broad categories—liberal democrats, liberal left, hardliner left, regional parties, and conservatives. In addition to these mainstream political parties, there are a number of smaller parties representing the various regional and ethnic groups in Nepal.

The Nepali National Congress (NNC) is one of the oldest political parties in Nepal, having being formed by a group of Nepali exiles in Banaras, India in 1947.[2] Two years later the Nepali Democratic Congress (NDC) was formed in Calcutta. In 1950, the NNC and NDC merged to form the Nepali Congress (NC) and joined hands with the palace to end the Rana regime.

## Political parties

| Party | Description |
| --- | --- |
| Nepal Sadhvawana Party, Madhesi People's Right Forum, and Rastriya Jana Mukti Party | Identity-based parties of Madhesi and indigenous nationalities. |
| Nepali Congress (NC) | Left leaning in early years, slightly right leaning today. |
| Nepal Sadbhavana Party (NSP) | Regional party representing the plain region. |
| National Democratic Party (or Rastriya Prajatantra Party) | Conservative associated with the Panchayat regime. |
| United People's Front (UPF) | Radical left-wing. |
| Communist Party of Nepal (United Marxist-Leninist) | Radical left-wing transformed into Liberal left (social democratic). |
| Communist Party of Nepal (Maoist) | Radical left–Maoist. |

The NC in its earlier years was a left-leaning party that espoused land reforms and changes in the caste system. It also promoted an ideology of democratic socialism. Since the 1990s, however, the party has transformed into a right-of-center party promoting market liberalization and resisting major social reforms. Though it has repeatedly fought against autocratic regimes to introduce or restore democracy, it lacks democratization within the party as most of the important decisions are taken by the top leaders. The Koirala clan has dominated it since its early years, producing four prime ministers from the family.

The NC has been successful in winning elections and governing the country. For instance, the NC came to power with a two-third majority in the first general election of 1959 but survived only 18 months because the king dissolved parliament on December 19, 1960. The party ruled the country during the 1990s with its own majority or as head of coalitions. In 2013, it again won the largest number of seats and is currently heading a coalition government. The party's vote share, however, dipped in the 2008 and 2013 elections, partly because Madhesi supporters deserted it in considerable numbers given its lack of support for Madhesi autonomy.

There is a strong popular support for political parties that call themselves communists. Such parties collectively won more than 50 percent of vote in the 2008 elections. Their mother party, the Communist Party of Nepal (CPN), which was founded in 1949, won four seats during the first parliamentary elections in 1959.

Intraparty factionalism has been rife within communist parties. The first major division emerged between those who wanted to oppose King Mahendra's intervention in 1960 and those who did not. Further splits occurred within these factions as well. Another new fault line appeared among those who wanted to launch rebellion immediately and those who argued that the objective conditions for such action were not right.

In 1975 various factions from across the country came together under the Jhapalis, who had initiated a violent class action in eastern Nepal in the style of Naxalites/Maoists in India, to form the All Nepal Communist Revolutionary Coordination Committee (Marxist-Leninist). Though the violent movement in Jhapa was brutally repressed, it appeared to attract considerable radical communist factions and leaders. In 1978, the Communist Party of Nepal (Marxist-Leninist) or CPN (M-L) was established. In 1991, CPN (M-L) and CPN-M merged to form the Communist Party of Nepal (Unified Marxist-Leninist) or CPN (UML). In 1993, the party adopted multiparty democracy as its main agenda and redefined its constitution (Hachhethu 2002).

In 1994, the CPN (UML) won plural seats and was invited to form a minority government when no party won a clear majority during the mid-term elections. Man Mohan Adhikari of the party became the first communist prime minster of Nepal. In 1998 the party split into CPN (UML) and CPN (M-L) but the two reunified in 2002 after King Gyanendra started acting autocratically[3]. CPN (UML) was one of the major participants in the April 2006 movement that ousted King Gyanendra and emerged as the third largest party in the Constituent Assembly elections held in 2008. In the 2013 election, it again emerged as the main communist party. It is important to recognize that despite its appellation, the party operates mainly as a social democratic entity today.

The Communist Party of Nepal (Maoist) (CPN-M) is a splinter radical faction of the Communist Party of Nepal (CPN). After the dissolution of multiparty system in 1960, the CPN was divided into three factions, one of which came to be known as CPN (Masal) in 1983. In 1985, the party broke up into CPN (Masal) and CPN (Mashal). Pushpa Kamal Dahal (Prachanda) became the general secretary of CPN (Mashal).

In 1990, the CPN (Unity Center) was formed bringing together various radical communist parties with Prachanda as the general secretary. The party's political wing, called United People's Front Nepal (UPFN), contested the 1991 general election from 69 constituencies, elected 9 members in the 205-member House of Representatives, and emerged as the third largest party in the parliament. In 1994, the Unity Center and the UPFN came together and changed the name of the party to the Communist Party of Nepal (Maoist). In 1996, the party launched an armed rebellion that lasted until 2006. CPN-M emerged as the larger party during the elections to the Constituent Assembly held in 2008. Overt and covert threats and people's aspiration for peace and change contributed to the Maoist electoral success (Lawoti 2009). The Maoist, however, dropped to a third position in 2013. The unfulfilled promises (such as lack of land reforms, ambivalence on identity-based autonomy, and the like), corruption charges, as well as anti-incumbency sentiment contributed to the party's loss. Anti-incumbency is significant in Nepal as no party has been able to win majorities or retain its pluralist position in successive elections (Lawoti 2014).

The conservative parties have not fared well in electoral politics. They emerged a distant fourth in 1991, third in 1994 and 1999, and second in 1959. Their vote base has now further eroded when compared to their standing in the 1990s, although the parties performed better in 2013 than in 2008. Their support toward autocratic regimes is a major reason for their lackluster performance, and their recent decline may also be due to the Nepali Congress (NC) winning over conservative votes (Lawoti 2014).

Regional- and identity-based parties also have a long history in Nepal and their support base has increased in recent years. A regional party, the Nepal Tarai Congress that espouses the interests of the Madhesi, was formed in the 1950s but disappeared after its leaders were coopted by King Mahendra after 1960. The Nepal Sadhvawana Party (NSP) was formed in 1990 to represent the interests of Madhesi people. Political parties representing the interests of the indigenous nationalities, such as the Rastriya Janamukti Party and Mongol National Organization, emerged in early 1990 and a Dalit party emerged in late 1990s. New Madhesh-based parties, such as the Madhesi People's Rights Forum, Nepal and Tarai Madhesh Loktantrik Party, and new indigenous nationalities and Dalit parties were also formed after the end of Maoist insurgency in 2006.

Except for the Nepal Sadhvawana Party, no other Madhesi party was able to win seats during the 1990s. However, the identity-based parties continue to expand. In 1959, the Nepal Tarai Congress won 2.1 percent of popular vote while during the 1990s the identity-based political parties received around 5 percent of vote. In 2008 they collectively garnered 13 percent of popular votes while in 2013 they obtained more than 15 percent of votes. The continued expansion of explicitly identity-based parties is partly due to the electoral reforms that introduced a proportional representation system for more than half the seats. However, the major reason for the rise of the identity-based parties is because the major parties, NC and CPN (UML), represent the dominant hill community and because they have failed to accommodate the demands of those who have long felt marginalized (Lawoti 2012b; Lawoti 2014).

## Managing conflict

Nepal has witnessed both class-based and ethnic conflicts in recent years—the Maoist rebellion and identity-based conflicts involving the marginalized caste, ethnic, and regional groups. Beginning in 1996, Nepal went through a decade-long armed rebellion led by the Communist Party of Nepal (Maoist). The conflict ended in 2006 with the signing of a Comprehensive Peace Accord. The following section first chronicles the rise and spread of Maoist rebellion in Nepal and thereafter discusses identity-based conflict in the country.

### Class-based conflict

Although the exact cause of the insurgency is still being debated, most existing literature tends to argue that accumulation of resentment stemming from Nepal's feudal past and failure by the governments formed after 1990 to address grievances of ethnic minorities gave rise to the conflict. Most development activities came to be centered in Kathmandu to serve the interests of the ruling elites while development activities in the periphery were virtually absent (see Adhikari and Samford 2013 for details).

When democracy was restored in 1990, the interim government was tasked with the responsibility to address a host of demands stemming from a history of authoritarianism. These included ending the discriminatory caste system, declaring Nepal a secular state, and recognizing the rights of ethnic minorities through such provisions as federalism, secularism, reservation of seats in the parliaments, and quotas in government jobs. The minority population had hoped that the new constitution would recognize the plurality of Nepali society by addressing these demands (Thapa and Sijapati 2004). However, framers of the 1990 constitution completely ignored these demands of the minorities. The 1990 constitution declared Nepal a Hindu state, dashing the hope of addressing minorities' demands for a secular state. This aggravated the grievances of the non-Hindu and other ethnic minorities.

Several radical but small parties came together to form a new left party called the Communist Party of Nepal (Unity Center) in November 1990 with Prachanda as general secretary. The Unity Center had passed a resolution in December 1991 to initiate a people's war to bring about a new democratic revolution in Nepal. They changed the name of the party to the Communist Party of Nepal (Maoist) and started preparing for a violent revolution. The party boycotted the mid-term elections held in 1994. In September 1995, the party publicly announced plans for a protracted "People's War" with a stated objective to abolishing feudalism and establishing people's democracy. The party sought to mobilize support from marginalized sections of society and developed a list of demands that resonated with minority grievances.

Initially, the government considered the Maoist rebellion as a law-and-order problem and mobilized police force to suppress the mass uprising. In September 1995, the CPN-M began making preparations to launch a People's War in the mountainous districts of Rolpa and Rukum in western Nepal. In November, these activities came to the attention of the government, which mobilized the police to launch Operation Romeo to repress the uprising. Operation Romeo was "characterized by random arrests, torture, rape, and extra-judicial killings" (Thapa and Sijapati 2004, 48). The use of blunt force resulted in further antagonizing the rural masses. When the party submitted a 40-point demand to the government on February 4, 1996 with a warning to launch an armed struggle should the government fail to address their demands, the government paid no attention to these demands, instead sending its prime minister on February 11 for a state visit to India.

In May 1998, the government launched a search-and-kill operation called "Kilo Sierra Two" with the objective to suppress the Maoist movement across the country. This operation was conducted by a poorly trained police force that relied on the use of force. Over 500 people were killed during the operation, including women and children (INSEC 1999). One might wonder why the political parties failed to notice the seriousness of the rebellion in Nepal. The answer lies elsewhere in Kathmandu where political parties were engaged in maintaining their hold on power.

In December 1999, Prime Minister K.P. Bhattarai's government set up the High-Level Committee to Provide Suggestions to solve the Maoist Problem. This was the first time that the government seemed interested in understanding the cause of the rebellion. Less than a year later, G.P. Koirala from the same Nepali Congress Party ousted Bhattarai and became prime minister. The Committee submitted its report in November 1999 with a suggestion to engage the Maoists in talks while continuing with police operations. However, the Koirala government was too busy patching factionalism within his own Nepali Congress Party and paid little or no attention to the Committee's recommendations.

Political instability in Kathmandu benefited the Maoists in intensifying their attacks. In 2000, the party renewed its strategy to remove government presence from the countryside.

In September, Maoists rebels captured the district headquarters of Dolpa. In January 2001 the Koirala government created a paramilitary force called Armed Police Force (APF) to fight the insurgency as the king was reluctant to deploy the army against the rebels. In July 2001 the Maoist attacked a police post in Hoileri in Rolpa district and took 71 policemen as prisoners. Prime Minister G.P. Koirala tried mobilizing the Royal Nepalese Army (RNA) to fight the insurgency. However, lack of understanding between the prime minister and the palace prevented the PM from using the army.[4] Koirala resigned following his inability to mobilize the RNA.

The next government, headed by Sher Bahadur Deuba, declared a ceasefire and invited the Maoists for a dialogue for the first time. Three rounds of peace talks were held between August and November 2001. On November 21, the Maoists ended the ceasefire stating "our bid to establish peace has been rendered unsuccessful by reactionary and fascist forces" (Thapa and Sijapati 2004, 121). Two days later, the rebels launched their first ever attack on the army.

In response to the attack, the government declared a state of emergency and mobilized the Royal Nepalese Army to fight the insurgents. The government also enacted a Terrorist and Disruptive Activities (Control and Punishment) Ordinance (TADO), suspended freedoms of speech and peaceful assembly, among other rights, and started censoring the media. In May 2002 the PM dissolved parliament. In October the king sacked the popularly elected government and began handpicking prime ministers and cabinet ministers of his choice; in November 2003 the government publicly announced creation of village-based government-sponsored militias to counter the Maoist uprising; and in February 2005 King Gyanendra took direct control of the state.

King Gyanendra's authoritarian steps brought together the Maoists and political parties, who had launched a mass movement seeking to revive democracy. The seven political parties and the Maoists met in Delhi and signed a 12-point understanding to fight the "autocratic monarchy" in November 21, 2005. This culminated into what came to be known as the "People's Movement II," when in April 2006 millions of Nepalis gathered in the streets of Kathmandu and forced King Gyanendra to give up power and reinstate the House of Representatives, dissolved in 2002. The rebellion ended in November 21, 2006 with the signing of a Comprehensive Peace Accord (CPA) between the Maoists and the government. Among other things, the parties agreed to hold elections for a constituent assembly that would write a new constitution for Nepal and create several autonomous regions to accommodate ethnic minorities.

Elections to the constituent assembly were finally conducted in 2008. The CPN-M emerged as the largest party in the assembly. In May 2008, the first sitting of the assembly declared Nepal a republic, thereby abolishing the 240-year-old monarchy. As per the terms of the CPA, the constituent assembly was to finish writing a new constitution within two years of the election. However, the deadline was postponed four times before the assembly itself was finally dissolved in May 2012. Elections for a new constituent assembly were held in November 2013 but the parties have yet to agree on a new constitution for Nepal.

### Identity-based conflicts[5]

Nepal is a complex territory with over a hundred different castes, and ethnic groups that speak more than a hundred different languages, with multiple religious groups and regional groups. In their effort to consolidate autocratic rule, the Shahs and Ranas introduced several divisive policies. The most notable ones are a feudal bureaucracy, the Hindu state and reinforcement and spread of Hindu caste system, and introduction and imposition of Nepali as the national language. These policies resulted in the concentration of wealth and power in the hands of Nepali-speaking elites in Kathmandu and marginalization of ethnic minorities and lower-caste citizens living in rural Nepal. This laid conditions for violent ethnic conflicts to emerge. The irony of the 2006 peace settlement is that while it ended the Maoist armed conflict it unleashed violent armed ethnic mobilization and identity based conflicts.

Violent ethnic conflicts could emerge over time if grievances or perceived disadvantages and threats are not addressed. The Madhesis and indigenous nationalities but also those belonging to the dominant community have asserted themselves in recent decades. For the first time in Nepal's modern history, an ethnic armed group, Kirat Workers Party (KWP), appeared in 1997 and such groups have proliferated since the turn of the century. Madhesis have more armed groups than indigenous nationalities or Dalits. More than three dozen armed groups operated in the Tarai in 2008 and 2009. The Janatantrik Tarai Mukti Morcha (Tarai People's Liberation Front) Goit and Jwala Singh (TPLF-G and TPLF-J) factions are the most active and well known. Some of these organizations have demanded secession. Data on killings specifically by ethnic organizations, collected by the Informal Sector Service Centre (INSEC), show that the Madhesi organizations are involved in the most killings, with a high of 108 in 2007, 75 in 2008, 22 in 2009, and 29 in 2010. The extremist Hindu organizations rank second in killings (Lawoti 2012a).

After 2006, several Limbu political parties and factions maintained armies and army camps. The Limbu organizations at present only claim to have volunteer forces that provide security during public meetings. A Limbu organization, the Pallo Kirat Limbuwan Rastriya Manch (Pallo Kirat Limbuwan National Forum, PKLNF), declared Limbuwan as an independent state on March 23, 2008 arguing that with the end of monarchy, the treaty the Limbus had with King Prithvi Narayan Shah to remain as part of the House of Gorkha became void. Some other indigenous groups like the Tharu, Tamang, and Khambu/Rai have demonstrated armies to the media and KWP, a Khambu/Rai organization, is engaged in an underground armed movement. The Dalits did engage in the rhetoric of armed rebellion in public forums as early as 2000 but this has not resulted in extreme demands or an armed movement.

The second type of violence, such as riots and attacks, often instigated and launched by the extremist organizations of the dominant group against minority religious groups and marginalized communities but occasionally also by marginalized groups against the dominant group, have also increased. While the country witnessed around six violent conflicts between ethnic groups (violent protests, attacks, and riots but excluding the violent activities of armed groups) during the four decades from 1951 to 1990, the last two decades (1990–2010) witnessed 10 violent ethnic riots. The riots have spread after the turn of the century to different parts of the country. The Hindu-Muslim riots during 1958–59 and 1971 were confined to the central Tarai districts and its vicinity and all the five violent riots in 1990s were confined to Nepalganj where a considerable Muslim population lives. After the turn of the century, riots spread to Kathmandu and eastern, central, and western districts in the Tarai (Lawoti 2012b).

To stem and manage the violent conflicts, grievances of the marginalized groups have to be addressed. Some of the demands made by the marginalized groups have been met. The state has become more representative compared to earlier years. The 2008 and 2013 elections to the Constituent Assembly were held after the delineation of electoral constituencies to reduce the under-representation of the populous Tarai region and with a mixed electoral method, which contributed to the higher representation of most of the previously excluded groups, including women.

The country went through significant legal changes in important arenas with the Interim Constitution of 2007. It has become a secular republic from a Hindu kingdom. The recognition of multiple languages indicates that the formal domination of *Khas-kura*/Nepali has waned to some extent. The Interim Constitution of 2007 bestowed more recognition by calling all mother tongues with the same designation even though it still declared *Khas*-Nepali as the only official language.

The hegemony of the "upper" caste hill culture has significantly diminished. The old national anthem that glorified the Hindu king was replaced by the post-2006 government with a new anthem that recognized the country's ethnic and geographic diversity. Hill-centric nationalism has also weakened, largely due to the Madhesi Movements of 2007 and 2008. Citizenship provisions have been relaxed, and around two and a half million Nepalis—mostly Madhesis but others as well—received citizenship certificates in 2007 (Guneratne and Lawoti 2010). The Madhesi Movement also forced the government in 2007 to amend the Interim Constitution to commit towards federalism.

Despite the ongoing transformations and the declared-to-be-secular state, Hindu norms and values continue to dominate. Similarly, many symbols of the dominant group still prevail. The old national flag, which is composed of two juxtaposed triangles of red and blue, criticized as representing the Hindus, was retained in the Interim Constitution and the draft of the new constitution as well. Despite declaring public holidays during festivals of ethnic and religious groups, the hill Hindu public holidays still dominate disproportionately (Lawoti 2014).

Likewise, despite the higher inclusion of various groups in some state organizations, exclusion still continues in other sectors. For instance, the ethnic and caste gap in the top level of bureaucracy widened in 2005 and 2009 (85 and 84 percent respectively) (Lawoti 2012a). Similarly, all three major political parties are led by dominant-group members and the representation of indigenous nationalities, Madhesis, Muslims, and Dalits in top-party positions is minimal. The Madhesi also have very minimal representation in the army.

The political transformation to date has promoted more inclusion of those hitherto marginalized, but the dominant group still controls the polity and state. Federalism that grants autonomy to marginalized groups could substantially alter the power balance but the autonomy of the Madhesi and indigenous nationalities is still not guaranteed. The dominant group launched a movement against doing so in the media, academia, and through limited mass mobilization. Federalism that provides autonomy to different groups could manage conflict related to indigenous nationalities and Madhesi. However, the major political parties like the NC and CPN (UML) are against it, claiming this could lead to violent conflict and even disintegration of the country. The main reason behind the resistance is the fear that devolution would reduce their ability to continue to dominate other communities.

More than two-thirds of the first Constituent Assembly (CA) members supported the identity-based federal model. However, top Bahun leaders of the parties allowed CA to dissolve because they did not want an identity-based federal model to be adopted. The dissolution deprived the country not only of identity-based federalism but also a new constitution. The second CA, where anti-identity federalists have gained more seats, may not embrace identity-based federalism, although it is also possible that it may be coaxed into doing so by Madhesi and indigenous nationalities movements.

## Economy

Nepal remained closed to the outside world until 1950 for trade and commerce. Before the conquest of Nepal, Kathmandu and Tibet had a strong trade relationship.[6] However, when

Prithvi Narayan Shah invaded Kathmandu in 1768, he grew suspicious of the motives of the East India Company and introduced a closed economic policy for Nepal, expelled foreigners from Kathmandu, and discouraged imports. This led to a decline in the country's foreign trade with Tibet and India, which were then Nepal's major trading partners. Shah promoted a completely self-reliant economic policy. Consequently, land became the principal resource of livelihood for the citizens and the main source of revenue for an autocratic regime. Civil servants and military personnel serving the royal army were given land grants as remuneration during their tenure. In addition, a variety of land grants were introduced to reward those who supported the autocratic regime (see Mahat 2005 for details). This model led to land being concentrated in the hands of those serving the royal court.

While Jung Bahadur was keen on establishing peaceful relations with the British, he was always suspicious of their political motives. This lack of trust led the Ranas to maintain a closed economic policy for Nepal with emphasis on increasing export. The Ranas exported timber and rice to the British East India Company and generated revenues to feed their army. The Ranas continued with the policy of land grants introduced by the Shahs. The oligarchic regime lavishly exploited state resources, and aggrandizement continued under the hereditary fiefdom (Regmi 1978).

The end of the Rana regime marked the opening of Nepal to the outside world. The first challenge of the newly formed government was to clean up the wreckage created by the Shahs and Ranas. By the time the interim government came to office in 1950, the country had one airfield, one college, 11 secondary schools, about 50 doctors, and 649 hospital beds (Mahat 2005). The challenges before the new government were daunting and the resources available were extremely low.

When Nepal began receiving foreign aid, the United States provided technical assistance in agriculture, health, mining, education, and malaria eradication (Mahat 2005). India provided support for building an airport in Kathmandu and constructed a highway linking Kathmandu with the bordering town of Raxual. Many other countries, including China, the Soviet Union, and Switzerland, started providing assistance to Nepal. It was during this period that Nepal initiated development planning with assistance from the United Nations. The first Five-Year Plan (1956/57–1960/61) was implemented in 1956 laying a foundation for planned economic development in the country. In 1956, the Central Bank of Nepal was established and Nepal started using its own currency.

The Panchayat regime (1960–90), led by an active monarch, banned political parties and reversed the democratic process, but continued with the planned economic model introduced by the interim government. Priority was given to increasing national production by boosting growth in agriculture, industry, forestry, hydropower, and related sectors. To mobilize surplus manpower from agriculture to the industrial sector, the royal government emphasized creating employment opportunities in the industrial sector. With the objective of achieving social justice, the government identified "minimum basic needs" of the people and made budgetary allocations to meeting those needs. The government also recognized the importance of achieving sustainable growth for the economy and started investing in physical infrastructure such as roads and electricity.

The royal regime divided the country into five economic regions—eastern, central, western, midwestern, and far western—and initiated the process of allocating development budgets accordingly. Emphasis was also given to linking the three geographical regions of the country—mountains, hills, and plains—through the introduction of projects such as roads (Mahat 2005). Beginning in 1987, the World Bank started providing loans for a structural adjustment program.

When democracy was reinstated in 1990, over 40 percent of Nepalis were living in poverty, the private sector was yet to be conceived, a few sick state-owned enterprises dominated the industrial sector, and there were no private schools in the country. The entire economic system was ready for an overhaul and the challenges facing the interim government were enormous. The most immediate challenge facing the new government was renewing a trade treaty with India. Much of landlocked Nepal's trade with the rest of the world passes through India. In 1950, Nepal and India had signed a treaty of trade and transit that allowed Nepal to use Indian highways and harbor for accessing the sea. In 1978, this treaty was split into two separate treaties—Treaty of Trade and Treaty of Transit. In 1989, India suspended the treaties demanding that they be combined into a single document. The interim government renewed these treaties in 1991, though the two documents were not combined as demanded by India. The trade impasse had essentially blocked Nepal's trade with the rest of the world and the treaty's renewal brought big relief to the lives of everyday citizens.

After the general elections in 1991, the Nepali Congress government embarked on a fast-track reform path. A number of economic reform policies were introduced. In 1991, the national planning commission was charged with the task to formulate long-term economic policy for the country. In 1992, the new government strengthened a neoliberal economic reform program with support from the IMF. State-owned enterprises were privatized and import and export procedures simplified with the rationalization of tariffs. In 1992, the government introduced a foreign direct investment and technology transfer act, permitting foreign investment to come in. In 1997, a Value Added Tax (VAT) was introduced to boost revenue collection. By the end of 2001, over 660 joint-venture industries had arrived in Nepal bringing in 886 million Nepali Rupees in FDI. Nepal joined the World Trade Organization in 2004.

Significant achievements were made during the 1990s. Between 1990 and 2000, Nepal's GDP grew at an average annual rate of 4.7 percent with the non-agriculture sector taking the lead. Led by a robust growth in exportable items such as garments and rugs, exports grew at an average annual rate of 15 percent during the 1990s. However, inequality between rural and urban people, poor and wealthy, and among various regions widened.

If the Maoist rebellion disrupted economic growth, King Gyanendra's autocratic rule further exacerbated the economic picture. The economic growth rate started improving after the insurgency ended in 2006. A large youth force that has gone abroad (mainly the Middle East) to work has also contributed immensely to the country's foreign currency income and the overall economy.

## Regional and international relations

Nepal joined the United Nations in 1955 and is party to almost all major human rights treaties. The Nepali army has participated in UN peacekeeping missions since 1958 and the country maintained a neutral position during the Cold War. This was evidenced by the country joining the Non-Aligned Movement (NAM) when the organization was created in 1961.

The secretariat of the South Asian Association for Regional Cooperation (SAARC) is located in Kathmandu. During the late 1970s, King Birendra initiated a proposal to declare Nepal a "Zone of Peace" but the project failed after India's refusal to endorse it.

India remains Nepal's most important neighbor, although the relationship has had its fair share of tensions. The countries share a unique relationship that was formalized by the 1950 Treaty of Peace and Friendship. Under the terms of the treaty, nationals of one country are given the same privileges in the other's territory with regard to residency, ownership of property, participation in trade and commerce, and movement across borders (so that Nepalis and Indians do not need visas to visit and work in each other's country). The open movement of people across the 1,700-kilometer-long border has had a tremendous impact on the two states' economy, culture, and society.

India played an important role in ending the *panchayati* regime in 1990 when it refused to renew the trade and transit treaty mentioned above, probably due to the ego clash between the Shahs and Gandhis. Nepal was forced to import essential items like food and petrol via airplane. This led to a dramatic increase in food prices and adversely affected ordinary citizens.

India also played a crucial role in ending the Maoist insurgency in 2006. Several rounds of meetings were held between the rebel leaders and representatives of political parties in New Delhi. India facilitated a 12-point understanding between the two parties that laid the groundwork for signing the Comprehensive Peace Agreement, which ended the Maoist civil war in Nepal.

As noted above, India especially played a key role in establishing democracy in the country by facilitating a tripartite agreement between the Ranas, Shahs, and various political parties. However, Nepalis have a love-hate relationship with India. Nepali nationalism is to a certain extent based on India-bashing because the country relies significantly on Indian aid even as Nepalese feel strongly that India frequently interferes in the country's domestic affairs.

At the regional level, Nepal has friendly diplomatic relations with all countries in South Asia as well as China. Interestingly, Nepal has benefited from the border disputes between China and India. King Mahendra, for instance, sought support from China to counter-balance India's opposition to the royal takeover of 1960 when democracy was dismantled. China supported the king by providing economic assistance. China is considered a good neighbor since it has provided aid to Nepal but does not appear to be interfering. As long as the Tibetan refugees in Nepal are firmly monitored and controlled, China appears satisfied. China, however, has increased its activities and influence in Nepal since the monarchy's end. After coming to power in 2008 leaders of the Communist Party of Nepal (Maoist) have made repeated efforts to harness this so called "China card." Nepal has also tried to leverage the rivalry between India and Pakistan, though its gains in this regard from Pakistan are less conspicuous than advantages acquired through China.

## Opportunities and constraints

In 2006, Nepal emerged from a decade-long Maoist insurgency and 240 years of monarchy. The military was also placed under "civilian control" but enjoys considerable autonomy due to being the most stable state institution in the country. Nepal is now officially a republic for the first time. These are remarkable accomplishments that offer tremendous opportunities for Nepal in the twenty-first century. However, what has *not* been done in the past seven years is alarming. Since 2008, political parties have been trying to lay a foundation for a more stable Nepal that could potentially address demands of a critically conscious peasantry, minorities, and civil society. Addressing grievances of the peasantry necessitates restructuring the state in a manner that remedies regional disparities and structural inequalities in Nepal. So far the parties have performed poorly on these difficult tasks. Elections to the constituent assembly were finally conducted in 2008, a task that was long overdue since 1950. However, political parties have failed to write a constitution that would codify the achievements made during the civil war. Negotiations began in 2009 on an arrangement that would end the century-old model of Kathmandu-based feudalistic and centralized polity. As per the spirit of the CPA and the Interim Constitution of 2007, an agreement was to be reached on the federal structure of the state, which would then be codified in a constitution written by the constituent assembly. The constitution-writing process has been stalled largely due to disagreement on the nature of federalism.

The proposed two main models of federalism, both of which have been rejected by opposing major political parties, are identity-based federalism (that provides autonomy and sub-autonomy to around three dozen groups) and resource-based federalism (autonomy is denied and the dominant group dominates all or most provinces). The identity-based federalism is conceived along ethnic and regional lines. This model proposes dividing Nepal into dozens of federated units and around two dozen sub-autonomous areas based on concentration of ethnic population.

The alternative model proposes dividing Nepal vertically along the country's three geographic regions: mountains, mid-hills and the southern plain. Southern Nepal has fertile land conducive to agriculture, the mountains attract tourists, and the mid-hills are well suited for horticulture. This resource-based model, however, has been rejected by the indigenous nationalities and Madhesi. People living in southern Nepal, who have long argued that they have been unfairly excluded from the polity in Kathmandu, are the most vocal in opposing the resource-based model because in such a model the dominant group will continue to dominate all or most provinces (Lawoti 2014).

Currently the Second Constitution Assembly is debating and discussing what form of governance (presidential, semi-presidential, and reformed parliamentary system) and model of federalism to institute. The manner in which the structure of the Nepali state is agreed upon will have a huge bearing on the country's socio-political and economic trajectories.

## Political chronology

| | |
|---|---|
| 1768–69: | Prithvi Narayan Shah conquers Kathmandu Valley and lays the foundation to conquer other areas by him and his descendants. |
| 1814–16: | Anglo-Nepal War, Sugauli Treaty signed in 1846, Nepal concedes defeat. |
| 1846: | Kot Massacre takes places and Jung Bahadur Rana takes absolute control of the state, establishing a hereditary Rana prime ministerial system. |
| 1854: | Muluki Ain (Country Code) that codified caste system. |
| 1923: | Britain declares Nepal an independent state. |
| 1948: | First constitution. |
| 1951: | Rana regime ends, King Tribhuvan Shah returns to throne, multiparty democracy instituted for the first time. Interim Constitution. |
| 1955: | Mahendra Shah becomes new King of Nepal. |
| 1959: | A new constitution is promulgated, first general elections held, B.P. Koirala becomes first elected prime minister of Nepal. |
| 1960: | King Mahendra Shah dissolves parliament and bans multiparty system. |
| 1962: | King Mahendra Shah issues a new constitution and starts a guided democracy called Panchayat system. |
| 1990: | Panchayat system comes to an end and multiparty democracy is restored. |
| 1996: | The Communist Party of Nepal (Maoist) launches a "People's War". |
| 2001: | Royal Massacre takes place on June 1 and King Birendra Shah and his entire family are killed by the crown prince Dipendra Shah. |

| 2002: | Parliament dissolved and the government is subsequently sacked by King Gyanendra. |
| 2005 February: | King Gyanendra Shah imposes emergency and assumes full control of the state. |
| 2005 November: | Delhi Understanding between the Maoists and Seven Party Alliance. |
| 2006 April: | Peoples Movement II takes places in Kathmandu, democracy reinstated; Maoist insurgency ends; declaration of secular state. |
| 2006 November: | Comprehensive Peace Agreement signed between the Maoist and government of Nepal; 2007 Interim Constitution; Madhesi Movement. |
| 2008 April: | Elections to a Constituent Assembly (CA) held, Maoist Party wins largest share of votes. |
| 2008 May: | Monarchy comes to an end and Nepal becomes a Republic. |
| 2010 May: | Ruling and opposition parties extend deadline for drafting of new constitution to May 2011. |
| 2012 May: | Constituent Assembly dissolved. |
| 2013 November: | Elections for Constituent Assembly held, no party wins majority. |
| 2014 February: | Sushil Koirala from the Nepali Congress party becomes prime minister. |
| 2015 February: | Government sets up two commissions—Truth and Reconciliation Commission and Commission for Enquiry on Enforced Disappearance to investigate war crimes committed during the Maoist insurgency. |
| 2015 April: | Major earthquake strikes Nepal killing over 8,000 people. |

Sources: Whelpton (2005); Thapa and Sijapati (2004)

## Notes

1 The majority of the population is Hindu (81.3 percent) followed by Buddhists (9 percent), Muslims (4.4 percent), Kirats (3.1 percent), Christians (1.4 percent) and others such as Jains, Bahais and Sikhs.
2 Nepal Praja Parishad, formed in 1939, was the first political party in the country. However, the party was dissolved following the execution of its top leaders by a Rana tribunal in 1941. Remaining members of the Parishad thereafter joined the NC party.
3 Despite the merger, Chandra Prakash Mainali, one of the two major leaders of the breakaway faction, refused to go along with the merger and reestablished the CPN (M-L).
4 Under the 1990 Constitution, the King was the commander-in-chief of the army.
5 This section draws heavily from Lawoti 2012a and Lawoti 2012b.
6 Most people lived on subsistence farming during that period and land was the principal resource. People living in the Himalayan region were engaged in animal husbandry dealing mainly with yak and sheep and trading them for basic commodities such as paper and salt with Tibet. The southern part of Nepal, which borders India, is rich in agricultural land. People living in the plains produced commodities such as rice and cotton and exported them to India. Meanwhile, the capital of Kathmandu served as a link between Indo-Tibetan trade because of its strategic location. Before the opening of a direct trade link between India and Tibet in 1902, Kathmandu was the only route linking India and Tibet. All trade between the East India Company and Tibet took place via Kathmandu.

## Works cited

Adhikari, Prakash, and Steven Samford. 2013. "The Dynamics of the Maoist Insurgency in Nepal." *Studies in Comparative International Development* 48 (4): 457–481.
Guneratne, Arjun, and Mahendra Lawoti. 2010. *Ethnicity, Inequality and Politics in Nepal*. Lalitpur, Nepal: Himal Books.

Hachhethu, Krishna. 2002. *Party Building in Nepal: Organization, Leadership and People: A Comparative Study of the Nepali Congress and the Communist Party of Nepal (Unified Marxist-Leninist)*. Kathmandu: Mandala Book Point.

Informal Sector Service Center (INSEC). 1999. *Nepal Human Rights Yearbook 2009*. Kathmandu: INSEC.

Joshi, Bhuwan Lal, and Leo E. Rose. 1966. *Democratic Innovations in Nepal: A Case Study of Political Acculturation*. Los Angeles: University of California Press.

Lawoti, Mahendra. 2005. *Towards a Democratic Nepal: Inclusive Political Institutions for a Multicultural Society*. New Delhi: Sage.

Lawoti, Mahendra. 2009. *Federal State-Building: Challenges in Framing the Nepali Constitution*. Kathmandu: Bhrikuti Academic.

Lawoti, Mahendra. 2012a. "Ethnic Politics and the Building of an Inclusive State." In *Nepal in Transition*, edited by Sebastian von Einsiedel, David M Malone, and Suman Pradhan. Cambridge: Cambridge University Press.

Lawoti, Mahendra. 2012b. "Dynamics of Mobilization" in *Nationalism and Ethnic Conflict*, edited by Mahendra Lawoti and Susan Hangen, pp. 193–225. London: Routledge.

Lawoti, Mahendra. 2014. "Reform and Resistance in Nepal," *Journal of Democracy* 25 (2): 131–145.

Lawoti, Mahendra, and Anup K. Pahari. 2009. *The Maoist Insurgency in Nepal: Revolution in the Twenty-first Century*. London: Routledge.

Lawoti, Mahendra, and Susan Hangen. 2013. *Nationalism and Ethnic Conflict in Nepal*. London: Routledge.

Mahat, Ram Sharan. 2005. *In Defense of Democracy: Dynamics and Fault Lines of Nepal's Political Economy*. New Delhi: Adroit.

Regmi, Mahesh C. 1978. *Thatched Huts and Stucco Palaces: Peasants and Landlords in 19th Century Nepal*. New Delhi: Vikas.

Thapa, Manjushree. 2005. *Forget Kathmandu: An Elegy for Democracy*. New Delhi: Penguin Books.

Thapa, Deepak, and Sijapati, Bandita. 2004. *A Kingdom Under Siege: Nepal's Maoist Insurgency, 1996 to 2004*. Kathmandu: The Printhouse.

Whelpton, John. 2005. *A History of Nepal*. Cambridge: Cambridge University Press.

## Recommended texts

Baral, Lok Raj. 1977. *Opposition Politics in Nepal*. New Delhi: Abhinav.

Bista, Dor Bahadur. 1991. *Fatalism and Development: Nepal's Struggle for Modernization*. Bangalore, India: Orient Longman Private Limited.

Hagen, Susan I. 2010. *The Rise of Ethnic Politics in Nepal: Democracy in the Margins*. London: Routledge.

Joshi, Bhuwan Lal, and Leo E. Rose. 1966. *Democratic Innovations in Nepal: A Case Study of Political Acculturation*. Los Angeles: University of California Press.

Lawoti, Mahendra. 2005. *Towards a Democratic Nepal: Inclusive Political Institutions for a Multicultural Society*. New Delhi: Sage.

Rose, Leo. 1971. *Nepal: Strategy for Survival*. Berkeley: University of California Press

Thapa, Deepak, and Sijapati, Bandita. 2003. *A Kingdom Under Siege: Nepal's Maoist Insurgency, 1996 to 2003*. Kathmandu: The Printhouse.

Whelpton, John. 2005. *A History of Nepal*. Cambridge: Cambridge University Press.

# 7  Afghanistan

*Vikash Yadav*

The challenges Afghanistan faces today are mostly due to a legacy of tense relations between the state and a range of ethno-national groups; the failure to pacify or eliminate rival challengers to the new state's monopoly on the legitimate use of violence; and the failed emergence of balanced and robust political institutions after the Taliban regime was toppled in late 2001.

Power in the new Afghan state is centralized but weak, sparse, and neo-patrimonial.[1] President Hamid Karzai was an ineffective leader given to populist rhetoric and the politics of patronage, with few substantive accomplishments to show after a decade in power. The parliament has failed to develop as an institution that can balance the executive branch or act decisively to make effective laws. The population has little faith in the state's court system, preferring instead traditional local councils or even the informal courts of the insurgents (Fleschenberg 2009). And although the Afghan National Army has experienced rapid growth and is widely considered to be the most capable bureaucratic organization within the state, the military remains fragmented and politicized.

The various groups fighting under the banner of the insurgency have not been defeated or demoralized by the International Security Assistance Force (ISAF) that occupied the country for over a decade. Meanwhile, warlords from the Anti-Soviet War era have penetrated the new state but have not been transformed into parliamentarians (Giustozzi 2009). The narcotics trade, a major source of funding for insurgents and warlords (Felbab-Brown 2005), has not been successfully marginalized and replaced with conventional agricultural practices. The incentives for regional powers to intervene in Afghanistan's internal affairs, which have resulted in nearly constant warfare since 1978, have not been altered significantly. The puzzle is to explain all these failures in light of overwhelming foreign aid and security assistance to Afghanistan for over a decade.

## History and political development

Far from being a peripheral backwater, the land that is now Afghanistan was a significant crossroad for armies, merchants, and monks for centuries. The site of modern Afghanistan has probably been continuously inhabited for 50,000 years (Dupree 1997). There is archaeological evidence indicating trade links with Greek and the Indus Valley civilizations dating back to the fourth millennium BCE. Throughout the ages, this land has witnessed numerous conquests (e.g. Greek, Mauryan, Mongol, Turco-Mongol, Mughal, British) and it has served as the seat of several empires (e.g. the Kushan, Ghaznavids, Ghorids). This land was also once a prominent Buddhist center and overland trade route. For instance, the famed itinerant Chinese monk, Xuanzang, passed by the Buddhist colossi of Bamiyan around 634 CE en route from China to the famed Nalanda monastery in northern India. The arrival of Islam from the mid-seventh to the ninth century CE revolutionized Afghan society and culture, and by the end of the nineteenth century nearly all Afghans were Muslim. Today, Islam is the common link in an otherwise very diverse society.

Throughout the sixteenth to the seventeenth centuries, much of the area that is present day Afghanistan was contested between the empires of the Persian Safavids and the Indian Mughals. In 1747, during a period of disarray and decline in the Afsharid (Persian) and Mughal (Indian) empires, respectively, a famed local commander, Ahmad Shah Durrani, was crowned emperor in Kandahar by a confederation of Pashtun tribes. The Durrani empire would lay the foundation for the Afghan state.

Although never directly colonized, Afghanistan was gradually and quite literally drawn into the middle of a conflict between the tsarist Russian empire and the British empire. In order to secure and sustain a buffer zone, the British thrice fought in Afghanistan (1839, 1878, and 1919) so as to protect their most important possession and the heart of their empire, British India, from what they perceived as an expansionist Russian empire.

Inter-imperial rivalry, intervention, and cooperation ultimately shaped Afghanistan's present southern (Durand Line Agreement of 1893) and northern boundaries (Anglo-Russian Agreement of 1873; and the Anglo-Russian Agreement of 1895). Under a series of monarchs from 1880 (Abdur Rahman Khan) until 1973 (Mohammed Zahir Shah), the modern Afghan state gradually evolved and spread its influence over the different ethno-linguistic groups and tribes. The modern state sought to forge not an empire, but a nation-state, from the outline drawn by the British and Russian empires. To a great extent, the rulers of Afghanistan had little choice but to cultivate a nation-state since the British controlled their foreign relations until 1919. Like many other states in Asia and Africa, Afghanistan's mode and chronology of incorporation into the international system has "left a lasting imprint on the pattern of politics in these states" (Rubin 1995, 16).

### *Identity politics*

Afghanistan is often mistakenly portrayed as a predominantly tribal society. However, more than half its population is non-tribal. Moreover, even in areas where tribes are present, the tribe or sub-tribe may not be the most salient form of political identification. The Durranis in western Afghanistan, for example, have identified with the structures of the state far more than their tribal grouping even though the Durrani tribe is considered to be one of the most important among Pashtuns (Roy 1990). Moreover, the meaning and influence of tribes has waxed and waned over time and may be structured by state policies and administrative boundaries. For example, before the communist Saur Revolution in 1978 and subsequent tribal revolts, tribes (with the exception of some eastern Pashtuns) had been largely disarmed and tribal structures were hardly seen as threatening the state (Dorronsoro 2005).

Afghans may find their *qawm* (solidarity group), city-of-origin, region, ideology, ethno-national and ethno-linguistic group, or membership in the *ummah* (community of Muslims) to be the most important form of identity in a given social situation. As in any society, all forms of politically meaningful identity must be shaped and activated by political entrepreneurs and organizations; there is no primordial or pre-political form of identity.

The Pashtuns are the largest ethno-national group and are estimated to constitute between 38 to 42 percent of the population. While Pashtuns have historically been a dominant group in the domestic politics of Afghanistan, the majority of the Pashtun people actually live in neighboring Pakistan. Most Pashtuns speak Pashto and are Sunni Muslims, except the Turi who are Shia. The Tajiks are the second largest ethno-national group; however the category "Tajik" covers a range of linguistic, sectarian, and behavioral criteria and is not usually a basis for political mobilization. Other significant ethnic groups include the Hazara, Uzbek, Aimaq, Turkmen, Baluchi, Kyrgyz, Pashai, Nuristanis, Brahui, and Pamiri.

Half of the population speaks Dari (which includes Hazaragi and Tajiki as dialects) and over a third speak Pashto. Turkic languages (Uzbek/Jagatai and Turkmen) are spoken by a tenth of the population, and there are also speakers of Baluchi, Pashai, Nuristani/Kafiri, Dardic, Pamiri, and more. Only just over a quarter of the population is literate.

## The modernizing project

As M. Nazif Shahrani argues, the history of the modern Afghan state from 1880 onward has been characterized by a remarkable thematic consistency: the state has been almost exclusively dominated by elites from the Pashtun ethno-linguistic group and oriented toward pursuing a "modernizing project of internal colonialism" (Shahrani 2008, 155–56). He notes that the modern Afghan state has shown consistent hostility toward its subjects in general, and to the Uzbek, Turkmen, and Tajik peoples of western, northern, and central Afghanistan in particular (Shahrani 2008). Shahrani documents a range of abuses and efforts to marginalize non-Pashtun communities. The lands of minority communities were frequently seized by the state and distributed to Pashtun tribal settlers from southern and eastern Afghanistan in a systematic internal colonization policy from the 1930s to the 1970s (Edwards 2002). Even place names such as Afghan Turkestan, which was once a common term referring to northern Afghanistan, were removed from official use (Shahrani 2008).

Shahrani contends that the roots of ethno-linguistic factionalism and contempt can be traced to the "Iron Amir," Abdur Rahman Khan, who ruled from 1880 to 1901. It was the Iron Amir who set forth what became the hegemonic discourse of Afghanistan's Pashtun rulers. He emphasized the creation of a centralized, unified, and socially stratified state. The unified state was not meant to be a reflection of Afghanistan's multi-ethnic polity. The state displayed the consolidation of power by a single royal family, buttressed by the tribal elders of the Barakzai clan, and the leaders of other Pashtun tribes. In other words, this ethnically diverse state was meant to be ruled only by the royal family of the Barakzai clan of the Durrani Confederation of the Pashtun ethno-linguistic group. All others were to be treated as subjects at best, but were often portrayed as merely "cattle, beasts of burden, and chattel" (Shahrani 2008, 165–166). Efforts at local autonomy or self-governance by inferior minority communities were to be resisted aggressively through a policy of internal colonialism that included physical repression, land appropriation, and population resettlement.

The driving force behind the policy of internal colonialism is the contradiction between Pashtun leaders who rely on tribal networks to achieve power and their need to surpass the kinship network in order to gain independent access to reliable and renewable resources to sustain an autocratic and patrimonial political order. In essence, Shahrani argues that internal colonialism is driven by a limitation within the political economy of Afghanistan.

Before the Afghan state was confined to its modern boundaries by the British and Russian empires, Afghan rulers were able to secure resources by attacking non-Muslim populations in the Indian subcontinent. Once the state was confined within its present borders, greater pressure was exerted against non-Pashtun communities. Some of the pressure on the policy on internal colonialism eased through the supply of foreign assistance by patron states. Nevertheless, foreign support also prolonged the ability of state leaders to avoid shifting from authoritarian rule to "broader, more inclusive, participatory national politics based on the development of modern and democratic national institutions and rules of governance" (Shahrani 2008, 160–161). In other words, foreign support impeded the fulfillment of a democratic nation-building project and enabled (a sometimes brutal) authoritarianism built on a policy of divide and conquer. Even nominal efforts at creating a constitutional monarchy by Amir Amanullah Khan in 1923 and King Nadir Shah in 1931 mainly affirmed the absolute power of the monarch and the rubber-stamp role of the *Loya Jirga* (Grand Assembly). More liberal constitutions initiated by rulers in 1964, 1977, and 1990 did not outlast the reign of their promulgators. Regardless of the content of the constitutions, the only parts that were enforced related to the rights and duties of rulers and the government, not the rights of subjects (Shahrani 2008).

Efforts to catch up quickly with the West by imposing Western institutions and norms in the early twentieth century, including the creation of a secular, written constitution, education for girls, legal rights for women, abolition of slavery, and the like generated a severe internal backlash from traditional religious leaders in the Afghan society. There were a series of revolts by tribesmen to the pace of reforms and particularly to new taxes implemented by the state. Ultimately, King Amanullah was overthrown in 1929 by a Tajik rebel known as Bacha-e Saqao (son of the water carrier) with the backing of the *'ulama* (Islamic legal scholars). The traditionalist regime that came to power for nine months has been compared to the scripturalist Taliban regime and for some scholars there are interesting historical parallels in the dynamics between modernizers and their opponents in Afghanistan then and now.

Nadir Shah, a member of the royal family who eventually overthrew the usurper a few months later, charted a middle course between talking about modernization while reinforcing traditional rules and social norms. Nadir and his son Zahir Shah ruled Afghanistan until 1973, when the push for modernization began again and subsequently resulted in more instability.

## Coups and revolutions

In 1973, Sardar Mohammed Daoud, a former prime minister and close relative of the king, overthrew the monarchy in a bloodless *coup d'etat*. He established a republic with the backing of the Communist Party of Afghanistan (also known as the People's Democratic Party of Afghanistan [PDPA]). The five-year-long republic witnessed three coup attempts against the head of state. Daoud, a fervent Pashtun nationalist, sought to create a one-party state and to use the Communists to eliminate Islamist factions (Dorronsoro 2005). However, he was unable to balance against the Communist Party and his foreign policy overtures to non-communist countries alarmed the Soviet Union.

In 1978, with the assistance of the USSR, the two main factions (i.e. Parcham and Khalq) of the Communist Party overthrew Daoud's republic. Almost immediately, the two factions began squabbling for power with each other and within their own cliques. After the Soviet-backed President Nur Mohammed Taraqi was strangled to death in a prison cell in September 1979 by the henchmen of Taraqi's subordinate, Hafizullah Amin, the Soviet military intervened. The Soviets killed Amin in December 1979, and installed Babrak Karmal as President. The communists' zeal and determination to restructure rural Afghan society sparked revolts and instability in three-quarters of the country. The resistance in rural areas initially reflected a traditional anti-state response by the peasantry to the application of certain alien aspects of the Communist party's rural reform agenda. However, once the Soviet Union intervened militarily, the rebellion transformed into a national liberation movement (Roy 1990; Dorronsoro 2005).

Resistance groups formed in Pakistan (as well as Iran) to expel the Soviet Union. The groups that fought back were loosely organized around "fronts" with well-known rebel commanders. The parties were primarily conduits for the distribution of patronage (i.e. weapons) to clients (i.e. rebels) with little coordination or cooperation among them. Eventually many of the Sunni fronts would come to be organized by Pakistan's intelligence services into seven major parties (Roy 1990). Three of the resistance groups were traditionalist (*Harakat, Mahaz, Jabha*) in ideological orientation and gravitated toward supporting a royalist position; the other four were Islamists (*Jamiat-e Islami, Hezb-e Islami Hekmatyar, Hezb-e Islami Khalis, Ittehad-e Islami*). The remnants of the Anti-Soviet resistance parties (the *mujahideen*) continue to operate at an important level in contemporary Afghanistan.

The United States, Saudi Arabia, and other countries funded and armed the *mujahideen*. Initial levels of funding were nominal so as to avoid provoking the USSR into expanding the conflict into neighboring states. As the conflict intensified, the United States supplied the rebels with state of the art surface-to-air "Stinger" missiles; however, the USSR also transferred thousands of tactical ballistic "SCUD" missiles to the Afghan government. The USSR did somewhat escalate the conflict with Pakistan from 1986 to 1989 through airstrikes and artillery barrages.

Although the Soviets withdrew in 1989, their client regime headed by Mohammed Najibullah hung on to power for a couple more years. Unfortunately, the final collapse of the Communist regime in Afghanistan heralded a complete collapse of the state in 1992. It is important to understand the context that led to this dramatic development if one hopes to comprehend the challenges that continue to beset Afghanistan more than 20 years later.

When Kabul finally fell on April 25, 1992, it was a coalition of the Iranian coordinated forces, composed of Abdul Rashid Dostum (a former Uzbek general in the communist Afghan regime and a leader of a very large militia), Ahmad Shah Massoud (a Tajik resistance commander from the Panjshir Valley), the Hazara community's *Hezb-e Wahdat*, Shi'a militias within Kabul, and some PDPA Parchamis that toppled the PDPA Khalqis of the pro-Soviet Najibullah regime. However, the flow of other *mujahideen* forces into Kabul shortly thereafter, particularly Islamist groups backed by Pakistan and Saudi Arabia, led to clashes and chaos that ultimately devastated the capital city. Gulbuddin Hekmatyar, the leader of the majority faction of *Hezb-e Islami*, refused to accept the new government in Kabul once Ahmad Shah Massoud was appointed Defense Minister. When Massoud eventually turned on some of the Shi'a militias in control of Kabul University, and an alliance was forged between *Hezb-e Wahdat*, Dostum's militia, and Hekmatyar's forces, the possibility of a peaceful solution ended. By 1993 there were direct clashes between the Iranian-backed *Hezb-e Wahdat* and the Saudi-backed *Ittehad-e Islami* headed by Abdul Rasoul Sayyaf. Hundreds of thousands perished in the ensuing anarchy and civil war.

### *Explaining prolonged state collapse*

The state that effectively collapsed in 1992 would not be resurrected until the rise of the de facto Taliban regime in 1996. The revival of a modern (Weberian) state was not actually attempted until 2002. There are multiple interrelated factors that may explain the state's prolonged collapse: the social transformations wrought by the duration and intensity of the Soviet occupation; geo-politics among the super powers in the international system; the preferences of minority parties that viewed the post-Najibullah regime as potentially hostile to their regional autonomy; and the influence of regional powers (Goodson 2001).

Afghanistan was physically destroyed and transformed socially and culturally by the Anti-Soviet War. Socially, the protracted war led to the departure and decline of the traditional elites, the *khans* (agrarian landlord class), in many regions; the rise of a large cadre of young Islamists; and the imposition of *shari'at* by the *'ulama* (Islamic legal scholars) (Roy 1990). Culturally, Olivier Roy has argued that there was a "re-traditionalization" of Afghan society in the wake of the Soviet withdrawal (Roy 1990, 215). Relations between the Resistance Parties in Afghanistan also became "de-ideologized" once the Soviets withdrew and the militias turned on one another. The dramatic transformation of the society, particularly the decline of the old elite, prolonged the state's collapse as a new ruling elite emerged slowly.

Due to these social and cultural transformations, Afghan society could not immediately supply the basis for a new model of state and society. Traditional power relations came to be channeled through the political parties. In essence, the Resistance Parties' commanders became the new *khans*. They tried to adopt modern political structures onto traditional social patterns (Roy 1990). They used their party affiliation to enhance their local status rather than aiming to acquire a national platform grounded in ideology. This new class was oriented toward rising above their equals rather than seeking to challenge or capture the state.

The emergence of *amirs* (regional warlords), who represented the synthesis of political and military power and to whom commanders and local notables were subordinate, was also new. Of course, the power of the *amir* is not based on tradition, but on charisma and/or religion. Simultaneously, there was a decline of the intellectual class through emigration abroad. Thus, the leaders who emerged from the anti-Soviet campaign were often less educated and less politically and ideologically minded than their predecessors (Roy 1990).

Afghanistan thus began tilting toward fragmentation after the Soviets withdrew. This process was accelerated because by the 1990s Afghanistan was already flooded with weapons and narcotics. Weapons were often collected and re-distributed by local field commanders as a way to earn legitimacy. One might have supposed that the anti-Soviet parties would have been able to cooperate to form a new state after the Soviets withdrew. The United States certainly hoped that these parties would put together a shadow government. The Pakistanis also hoped to unite the groups so as to retain a measure of leverage over field commanders. However, the Resistance Parties generally succumbed to competitive clientele-ism in the absence of an external enemy.

The collapse of the Afghan state was also a product of the relations between the super powers toward the end of the Cold War. In short, Afghanistan's failure was not inevitable. A strategy of positive symmetry (or mutual lack of restraint) between the United States and the USSR set the stage for the breakdown of order. Mistrust and misperception between the superpowers were the main reasons for this outcome. For instance, while the Soviets advanced a second track of diplomacy to facilitate their withdrawal and stabilization of post-occupation Afghanistan, the Americans and Pakistanis continued to believe that Soviet gestures were part of a ploy to stall for time (Rubin 1995).

Certain Afghan resistance parties and regional powers also did not have an interest in peace after the collapse of the Najibullah regime. The forces opposed to resolving the civil war were Dostum's *Junbish* and the Hazara Shi'a dominated *Hezb-e Wahdat*. The Hazara Shi'a and *Hezb-e Wahdat* demanded federalism and autonomy in the new regime, which the Sunni parties promptly rejected (Dorronsoro 2005).

Pakistan wanted to ensure an Islamist regime in Afghanistan, which would operate as its client. Pakistan initially backed *Hezb-e Islami* led by Gulbuddin Hekmatyar. After the Soviet withdrawal, the Pakistani military and intelligence services provided Hekmatyar's front with logistical support in the ill-fated Battle of Jalalabad in 1989 (Dorronsoro 2005). Unfortunately, Pakistan came to realize that Hekmatyar might not be as skilled of a commander as they had hoped. Eventually, Pakistan shifted its support from Hekmatyar to a new group, the Taliban.

It is also worth noting that Pakistan rejected "enthroning" or empowering Massoud despite his charismatic reputation, specifically because Massoud was not pliable to the Pakistani intelligence service (Inter-Services Intelligence [ISI]). Massoud insisted on developing his own strategies and using his own intelligence agents. Massoud also maintained his own offices in London and Paris, which were staffed by his brothers. Massoud even attempted to reach out to the United States (with varied success at different times), because he assumed it would eventually turn against Pakistan and its clients. Because Massoud's base of operation was in the remote Panjshir Valley, the ISI could not easily undermine him. Hence, the ISI tried to use Hekmatyar to knock out Massoud and his militia. In response to Pakistani machinations, Massoud negotiated a truce with the USSR in 1983, so the Soviets could concentrate on attacking Hekmatyar (Rubin 1995).

In essence, the efforts of internal and external powers to shape the "end game" in Afghanistan may have prolonged the resolution of the crisis. The anarchic environment that resulted from the final collapse of the communist state would give birth to a new and ruthlessly puritanical movement, the Taliban.

### *The Taliban regime*

The history of the scripturalist Taliban movement and their elusive leader, Mullah Omar, are disputed. It appears that the militant group emerged from a band of *madrassah* (a school attached to a mosque) students who sought to restore order and impose an austere form of morality following the collapse of the Afghan state. Pakistan's Inter-Services Intelligence (ISI) helped to fund and enhance the military and logistical capabilities of the organization. From 1994 to 1996, the Taliban won some stunning military victories and negotiated surrenders of key cities and towns, so that by 2001 the group controlled at least 85 percent of Afghanistan's territory. The only militia holding out against the regime, the Northern Alliance, which was supported by India, Russia, and Iran, appeared to be a lost cause.

### Box 7.1: Mullah Omar

While the head of the Taliban, Mullah Omar, shares the ethnic and tribal heritage as well as the religious training of his senior leaders, his lineage is not considered to be distinguished. Moreover, as a mullah, he is not considered a traditional tribal leader (Roy 1990). So how was he able to create and lead such a centralized regime?

Mullah Omar's success is best explained by his charisma. He has claimed divine grace from the earliest days of the movement. He is said to have been inspired in the mid-1990s to lead the Taliban by a dream in which the Prophet Muhammad told him that he would bring peace to Afghanistan. His ability to articulate this vision and to present himself and his organization as credible purveyors of the vision helped him to woo support across Pashtun areas of Afghanistan (Sinno 2008). Mullah Omar assumed the title of *Amir al-mu'minin* (Commander of the Faithful) after donning a relic purported to be the cloak of the Prophet Muhammad in Kandahar in 1994. In the Afghan context, the title was synonymous with the political status of a Caliph (or *Khalifah*) and implied compulsory obedience from the faithful (Nojumi 2002). Although the one-eyed Mullah is only semi-literate and lacks a sophisticated understanding of international relations, he is "adored" by most of his followers who are willing to kill and die for him. Presently, as he stages one of the greatest insurgency campaigns in history, he would certainly appear to his followers to be endowed with charisma or the gift of grace (Shane 2009).

Nevertheless, his charismatic leadership should not be overemphasized (Porter 2009). If he succeeds, his charisma will be routinized through the development of a state bureaucracy. If he is killed, he will become a martyr, but the movement is likely to fight on.

The original governing structure of the Taliban regime consisted of a series of *shuras* (councils), including a 6–10-member Supreme Council and a subordinate nine-member council (later expanded to 22). In addition to being the head of state, Mullah Omar was also the head of the Supreme Council. The model of government, although seemingly Quranic in inspiration, was apparently taken from the PDPA and the National Security Council under President Mohammed Daoud in the mid-1970s (Nojumi 2002). Mullah Omar regularly changed the personnel in the Supreme Council. The Council members were generally drawn from the "bottom to the middle of the *ulema*," and almost all were Kandahari Pashtuns (U.S. Embassy in Islamabad 1995, 81).

Once the movement took power in Kabul in 1996, a seven-member Kabul *shura* was established in the capital and the governing structure began to change to include conventional ministries. By 1998 Mullah Omar invested the lion's share of power in the notorious Ministry for the Enforcement of Virtue and Suppression of Vice (*'Amr bil-Ma'rouf wal Nahi 'an al-Munkar*), which was charged with implementing the decrees of the head of state, by violence if necessary, and collecting taxes (*zakat* and *'ushr*). The ministry acted not only to discipline the civilian population but also to keep the Taliban troops in line. Thus, Mullah Omar retained supreme control (Rubin, 1999). In fact, Abdulkader H. Sinno argues that Mullah Omar had centralized power in his own hands to such a degree that by October 2001, "Taliban field commanders would fear taking the initiative without his permission" (Sinno 2008, 247).

## Box 7.2: The Taliban movement

The senior leadership of the original Taliban, with very few exceptions, was drawn from the same *qawm* of the Hotak sub-tribe of the Ghilzai tribal confederation of the Pashtun ethno-linguistic group. The Taliban is nevertheless best understood as "post-tribal" in important respects as its membership regularly and intentionally attempts to transcend tribal distinctions, particularly within combat units.

The Taliban is also an ideological movement. Its ideology is grounded in the scripturalist Deobandi tradition, which is distinct from but tolerant of similar scripturalists and unitarians like the Wahhabis (*Muwahiddun*) and *Ikhwani* (Muslim Brotherhood) ideologies (Nojumi 2002). The Deobandi school of thought is part of the Sunni (Hanafi) stream of Islam that embraces *taqlid* (imitation or tradition) and rejects *ijtihad* (independent interpretation) of the Quran and the sayings/habits of the Prophet Mohammad. In terms of education, most of the original Taliban leaders came from *madaris* run by Fazl-ul-Rahman's *Jammat-e-Ulema-e-Islami* (JUI). In fact, three of the senior Taliban leaders, including the leader of the organization Mullah Muhammad Omar Mujahid, hail from one large Deobandi *madrassa*, *Jamiat-ul-Uloom-al-Islamiyyah*, that is located in New Town, Karachi (Nojumi 2002). The students who studied at JUI schools became more linked to JUI Pakistani leaders and to one another than to the Afghan *mujahideen* leadership during the Soviet occupation. A possible reason is that the curriculum of the JUI *madaris* was substantively different from that taught in *madaris* run by Afghans (Nojumi 2002).

The Taliban regime was quickly toppled and dispersed by the United States and the Northern Alliance following Mullah Omar's refusal to extradite Osama bin Laden and members of the Al Qaeda terrorist network post-September 11, 2001. However, the highly centralized Taliban regime rapidly reorganized itself to return to fight in Afghanistan as an insurgency. The Taliban shifted from a tightly centralized organization to a "brand name" or a decentralized group of affiliated organizations, networks, and mercenaries popularly labeled the "Neo-Taliban."

It is believed that the largest segment of the "Neo-Taliban" insurgency is still loyal to the Supreme Council (also known as the *Rahbari Shura* or *Quetta Shura*) led by Mullah Omar. However, there are also a number of other affiliated groups that are also often labeled "Taliban" by the media, such as the Haqqani Network, Hekmatyar's *Hezb-e Islami*, and Hafiz Gul Bahadur's *Tehrik-i-Taliban Pakistan* (Sulaiman and Bukhari 2009). Each of these affiliated groups, while pursuing a common goal of expelling foreign forces, relies on different sources of funding (Robinson 2009). There are also irregular fighters, individuals connected through loose networks, as well as a base of sympathizers and supporters (Kilcullen 2009). There is no chain of command linking the Taliban with its affiliated organizations (Cordesman 2009). Remarkably, even with this dramatic reorganization, the core Taliban organization remains united and potent.

Ultimately, while the Taliban regime had pacified much of Afghanistan before the US intervention, the Taliban had not succeeded in rebuilding Afghanistan. This meant that the Afghan state had to be rebuilt from scratch once the regime was overthrown.

### Box 7.3: US–Taliban relations

The United States initially supported and engaged the Taliban regime. On September 27, 1996, when the Taliban took Kabul by force, their first act of business was to raid a UN compound in order to seize, torture, castrate, and hang the former president of the Soviet-backed regime, Mohammad Najibullah. The initial US reaction to Najibullah's torture and execution was merely to state that it was "regrettable" (U.S. Department of State 1996a). While the US government was well aware of the Taliban's oppressive policies toward women, it would not sever ties with the organization

(U.S. Department of State 1996b). The United States was optimistic that the Taliban's policies could be moderated or that a moderate faction would emerge. The reason for optimism was most likely due to the fact that a State Department official had met with the Taliban's "Deputy Foreign Affairs Advisor" nine days before the fall of Kabul. He had assured the US representative that the Taliban would not provide refuge to Osama bin Laden (U.S. Department of State 2010, 2).

The State Department called for "national reconciliation" in Afghanistan shortly after the Taliban captured Kabul (Coll 2004, 14). The United States hoped that it could use the Taliban to extend its sphere of influence to Central Asia. Ahmed Rashid quotes one anonymous US diplomat who hoped that the US–Taliban relation would be similar to the US–Saudi "special relationship":

> The Taliban will probably develop like the Saudis did. There will be Aramco, pipelines, an emir, no parliament, and lots of Sharia law. We can live with that. (Rashid 2001, 179).

Despite this pragmatic outlook, the United States made no real progress in finding a moderate faction or in moderating the Taliban's policies (Yadav 2010). Ultimately, when the Taliban refused to extradite Osama bin Laden after the events of September 11, 2001, the United States chose to back the Northern Alliance with air support in order to topple the Taliban regime.

## Institutions, political parties, and elections

Despite significant improvements in the social, political, and economic lives of ordinary Afghans since the end of the Taliban regime, the political institutions, parties, and processes of the new Afghan state are unlikely to foster the development of a strong democratic regime.

### Elections and political parties

After the appointment of a transitional regime under the Bonn Agreement of December 2001,[2] a constitution was approved in January 2004. Democratic elections have been held in 2004 (presidential), 2005 (parliamentary and provincial), 2009 (presidential and provincial), 2010 (parliamentary), and 2014 (presidential). The election process, however, has been increasingly characterized by violence, widespread fraud, low turnout, and contested results.

The electoral system in Afghanistan is a Single Non-Transferable Vote (SNTV) in multi-member constituencies based on population size, which favors independent candidates as well as large, organized political parties. There are 249 seats in the lower house (*Wolesi Jirga*) and 102 seats in the upper house (*Meshrano Jirga*). In 2010, Pashtun legislators held 95 seats (38 percent), while Hazara and Shiites held 58 seats (23 percent) and Tajiks held 55 seats (22 percent) (Hazara.net 2011). Women are guaranteed at least 25 percent of the seats in Parliament.

The major political parties in Afghanistan today are mainly descendent from the seven military "fronts" and various Shia military factions during the anti-Soviet struggle. A few political parties have emerged from civil society organizations in the post-Taliban period.

On the whole, political parties are not yet a major force in Afghan politics, although larger parties do have extensive networks of supporters. In the 2010 Parliamentary elections, only 34 out of 2,577 candidates were registered with a party affiliation on the ballot (National Democratic Institute 2011). Most candidates run as independents and their legitimacy is based on their potential to redistribute patronage and to activate regional and/or ethno-linguistic identity among voters. Constitutionally, registered political parties are not permitted to organize on the basis of ethnicity, language, region, or religious sect. Nevertheless, party platforms are not heavily influenced by ideological concerns, with the exception of the Islamist parties. Most parties at least claim to reach out across ethnic lines and promote "national unity," with the exception of those parties strongly associated with minority Hazara, Uzbek, and Turkmen communities.

From 2001 to 2009 there were over a hundred registered political parties. After the passage of a new electoral reform law in 2009, which was designed to promote consolidation, political parties were required to re-register and demonstrate they had at least 10,000 members. In the 2010 election only five parties met the criteria. Currently, there are over 20 registered political parties in the Wolesi Jirga, the lower house of Parliament. However, most parties play only a marginal role in the overall political process. Only four of 18 candidates in the 2004 presidential election were affiliated with a political party. Likewise, in 2005 only 14 percent of 2,835 parliamentary candidates declared a party affiliation. At the provincial level, the overwhelming majority of candidates (80 percent) registered as independents in 2009. The National Front party, created in 2006 by leading members of the Northern Alliance (i.e. the United Islamic Front) that helped to topple the Taliban regime, constitutes one of the main multi-ethnic opposition parties to the incumbent Karzai regime. The National Democratic Front is another multi-ethnic organization that is composed of political parties with links dating back to the PDPA communist parties (National Democratic Institute 2011).

The President, Hamid Karzai, was installed by the United States as the interim President of the transitional regime in 2001. Karzai lacked an autonomous base of support in Afghan society. In fact, it was his weakness that made him an attractive compromise candidate to all of the major warlords in Afghanistan. More than a decade later, Karzai remained a decidedly weak leader. He allowed corruption and poor governance to erode the political capital he had accumulated after the generally free and fair 2004 presidential election. The blatantly fraudulent 2009 presidential election disillusioned many of his domestic and foreign supporters. Nevertheless, he continued to receive foreign backing, despite his erratic and emotional outbursts, mainly to ensure regime stability and continuity in the face of a strengthening insurgency.

Karzai is the son of the chief of the Popolzai sub-tribe of the Durrani tribal confederation within the Pashtun ethno-linguistic group. Although well educated, he lacked both charisma and autonomous leadership experience that would have allowed him to transcend his ethnic roots without substantial patronage. He served as the "Director of Information" for Sibghataullah Mojaddedi's *Jebh-e Najat-e Melli* resistance party during the anti-Soviet struggle and later as the Deputy Foreign Minister of International Humanitarian Help from 1992–1994 in the short-lived and rather nominal Peshawar Accord government of President Burhanuddin Rabbani. By his own admission, Karzai has never fired a weapon in combat. His main skill has always been his ability to interface with foreigners in fluent English. He was placed in power initially by US forces in 2001, who pushed aside the more popular King-in-Exile, Zahir Shah. Thus, Karzai was a weak and dependent leader who had a tenuous grasp on power in the absence of foreign support.

Karzai may be viewed as a Pashtun figurehead who oversaw a regime heavily influenced by Afghanistan's historically marginalized ethno-national groups. Since the Northern Alliance was critical to the overthrow of the Taliban regime in 2001, the Tajiks and Uzbeks who made up the Northern Alliance sought to retain their influence and limit the power of Pashtuns in the new government. Given the historic domination of the Pashtun ethno-linguistic group over all other minority groups in Afghanistan—not to mention the brutal Taliban regime, which was dominated by Pashtuns—it is not surprising that many Tajiks are resistant to sharing power with Pashtuns. Nevertheless, this resistance to power sharing meant a high level of distrust between former Northern Alliance members and President Karzai (Dorronsoro 2005). Having reached his two-term limit as the president of Afghanistan, Karzai promised to step down in 2014 to pave the way for a democratic transition in power.

However, the first democratic turnover in the history of the country was badly botched. The 2014 presidential run-off elections were marred by accusations of massive ballot stuffing and bias by the Independent Election Commission. The contest carried a hint of ethnic politics since Ghani, a former World Bank technocrat and Finance Minister in the Karzai regime, is ethnically a Pashtun. Abdullah, who is of Tajik and Pashtun heritage, was a former Foreign Minister in the Karzai regime and a protégé of the legendary Northern Alliance resistance commander, Ahmad Shah Massoud. The accusations of fraud led to large protests and rumors that the projected loser, Abdullah Abdullah, might form a separate government— a move that would likely have plunged the country into a civil war. After an intervention by US Secretary of State John Kerry, both presidential candidates agreed to an audit of all 8 million votes cast in the election with the promise that the winner of the election would form a unity government with their rival and (reportedly) initiate fundamental constitutional changes to shift the country toward a parliamentary system with a prime minister.

This led to Ashraf Ghani becoming president and Abdullah Abdullah becoming Afghanistan's Chief Executive Officer. As part of their agreement, the country's constitution was to be amended within two years following parliamentary elections. But President Ghani's inability to institute a full cabinet and other important positions (such as Attorney General and Chief Justice of the Supreme Court) and his proclivity to centralize power through his associates have undermined relations between the two men and led to accusations that he was veering towards authoritarianism. It also led to parliament's term, which expired in June 2015, being extended, notwithstanding some holding that doing so was unconstitutional.

## *Parliament*

The legislature of Afghanistan has failed to develop as a strong national institution. Although Afghanistan has had parliamentary institutions dating back to 1919, Afghan rulers have regularly ignored or undermined the power of that institution. The current dynamic between parliament and the president is no exception (Emadi 2008). As Abdulkader Sinno notes, "Results of the parliamentary elections of September 2005 confirmed fears that the parliamentary electoral system (a single nontransferable vote) was chosen to produce a weak and fragmented parliament that cannot check Karzai's already overwhelming constitutional powers" (2008, 260–261). Thus, the Afghan state's power has remained highly centralized but weak, sparse, and neo-patrimonial (Sarwari and Crews 2008).[3]

Within parliament, an increasingly rigid conception of ethnic affiliation rather than negotiable policy positions is the major basis of organization, causing the legislature to frequently become deadlocked. As noted earlier, the political system lacks a strong party system.

The major political parties cluster around particular ethnicities and unite or fracture on the basis of prominent personalities as opposed to ideology (e.g. Khalili's *Hezb-e Wahdat*, Mohaqeq's *Hezb-e Wahdat*; Ahady's *Afghan Millat*, Shams's *Afghan Millat*; Abdullah's Coalition for Change and Hope/National Coalition of Afghanistan; Dostum's *Jombesh* Party; Sayyaf's *Ettehad/Tanzim*; Gailani's *Mahaz-e Melli*; the late Rabbani's *Jamiat-e Islami*) (*Economist* 2007; Faraso 2008).[4] There have actually been physical brawls on the floor of parliament along ethnic lines. Such ethnically tinged confrontations have resulted in constitutional crises and a complete stalemate between the legislative and executive branches of government.

From December 2010 to August 2011, the Afghan parliament was hamstrung by a disputed parliamentary election and the (constitutionally dubious) appointment of a Special Election Tribunal to determine whether any of the 413 parliamentary candidates that were disqualified (many of whom were from the Pashtun ethno-linguistic group) by the Independent Election Commission and the Electoral Complaints Commission should be reinstated. The Afghan attorney general also brought charges of corruption against individual election commissioners. The Special Election Tribunal ruled that the 62 disqualified candidates who "won" their seats should be reinstated by the attorney general and the election commissions. The sitting parliament responded by passing a vote of 'no confidence in the Attorney General' and the election commissioners refused to reinstate the disqualified candidates. The parliament also disqualified the chief justice and members of the Supreme Court.

There has also been internal deadlock within the parliament. In 2011, it took three months of balloting before a compromise candidate was elected to be the Speaker of the Parliament. A significant part of the stalemate that has gripped the Afghan parliament is attributable to ethno-linguistic and regional tensions between groups.

In the interim, President Karzai governed throughout 2011 without parliament and with a cabinet that had not been confirmed by parliament. Parliamentarians retaliated against the president's failure to allow confirmation hearings by staging silent protests and drumming their desks in protest. The cabinet appointees continued to sit in the cabinet in an acting capacity (Nordland and Rahimi 2011; Hasht-e Sobh 2011). The Karzai administration resorted to addressing controversial and highly complicated issues by holding national *jirgas* (assemblies), which are advisory bodies but lack the constitutional decision-making authority of parliament.

That the situation was unlikely to improve was perhaps clear given the politicking that led to the unity government between Ghani and Abdullah. Even post-agreement, the Ghani and Abdullah factions continue to accuse each other of the instability: Ghani's camp claims they had no choice but enter into the unity government so as to prevent instability and chaos, while the Abdulla camp continues to accuse the president and his allies of stealing the election (Mashal 2015). Consequently, the two rivals have not only been unable to coordinate a transition to better governance, the inability of parliament and president to agree on the list of cabinet ministers has led to Ghani centralizing power. Besides cabinet posts gone unfilled, various governors' posts have also been left vacant. Some fear that President Ghani, by claiming Afghanistan lacks governance capacity, is gradually moving toward being more authoritarian (Ahmed 2015). Parliament has been a major casualty in the process. While parliament's term has been postponed (because of the inability to agree on election reforms), many rightly believe that how the current crisis within the unity government gets solved will determine to a great extent whether Afghanistan muddles along or reverts to a new phase of instability.

## *The military*

The president is officially the commander-in-chief of the rapidly expanded Afghan National Army (ANA) and the Afghan National Army Air Corps (ANAAC), but the administration of the military is overseen by the Ministry of Defense and tactical operations are delegated to the chief of the general staff and his subordinates. In relative terms, the ANA is considered to be the most rational and capable bureaucracy in the state apparatus. Although the Afghan National Police (ANP) has been reformed as well, it still lags behind the ANA in terms of capabilities.

The military is not a strong, unified, national institution. Despite its growing personnel and reported popularity as an institution, the ANA is very poorly equipped, housed, and paid (Program for Culture & Conflict Studies at the Naval Postgraduate School n.d.; Younossi and et al. 2009),[5] and much of the force remains illiterate. Ethnic tension (Younossi et al. 2009),[6] predatory corruption and drug addiction is rampant within the ranks of the military (International Crisis Group 2010; Younossi et al. 2009). Although the United States has taken the lead in training most soldiers, parts of the military have been trained by different foreign governments with little coordination (until recently) between Kabul, Washington, and Brussels. The military remains a fragmented[7] institution that is politicized and not a neutral force to buttress the state's authority (International Crisis Group 2010; Younossi et al. 2009; Giustozzi 2008). Given its institutional weaknesses, the ANA is unlikely to help the Afghan state acquire a monopoly on the legitimate use of physical force in Afghanistan—a task which in any case has not been achieved even with substantial foreign military support for over a decade (Jalali 2002).[8] At best, the new Afghan army might help the state retain the delicate status quo after foreign forces withdraw, but even this will be a challenge without significant foreign funding as much of the ANA is currently unable to fight the insurgents on its own (Younossi et al. 2009).

The Ministry of Defense, which oversees the army, is itself characterized by micromanagement, ethnic factionalism, personal rivalries, patronage networks, and bureaucratic inertia (International Crisis Group 2010). In particular, the Defense Ministry has witnessed turf battles between General Wardak's clique dominated by Pashtuns and the clique of his former chief of staff, General Bismillah Khan, a Panjsheri Tajik with strong ties to the late charismatic Northern Alliance leader, Ahmad Shah Massoud and the former defense minister, Mohammed Fahim (International Crisis Group 2010; Harrison 2009).

It is important to note that a Panjsheri Tajik who was a Ministry of Defense official, Brigadier General Taleb Shah, was arrested and convicted in the plot to assassinate President Karzai in 2008. Some of the weapons used by assassins in the attack were linked to Taleb's weapons repair workshop. Several Ministry of Interior officials were also questioned in the investigation (International Crisis Group 2010; Gall 2008). The notion that a Tajik brigadier general would single-handedly collude with Taliban assassins to try to kill the president would be a rather suspicious conclusion. In 2005, gunmen fired on General Wardak's vehicle shortly after General Bismillah Khan's helicopter was forced to crash land (Baylough 2005). Neither man was injured in the separate incidents.

The Afghan army cannot serve as either an arbitrator or ruler of Afghanistan. The institution is not professional or prestigious enough to serve as the guardian of an "acceptable" civilian regime. Few civilians would believe that the military could lecture the civilian government on corruption. The military does not appear to have an independent ideology characteristic of ruler-type praetorian armies (Perlmutter 1969). The military and Ministry of Defense can scarcely claim with credibility to be the defenders of "the nation" (as the concept is underdeveloped in Afghanistan), or even "modernization" given the militia roots of many of its leaders.

## Managing conflict

The legacy of the failure to build political institutions that can overcome the internal contradictions of the Afghan political economy has been that "during its 250 years of statehood, Afghanistan has suffered through at least 100 years of fratricidal wars of succession and pacification" (Shahrani 2008, 161). Historically, minority communities have often been left alienated and distrustful of the central government. Moreover, these fratricidal wars have invited repeated foreign intervention by regional and global powers. Shahrani argues that although these conflicts have often been draped in ideological and religious garb, the underlying disputes often pit specific notables, great families, clans, sects, and ethno-linguistic groups against one another (Shahrani 2008). Religion and nationalism have been used to cover and distract from deep ethnic tensions and clashes between elite networks. Thus, if the past is prologue, enduring political solutions to deep divisions in Afghan society at the state level may be unlikely.

Decades of warfare have deeply damaged the society and its institutions for managing conflict. Tribal structures within Afghanistan were severely weakened by protracted conflict (Roy 1990), although tribalism remained strong among refugees. Unsurprisingly, the society that emerged in the wake of the Soviet withdrawal was characterized by violence and an openness to scripturalism (Roy 1990). And while scripturalist movements such as the Taliban were not an historical anomaly in Afghanistan, they did not mesh well with Afghan traditions, such as the celebration of *Nowruz* (i.e. the Persian new year) or the unwillingness to declare other Muslims as *kafirs* (apostates). Moreover, scripturalists have not usually been concerned to build state structures to manage conflict. Olivier Roy has argued (in a separate context) that scripturalists can weaken traditional modes of conflict resolution, increase social divisions, and fail to offer an alternate political model on which to rebuild Afghanistan (Roy 1990).

Even with the imposition of new and nominally democratic political institutions in the post-Taliban regime, the prospect for managing conflict through institutions remains remote. The Afghan Parliament remains a space in which elites defend their class interests as opposed to national interests. Hafizullah Emadi goes so far as to argue that even women, who have participated in the governance of Afghanistan since 1965 (although the female franchise was rescinded under the Taliban), generally only articulate the interest of other elite women in Parliament (Emadi 2008). More broadly, the Afghan state has struggled to compel obedience to its laws, provide quality public services, and ensure confidence in the police and courts (Jones 2008).

In this light, the sources of stability in contemporary Afghanistan may not be found at the level of exogenously imposed "democratic" institutions at the state level. In fact, exogenous actors such as ISAF or NGOs may have interests and restricted time horizons that work against the cohesion of the "nation" and local communities (Coburn 2011).

This is not to imply that stability can emerge completely in societal isolation from state institutions. The pre-Saur Revolution characterization of the Afghan state as deeply alienated from its society (Roy 1990) may no longer be completely accurate as greater integration and internal displacement of large segments of the population have reduced some of the rural isolation that once permitted strategies of evasion and resistance to the state. In any case, most Afghans value the rhetoric and symbols of their modern state. Afghans will continue to accord the state recognition as *a* source of legitimate authority but it is not *the* sole source of legitimate authority in the use of violence. The new Afghan state is unable to act as a container for all societal actors and their conflicts. Partly because it has limited ability to coerce or seduce a large number of actors in society. That noted, the state is not impotent; for as long as the state receives foreign financial support it has the power to intervene in most local conflicts given that it maintains a small presence in most towns. In short, the new Afghan state is too weak to be despotic but strong enough to check many rival militias and warlords. This is because while the state does not have a monopoly on the legitimate use of violence, it has enough capacity to inflict violence so as to keep opponents in check. The war weary people of Afghanistan are also unwilling to challenge openly the authority of the state because the state is a useful fiction whose existence permits foreign assistance to keep flowing and prevents the return of openly violent contestation for power in most areas (Coburn 2011). Thus the main source of conflict management or stability is not due to state institutions but the "masterly inactivity" of the Afghan people (Coburn 2011). Of course, much like the communist Najibullah regime, the current regime is dependent for its survival on external support.

## Economy

Afghanistan is extremely poor and has limited prospects to climb out of its status as a low-income country. With nearly continuous armed conflict since 1978, the country has a very low base of physical and human capital. Extensive political instability and entrenched corruption limit the state's ability to access what appears to be vast mineral resources and thereby promote equitable development.

In terms of the human capital and the labor force, government officals claim improvements in school enrollment since the overthrow of the Taliban regime, but the quality of education delivered is highly variable. Currently, less than a third of the population can read and write. About half of the country is involved in the agrarian sector. Almost a quarter of the population remains unemployed, which is one of the highest unemployment rates in the world. Less than half the population has access to safe drinking water and less than a tenth of the population has access to improved sanitation facilities.

Furthermore, the country suffered a major banking crisis in 2010 that undermined confidence in the new financial system set up by the United States. The arrival of foreign troops and development agencies in 2001 artificially inflated the economic performance of the country. However, the economic growth Afghanistan witnessed in the last decade is not sustainable; the economy is bound to decline when foreign forces depart and the international development industry loses interest in the country. Growth of investment in non-narcotic areas will be sparse due to political uncertainty and ongoing insurgency. Meanwhile, the production of opium continues to surge despite massive efforts by foreign powers to curb production, interdict flows, and incentivize farmers to switch crops.

Government revenue as a share of GDP is among the lowest in the world (Asian Development Bank 2014). The government will struggle to pay for the massive military and police force built up in the last decade. In recent years, more than half of the government's budget and trade deficit were supported by foreign donors. In 2010, it was estimated that foreign aid was equivalent to 98 percent of the country's GDP (Dominguez 2014). In essence, Afghanistan is a donor dependent country facing both a large (although not complete) withdrawal of foreign funding in the coming years and an ongoing armed conflict.

## Regional/international relations

After the Third Anglo-Afghan War in 1919, Afghanistan became a fully sovereign state capable of determining its own foreign policy. The most vexing aspect of Afghanistan's regional foreign relations relates to its relationship with Pakistan. At the regional level, it is this strained relationship that will shape the possibility for the emergence of a viable state in Afghanistan.

The roots of the Afghanistan-Pakistan conflict trace back to the Durand Line Agreement of 1893 between the Iron Amir and Sir Mortimer Durand, the Foreign Secretary of British India. The Durand Line artificially established the southern boundary of Afghanistan and separated the state from British India. However, this arbitrary line also divided the Pushtun ethno-linguistic group for the sake of securing British military control over key mountain passes.

Afghan (Pushtun) nationalists have refused to recognize the Durand Line as the legitimate international boundary. It is worth recalling that Afghanistan was the only state to object to Pakistan's admission into the United Nations in 1947. There have been border clashes between Afghanistan and Pakistan in 1960 and 1961 and diplomatic relations between the two states were suspended from 1960 to 1963. During the early Cold War, the USSR supported Afghanistan's position diplomatically in part to punish Pakistan for its gravitation toward the capitalist bloc.

The impact of Afghanistan's irredentist claims coupled with its traditionally warm friendship with India has deeply affected Pakistani strategic thinking. Eager to avoid the prospect of a two-front war, Pakistan's military developed its "strategic depth" doctrine that essentially entails the subordination of Afghanistan to the status of a client regime in order to preserve Pakistan's ability to deter the Indian military.

During the Anti-Soviet War, Pakistan was able to transform its traditional conflict with Afghanistan's Pashtun nationalists into an asset by directing nationalist fervor toward an external enemy. Pakistan's organization of the Sunni Resistance Parties during the Anti-Soviet War aimed to provide Pakistan with leverage over the group that ultimately formed the new government. In essence, Pakistan hoped that its role in the Anti-Soviet War would enable it to finally execute its "strategic depth" doctrine. When the *mujahideen* failed to transition from a guerilla force to a conventional army, Pakistan opted to fund a new organization, the Taliban.

Of course, the Taliban were never completely subordinate clients; however, Pakistan's ISI remained highly influential over the movement's leadership. Initially Pakistan had even secured tacit US support for the Taliban regime, but tensions developed as it became clear that the regime was unwilling to extradite Al Qaeda militants, including Osama bin Laden, based in Afghanistan. After the events of September 11, 2001, and the US-backed overthrow of the Taliban, it is widely rumored that Taliban fighters were offered sanctuary within Pakistan. The Pakistani security establishment is reluctant to move against the Afghan Taliban because it views the group as a useful asset for restoring strategic depth once US and NATO forces are withdrawn.

Pakistan is not the only important regional player in Afghanistan. India and Iran, in particular, are keen to help shape the political character of the new state and retain its friendship. India, a middle-income developing country, has pledged over two billion dollars in development assistance for Afghanistan in the last decade. India built the new Afghan parliament building and has helped to train some Afghan military officers in addition to investing in Afghan infrastructure and natural resource extraction. India hopes that a stable and sovereign

Afghanistan will prevent the strengthening of militant networks that target India. Despite its generous assistance and genuinely warm bilateral relationship, India is reluctant to step into the role of the departing Western security forces in order to ensure the success of its aid projects and investments. India's security policy community may fear that a robust presence in Afghanistan would agitate Pakistan. Similarly, Iran seeks greater economic integration with Afghanistan to promote the strength and political stability of the new state. The Iranian government would not like to see a resurgence of extremist Taliban dominance with its potential for increased flows of refugees and narcotics through Iran. Most importantly, Iran would like to eliminate the presence of foreign military troops on its border, particularly US forces, as America is one of Iran's archrivals (Barzeghar 2014). Although the departure of foreign troops may enhance Iranian security in the near future, Iran will still operate with great caution toward Afghanistan.

An example of this political engagement/security reluctance can be seen in a joint infrastructure project. From 2003 to 2009, India and Iran cooperated on a bold project to build a road from Delaram in southwestern Afghanistan to Zaranj near the Iranian border with the ultimate goal of linking Kandahar in southern Afghanistan and Herat in western Afghanistan to Iran's Chahbahar port along the Persian Gulf. The political and economic aim of this $110 million project was to reduce Afghanistan's dependence on Pakistan as a transit route for the majority of its trade and to weaken the Taliban insurgency by promoting greater economic development (Yadav and Barwa 2011). However, within two years of handing the new road over to the Afghan government, Taliban insurgents had seized control of the highway. Neither India nor Iran acted to regain their investment from the insurgents. While India and Iran would like to ensure that a sovereign and democratic Afghanistan succeeds, both states are reluctant to engage in overt military action to ensure their desired outcome.

It was clear that while India enjoyed good ties with Ashraf Ghani it preferred Abdullah Abdullah becoming president, given his and his family's close ties to the country (Samanta 2014, 57). India has watched with concern as Ghani has cultivated close links with Pakistan's ISI and military and also engaged in talks with the Taliban, even while ordering the Afghan military to crack down on anti-Pakistan elements operating within Afghanistan. Notwithstanding all the investments India has made in Afghanistan over the years, Ghani has refused India's offer to train Afghan officer cadets and has instead sent them to Pakistani military academies for training (Unnithan 2015, 43). At the same time, he has also allowed the United States a much freer hand than did President Karzai to conduct controversial raids against the Taliban, which has troubled many Afghans and foreign donors who question the efficacy of such raids. Much of what Ghani has done in his first year as president goes against the policies of his predecessor Karzai, and only time will tell if they will lead to a more stable Afghanistan.

## Opportunities and constraints

With the failure to install a set of dynamic and robust political institutions in Afghanistan, it is unlikely that the Afghan state will be able to effectively deter Pakistan's pursuit of strategic depth once foreign forces withdraw and foreign funding of the Afghan regime declines in the years ahead. Consequently, the future for Afghanistan, despite massive foreign assistance, looks pretty dim indeed.

The departure of American and European troops in the near future and ongoing negotiations with Iran might result in a "grand bargain" that simultaneously addresses Iran's legitimate security concerns and removes international sanctions in exchange for Iran's adherence to the provisions of the Nuclear Non-Proliferation Treaty. If this were to occur, Iran might be able to play a greater role in stabilizing and strengthening Afghanistan.

India is also unlikely to risk provoking a nuclear armed and hostile Pakistan by stepping up its military presence in Afghanistan. The presence of a significant number of Indian troops on Afghan soil would only strengthen the hand of the Pakistani military and undermine civilian government in Pakistan's domestic politics. While the presence of Indian troops would buttress the new Afghan state, such a scenario is highly improbable. Without a robust security presence, the weak Afghan state will not be able to secure Indian interests and investments on its own. The new Afghan state will struggle to maintain the status quo in which it is only able to check the advance of Taliban insurgents and other challengers to its authority.

## Political parties

- *National Coalition (Etelaf-e Milli)*: Founded in 2010 as the "Coalition for Hope and Change," this is the party of Abdullah Abdullah, a presidential candidate in 2009 and 2014. Mr. Abdullah, a former foreign minister, was a close advisor of the Anti-Soviet and Anti-Taliban, Tajik resistance fighter from the Panjshir Valley, Ahmad Shah Massoud.
- *New Afghanistan Party (Hezb-e Afghanistan Naween)*: Created in 2004, this is the party of the Vice President of Afghanistan and the former Speaker of the *Wolesi Jirga* (Lower House of Parliament), Yunus Qanuni, a Panjshiri Tajik leader also affiliated with Massoud.
- *Islamic Society (Jamiat-e Islami)*: A (gradualist) Islamist political party founded in 1968 by the late Professor Burhanuddin Rabbani at Kabul University. During the Anti-Soviet conflict, Rabbani would become the nominal President of Afghanistan from the collapse of the communist regime until the rise of the Taliban regime. With the assassination of Burhanuddin Rabbani in 2011, the party is now led by Rabbani's son, Salahuddin Rabbani. Ahmad Zia Massoud, the younger brother of the late Ahmad Shah Massoud, and the son-in-law of Burhanuddin Rabbani is also a prominent member of the party.
- *Islamic Party (Hezb-e Islami)*: The non-militant wing of this (radical) Islamist party, originally founded by Gulbuddin Hekmatyar in 1977, is a legal political party in Afghanistan. The militant wing of the party is called *Hezb-e Islami Gulbuddin* (or HIG) and has been linked to the Taliban and Al Qaeda. The moderate wing is headed by Abdul Hadi Arghandiwal, a former Finance Minister and Economic Minister in President Karzai's cabinet in 2010. The links between the two wings of the party are murky.
- *Islamic Unity Party (Hezb-e Wahdat Islami)*: This party which traced its lineage to the predominately Hazara Shia fronts during anti-Soviet period has fragmented into multiple parties organized around eminent leaders (e.g. Vice President Abdul Karim Khalili, Mohammad Mohaqiq's *Hezb-e Wahdat Islami Mardoum-e Afghanistan*).
- *National Islamic Movement of Afghanistan (Junbish-e Milli Islami Afghanistan)*: The party of the notorious Uzbek warlord, Abdul Rashid Dostum, is still influential in the northern provinces of Afghanistan near Turkmenistan and Uzbekistan.

## Political chronology

1747:        During a period of disarray and decline in the Afsharid (Persian) and Mughal (Indian) empires, respectively, a famed local commander, Ahmad Shah Durrani, was crowned emperor in Kandahar by a confederation of Pashtun tribes. The Durrani Empire laid the foundation for the Afghan state.

1826:        Dost Mohammed Khan, a Pashtun member of the Barakzai clan, acquires Kabul and begins to supplant the Durrani clan.

1839–1842:   The First Anglo-Afghan War results in the temporary overthrow of Dost Mohammed in favor of Shah Shuja Durrani. Shah Shuja is assassinated in 1842, paving the way for the return of Dost Mohammed.

1878–1880:   The defeat of Dost Mohammed's son, Sher Ali Khan, in the Second Anglo-Afghan War results in British control of Afghan foreign policy.

1880–1901:   Abdur Rahman Khan, the "Iron Amir," begins to create a centralized, unified, and socially stratified state.

1893:        The Durand Line Agreement establishes the southern boundary of Afghanistan with British India.

1901–1919:   The son of the Iron Amir, Habibullah Khan, comes to power.

1919:        Afghanistan declares its sovereign independence from British influence after the Third Anglo-Afghan War.

1919–1929:   King Amanullah Khan, the son of King Habibullah Khan, attempts to modernize Afghanistan by relying on internal sources of revenue.

1929:        The modernizing King Amanullah's regime is overthrown for nine months by an obscure Tajik rebel known as the "Bacha-e Saqqao," the son-of-the-water-carrier, who is backed by the *'ulama* (Islamic legal scholars). He is crowned as Habibullah Kalakani. Kalakani is in turn overthrown by Mohammed Nadir Shah, a member of the deposed royal family and a military general. King Nadir Shah's regime is legitimated by the *Loya Jirga* which insists that the new king must obtain their consent before imposing new property taxes.

1933:        The son of Mohammed Nadir Shah, Mohammed Zahir Shah becomes the king and attempts to restart the modernizing project with a focus on education, infrastructure, and industrialization.

1973:        Zahir Shah is overthrown by his relative and former Prime Minister, Prince Sardar Mohammed Daoud, who establishes a short-lived republic.

1978:        The Saur Revolution results in the overthrow of the republic and the establishment of a communist regime. The radical policies of the Communist government spark a revolt in the countryside that begins to spread.

1979:        The USSR enters Afghanistan to stabilize and consolidate the new communist regime that has fallen into bitter factional infighting. An anti-Soviet insurgency based mainly in Pakistan is organized and backed by the United States, Saudi Arabia, and other countries.

1989:        The USSR, led by the reformist Mikhail Gorbachev, withdraws from Afghanistan not due to military defeat (the insurgents failed to capture a single Soviet military base) but a desire to ease Cold War tensions and to focus on domestic restructuring. Nevertheless, distrust and lack of restraint between the US and USSR sets the stage for the breakdown of order in the coming years.

1992:     Following the collapse of its Soviet patron, the Communist regime of Dr. Mohammed Najibullah is toppled by a trio of resistance parties organized by Iran. Despite a power sharing agreement, the final collapse of the Afghan state unleashes a civil war between all of the major resistance factions that devastates the country.

1996:     An obscure, radical, scripturalist group of militants, backed by Pakistani intelligence services, calling itself the Taliban seizes Kabul. The US urges reconciliation and engagement with the new regime.

2001:     After the 9/11 terrorist attacks, and the refusal of the Taliban regime to extradite the leadership of Al Qaeda, the US invades and overthrows the Taliban regime. The Bonn Agreement creates an internationally recognized transitional government. The US maneuvers its client, Hamid Karzai, to become the Interim President.

2004:     Karzai is elected President of Afghanistan in generally free and fair elections.

2009:     Karzai is re-elected President in blatantly fraudulent elections.

2014:     After failing to either build a robust state or eliminate a growing insurgency by reinvigorated Taliban forces, the US and NATO forces withdraw active combat forces from Afghanistan. The country goes through a flawed Presidential election that exacerbates divisions. In September Ashraf Ghani and Abdullah Abdullah, the two rivals claiming the right to be president, agree to a US-brokered power-sharing agreement that leads to Ghani becoming president and Abdullah Afghanistan's Chief Executive Officer.

2015:     President Obama says the United States will delay pulling out troops from Afghanistan following a request from President Ashraf Ghani. Representatives of the new government and the Taliban hold peace talks in Qatar, with the latter demanding that all foreign troops leave the country.

## Notes

1  A neo-patrimonial state sustains itself through personal patronage while maintaining the façade of a legal-rational state (e.g. a formal bureaucracy). The instruments of the state are used to secure the loyalty of clients.

2  The Bonn Agreement was the end result of a one-week conference held in Bonn, Germany in December 2001. The aim of the conference, chaired by UN Special Representative Lakhdar Brahimi, was to create an internationally recognized interim government and draft a constitution after the US toppled the Taliban regime earlier that year.

3  The US actively resisted calls by Germany to create a federal system and insisted that Karzai have the right to appoint governors.

4  Candidates for parliament were not allowed to declare a party affiliation in the first election.

5  The average pay for a private in the ANA is approximately $150 to $170 per month; it is widely reported that the Taliban pay recruits approximately $300 per month.

6  Although the Pashtun ethno-linguistic group is represented roughly in line with its general portion of the population; Tajiks are overrepresented, while Uzbeks and Hazaras are underrepresented.

7  The ANA has really only existed since September 2003. The first version of the post-Taliban Afghan Army managed by the US, Afghan Military Forces (AMF) had to be completely disbanded because of poor performance in combat, internecine rivalry and politicization of units, and predatory corruption against the civilian population (Giustozzi 2009).

8  Historically, of course, the Afghan state has rarely achieved a monopoly on violence (except from 1959 to 1978), relying instead on popular uprisings and tribal forces to supplement the army during times of foreign invasion.

## Works cited

Ahmed, Azam. 2015. "Afghan Leader Said to Be Centralizing Power as Unity Government Plan Stalls." *New York Times* (March 20). Retrieved from www.nytimes.com/2015/03/21/world/asia/ghani-afghanistan-unity-government-plan.html. Accessed June 21, 2015.

Asian Development Bank. 2014. *Asian Development Outlook 2014: Fiscal Policy for Inclusive Growth: Afghanistan*. Manila: Asian Development Bank.

Barzeghar, Kayhan. 2014. "Iran's Foreign Policy in Post-Taliban Afghanistan." *The Washington Quarterly* 37 (2) (June): 119–137.

Baylough, Tim Albone. 2005. "51st US Soldier is Killed in Forgotten War." *Sunday Times* (September 11).

Coburn, Noah. 2011. *Bazaar Politics: Power and Pottery in an Afghan Market Town*. Stanford, CA: Stanford University Press.

Coll, Steve. 2004. *Ghost Wars: The Secret History of the CIA, Afghanistan, and Bin Laden, from the Soviet Invasion to September 10, 2001*. New York: Penguin Press.

Cordesman, Anthony. 2009. "Sanctum FATA." *National Interest* (May/June): 28–38.

Dominguez, Gabriel. 2014. "Afghan Economy at a Crossroads," *Deutsche Welle* (March 25). Retrieved from http://dw.de/p/1BKdR. Accessed July 16, 2014.

Dorronsoro, Gilles. 2005. *Revolution Unending: Afghanistan, 1979 to the Present*. New York: Columbia University Press.

Dupree, Louis. 1997. *Afghanistan*. Oxford: Oxford University Press.

*Economist*. "The Arrival at last of Party Politics." April 28, 2007: 46.

Edwards, David B. 2002. *Before Taliban: Genealogies of the Afghan Jihad*. Berkeley: University of California Press.

Emadi, Hafizaullah. 2008. "Establishment of Afghanistan's Parliament and the Role of Women Parliamentarians: Retrospect and Prospects." *International Quarterly for Asian Studies* 39 (1/2) (May): 5–19.

Faraso, Abas. 2008. "Challenges before the Parliament in Afghanistan." *Daily Afghanistan* (October 11).

Felbab-Brown, Vanda. 2005. "Afghanistan: When Counternarcotics Undermines Counterterrorism." *The Washington Quarterly* 28 (4): 55–72.

Fleschenberg, Andrea. 2009. *Afghanistan's Parliament in the Making: Gendered Understandings and Practices of Politics in a Transitional Country*. Berlin: Heinrich Boll Stiftung.

Gall, Carlotta. 2008. "Afghanistan Links Officers to Assassination Attempt." *New York Times* (May 6): 3.

Giustozzi, Antonio. 2007. "War and Peace Economies of Afghanistan's Strongmen." *International Peacekeeping* 14 (1) (January): 75–89.

———. 2008. *Koran, Kalashnikov, and Laptop: The Neo-Taliban Insurgency in Afghanistan*. New York: Columbia University Press.

———. 2009. *Empires of Mud: Wars and Warlords in Afghanistan*. New York: Columbia University Press.

Goodson, Larry. 2001. *Afghanistan's Endless Wars: State Failure, Regional Politics, and the Rise of the Taliban*. Seattle: University of Washington Press.

Harrison, Selig. 2009. "Pashtun Alienation." *International Herald Tribune* (August 17): 6.

Hasht-e Sobh. 2011. "Is a new Cabinet on the way?" *Hasht-e Sobh* (October 24).

Hazara.net. 2011. "Ethnic Composition of the Newly Elected—2010 Wolesi Jirga (Lower House) Islamic Republic of Afghanistan, 4 January 2011. Retrieved from www.hazara.net/downloads/afghanistan/afghanistan_ethnic_compositon_wolesi_jirga_2010.pdf. Accessed August 5, 2014.

International Crisis Group. 2010. *A Force in Fragments: Reconstituting the Afghan National Army*. Crisis Group Asia Report No. 190. London: International Crisis Group.

Jalali, Ali Ahmad. 2002. "Rebuilding Afghanistan's Army." *Parameters* (Autumn).

Jones, Seth G. 2008. "The Rise of Afghanistan's Insurgency: State Failure and Jihad." *International Security* 32 (4): 7–40.

Kilcullen, David. 2009. *The Accidental Guerilla: Fighting Small Wars in the Midst of a Big One*. Oxford: Oxford University Press.

Mashal, Mujib. 2015. "Afghan Parliament's Term is Extended After Squabbles Delay Elections." *New York Times* (June 19). Retrieved from www.nytimes.com/2015/06/20/world/asia/afghan-parliaments-term-is-extended-after-squabbles-delay-elections.html?_r=0. Accessed June 21, 2015.

National Democratic Institute. 2011. *Political Parties in Afghanistan: A Review of the State of Political Parties after the 2009 and 2010 Elections.* Washington, DC: National Democratic Institute.

Nojumi, Neamatollah. 2002. *The Rise of the Taliban in Afghanistan: Mass Mobilization, Civil War, and the Future of the Region.* New York: Palgrave.

Nordland, Rod, and Sangar Rahimi. 2011. "Afghan Court Ruling Seeks to Alter Election Results." *New York Times* (June 24): 9(A).

Perlmutter, Amos. 1969. "The Praetorian State and the Praetorian Army: Toward a Taxonomy of Civil-Military Relations in Developing Societies." *Comparative Politics* 1 (3): 382–404.

Porter, Patrick. 2009. *Military Orientalism: Eastern War Through Western Eyes.* New York: Columbia University Press.

Program for Culture & Conflict Studies at the Naval Postgraduate School. n.d. "Summary of the Afghan National Army." *Naval Postgraduate School.* Retrieved from www.nps.edu/programs/ccs/Docs/Pubs/ANA_Summary_Web.pdf. Accessed March 17, 2012.

Rashid, Ahmed. 2001. *Taliban: Militant Islam, Oil and Fundamentalism in Central Asia.* New Haven: Yale Nota Bene.

Robinson, Geoffrey. 2009. "The Great Gamble." *New Statesman* (October 6): 28–31.

Roy, Olivier. 1990. *Islam and Resistance in Afghanistan*, 2nd ed. Cambridge: Cambridge University Press.

Rubin, Barnett. 1995. *The Search for Peace in Afghanistan: From Buffer State to Failed State.* New Haven: Yale University Press.

———. 1999. "Afghanistan Under the Taliban." *Current History* (February 1): 79–91.

Samanta, Pranab Dhal. 2014. "The Importance of Being Ghani." *India Today* (July 21): 57.

Sarwari, Atiq, and Robert D. Crews. 2008. "Epilogue: Afghanistan and the Pax Americana." In *The Taliban and the Crisis of Afghanistan*, edited by Robert D. Crews and Amin Tarzi. Cambridge, MA: Harvard University Press.

Shahrani, M. Nazif. 2008. "Taliban and Talibanism in Historical Perspective." In *The Taliban and The Crisis of Afghanistan*, by Robert D. Crews and Amin Tarzi. Cambridge, MA: Harvard University Press.

Shane, Scott. 2009. "Taliban Leader, In a Comeback, Is Vexing U.S." *New York Times* (October 11): 1.

Sinno, Abdulkader H. 2008. *Organizations at War in Afghanistan and Beyond.* Ithaca, NY: Cornell University Press.

Sulaiman, Sadia, and Syed Adnan Ali Shah Bukhari. 2009. "Hafiz Gul Bahadur: A Profile of the Leader of the North Waziristan Taliban." *Terrorism Monitor* (April 10): 4–6.

Unnithan, Sandeep. 2015. "The Great Game of Balance." *India Today* (March 30): 43.

U.S. Department of State. 1996a. "State Department Briefing." Washington, DC: FDCH Political Transcripts (September 30).

———. 1996b. "State Department Briefing." Washington, DC: FDCH Political Transcripts (October 8).

———. 2010. "US Engagement with Taliban on Usama Bin Laden." *National Security Archive.* July 16, 2001. Retrieved from www.gwu.edu/~nsarchiv/NSAEBB/NSAEBB97/tal40.pdf. Accessed February 04, 2010.

U.S. Embassy in Islamabad. 1995. "Finally, A Talkative Talib: Origins and Membership of the Religious Students' Movement." (February 20): 4. *National Security Archive.* Retrieved from www.gwu.edu/~nsarchiv/NSAEBB/NSAEBB97/tal8.pdf. Accessed June 30, 2009.

Yadav, Vikash. 2010. "The Myth of the Moderate Taliban." *Asian Affairs: An American Review* 37 (3): 133–45.

Yadav, Vikash, and Conrad Barwa. 2011. "Relational Control: India's Grand Strategy in Afghanistan and Pakistan." *India Review* 10 (2): 93–125.

Younossi, Obaid, Peter Thruelsen, Jonathan Voccaro, Jerry Sollinger, and Brian Grady. 2009. *The Long March: Building an Afghan National Army.* Santa Monica, CA: RAND Corporation—National Defense Research Institute.

## Recommended texts

Coburn, Noah. 2011. *Bazaar Politics: Power and Pottery in an Afghan Market Town*. Stanford, CA: Stanford University Press.

Crews, Robert D., and Amin Tarzi, eds. 2008. *The Taliban and the Crisis of Afghanistan*. Cambridge, MA: Harvard University Press.

Dorronsoro, Gilles. 2005. *Revolution Unending: Afghanistan, 1979 to the Present*. New York: Columbia University Press.

Edwards, David B. 2002. *Before Taliban: Genealogies of the Afghan Jihad*. Berkeley: University of California Press.

Giustozzi, Antonio. 2009. *Empires of Mud: Wars and Warlords in Afghanistan*. New York: Columbia University Press.

Roy, Olivier. 1990. *Islam and Resistance in Afghanistan*, 2nd Edition. Cambridge: Cambridge University Press.

Rubin, Barnett R. 1995. *The Fragmentation of Afghanistan: State Formation and Collapse in the International System*, 2nd ed. New Haven, CT: Yale University Press.

Zaeef, Abdul Salam. 2010. *My Life with the Taliban*. New York: Columbia University Press.

# 8   Trends and prospects

*Neil DeVotta*

If it is true that the twenty-first century is to be Asia's century, then South Asia could play a leading role in global developments. The region is home to nearly 1.7 billion people, which is over 20 percent of the global population, and represents a huge market. This and changing international relations have led to major powers seeking influence in the region even as South Asian states grapple with numerous challenges stemming from contradictions rooted in interstate and ethno-religious tensions. Consequently, how South Asia manages to accommodate its people's aspirations will have a major impact on stability in the Asian region as a whole.

Achieving stability, however, will not be easy, given that a large percentage of the region's population comprise youth, which promotes conditions for a demographic dividend but also portends instability and conflict if this population's needs go unfulfilled. This is especially evident in India, which is set to be the world's fastest growing economy in the next few years but also needs to create a million jobs every month to accommodate those entering the labor force. Nearly 150 million Indians are between the age of 18 and 23; and half the population is under the age of 25, while two-thirds are under the age of 35.

The situation is no different in Pakistan, where nearly 20 percent of the population is under the age of 26 and nearly 48 percent are between the age of 18 and 35, which requires the country to create 1.5 million jobs a year to accommodate this youth bulge.[1] While Pakistan's fertility rates have come down, it still hovers around 2.9 births per woman, which contrasts with Sri Lanka's 2.1 births per woman.[2] Some projections suggest Pakistan's population could exceed 300 million by 2050. How Pakistan manages to absorb such a large number will have significant ramifications, given that youth that are marginalized are more likely to be swayed by extremism and Pakistan can ill afford to add to its already destabilizing extremist ranks.

Indeed, the evidence is strong that a high fertility rate in especially poor countries hampers development, because these states typically find it difficult to meet their population's health, education, and employment needs. And India and Pakistan are not the only countries facing stiff challenges in this regard. All South Asian states covered in this volume face equally daunting challenges stemming from population pressures. In Nepal, where 20 percent of the population is between the age of 15 and 30, the country needs to create approximately 350,000 jobs a year but only manages to accommodate about 10 percent entering the workforce. While Bangladesh has experienced a dramatic reduction in fertility rates, even here about 10 percent of the population are in their twenties and that figure keeps rising. And in Afghanistan over 42 percent of the population is under the age of 15, while in Sri Lanka, with approximately 21 million people, 23 percent is between the age of 15 and 29.[3] Employment in the Middle East—as drivers, laborers, and restaurant workers—has helped alleviate some pressures the region's governments face when seeking to accommodate this bulge in youth, but there is no substitute for jobs generated domestically and the extent to which the region's states succeed in this regard will determine South Asia's economic trajectory and stability.

At present South Asia's states are politically relatively stable. While Afghanistan labors to control spoiler elements within the country and Nepal continues to struggle to create a constitution that will restructure the state, all cases covered in this volume now have democratically elected governments (with Nepal's second elected Constituent Assembly serving as parliament). Democracy is appreciated within the region and democracy has also deepened over the years, and this includes Pakistan—where the military has ruled for about half the time the country has been independent—and Bangladesh—where notwithstanding military rule and the subsequent animus between the Awami League (AL) and Bangladesh National Party (BNP) Bangladeshis continue to place faith in the voting process. The same is true for Sri Lanka, Asia's oldest democracy, which used the vote in 2015 to oust a government that was propelling the island in an increasingly authoritarian direction.

But there is a democratic paradox to the region in that the spread and deepening of democracy has not been accompanied by good governance. There are multiple causes for the lack of good governance, and it includes corruption, identity politics accentuated by caste and ethno-religious extremism, rivalries exacerbated by dynastic politics, and disregard for the rule of law. All this will need to be rectified if South Asia is to achieve its potential, especially economically.

Regional and interstate rivalries have also colluded to slow development, and in that sense South Asia is a good example of how domestic and international politics feed off each other to impact stability and economic progress. For instance, India-Pakistan tensions and distrust and fear of India among the smaller states have caused the region to be among the least connected, which is evident to anyone who has tried to travel between South Asia's major cities. With India responsible for nearly 70 percent of South Asia's population, the region's smaller countries fear Indian superintendence, while India in turn is extra sensitive to how these states' relations with powers outside South Asia may compromise her security. India thus usually prefers bilateral dealings with fellow South Asian countries, while the latter in turn feel more secure negotiating with India through the South Asian Association for Regional Cooperation (SAARC). While SAARC was meant to promote trade and develop the region economically, intra-SAARC trades stands at just over one percent of South Asia's GDP. This is partly because certain Indian policies have hindered greater trade between it and the other countries, the lack of connectivity, and intra-SAARC rivalries. Part of the irony here is that while India wants to operate as South Asia's hegemon, some of its policies delegitimize India's status and undermine that very goal.

One major issue that has destabilized South Asia is the India-Pakistan dispute over Kashmir. Long festering, it has ruined relations and complicated all other possibilities for cooperation between the two states. Pakistan aspired to all of Kashmir, but controls only one-third, and does not feel complete without owning the rest of it; while India opposes letting go any part of the territory it controls even while laying claim to all of Kashmir. With its predominant Muslim population Kashmir allows India to play up its secular credentials even as Hindu extremists resort to various shenanigans that erode secularism. On the other hand, the dispute has, over the years, allowed Pakistan's military to strengthen itself at the expense of democracy and good governance and also provided Islamist extremists a reason to mobilize and expand to the point where some of these forces now threaten Pakistan itself. It has also led to a nuclear rivalry between India and Pakistan, with the latter especially dependent on nuclear weapons for its security given India's superior conventional capabilities, and caused many to worry about Islamist extremists getting their hands on such weapons. Though politically hard to sell, ultimately the current Line of Control in Kashmir is bound to become the international border separating India and Pakistan, and this is an outcome that the international community would welcome.

Another issue that has destabilized South Asia is foreign involvement in Afghanistan. The country's bedeviling domestic politics were exacerbated by the 1979 Soviet invasion, which led the United States to support mujahideen forces bent on jihad through Pakistan's Inter-Services Intelligence. The links created among the various foreign groups that joined the mujahideen together with Pakistani meddling enabled the rise of the Taliban, which eventually collaborated with Osama bin Laden's Al Qaeda, which in turn led to the US invasion of that unfortunate country following the attacks on 9/11. Given the unstable border with India in Kashmir, Pakistan feels it has to influence events in Afghanistan lest it end up with hostile forces on its western flank as well. India's significant aid to Afghanistan only increases such concerns and it has led Pakistan to follow a dangerous policy of tolerating anti-Indian Taliban while cracking down on anti-Pakistan Taliban. With President Ashraf Ghani having asked the United States to continue to maintain a presence in Afghanistan, and the dynamics among the Afghan government, Taliban, and pro-Pakistan extremists evolving, there is no reason to believe that stability will return to Afghanistan soon, which in turn does not bode well for the region.

A third issue that could potentially destabilize interstate relations in South Asia, although it also stands to drive the region's economy, is China's increased involvement in the region. China has dramatically increased its footprint across South Asia by resorting to economic diplomacy—whereby China uses its massive foreign currency reserves to finance much-needed infrastructure projects in the region—but this has led to Indian concerns and partly conditioned India's relations with fellow South Asian countries even as India-China trade keeps expanding and India–US relations reach new heights. Chinese infrastructure investments in Pakistan, Nepal, and Sri Lanka suggest that the country may be seeking to use economic relations for geostrategic positioning in the Indo-Pacific. This is understandable given that much of China's oil, gas, and trade pass through the Indian Ocean and China aspires to be a superpower. But India tends to think of the Indian Ocean as India's Ocean and is unlikely to stand idle if it felt threatened by China's activities—especially if they stray too far from the trading realm to the military realm.

Sri Lankan President Mahinda Rajapaksa's ouster in 2015 may have been related to such Indian concerns. Rajapaksa went out of his way to cultivate close relations with China in ways that India felt compromised her security interests, and reports suggest Indian intelligence played a role in supporting opposition forces to defeat Rajapaksa. The former president has claimed India's Research and Analysis Wing contributed to his defeat (although he has also blamed the Central Intelligence Agency and other Western governments, all of whom disapproved of Rajapaksa's authoritarianism and were concerned with the way he was interacting with China). We may never know the role India (and Western countries) played in the seminal January 2015 Sri Lanka elections, but what the subsequent reports suggest is that undue interference on the part of major powers in South Asia could lead to instability if such involvement threatened India's preponderant interests. China has the finances and wants to invest in South Asia (and elsewhere for that matter); and South Asia, including India, needs to improve its infrastructure and no country currently is able and willing to fund massive infrastructure projects like China. Consequently, achieving agreement on the disputed India-China border and a degree of trilateral cooperation among India, China, and respective South Asian states in seeking to develop their countries will go a long way in building the region's capabilities, although it is important that such cooperation be achieved in a manner that India, the region's dominant power, finds nonthreatening.

While interstate and international influences stand to impact South Asia's stability, so will countries' domestic politics rooted in ethno-religious extremism. In a real sense, such ethno-religious extremism is the biggest threat to the region's stability. Here Pakistan stands out, given the manifest Islamist extremism within its population. Corruption, ethnic rivalries, and gross malgovernance have contributed to Pakistan's inability to meet its people's expectations, including attaining a decent education, and this is a major reason for the rise in *madaris*, some of which have only specialized in radicalizing young men for jihad in Afghanistan and Kashmir.

Pakistan is not the only country in South Asia to be adversely affected by religious extremism. Sri Lanka and India are also prominent examples of how religion has been manipulated to fan nationalism and persecute minorities, especially Muslims and Christians. If Islamist extremism discredits Islam and has been a blight on Pakistan, Hindu extremism in India and Buddhist extremism in Sri Lanka in turn have targeted Muslims and Christians and compromised both countries' democracies.

In Sri Lanka, Sinhalese Buddhist nationalism played a leading role in laying the foundation for a civil war between the majority Sinhalese and minority Tamils that lasted nearly three decades. The war's end, rather than convincing nationalists about the dangers of marginalizing minorities, led to triumphalism that soon thereafter targeted Christians and especially Muslims. For instance, the Bodu Bala Sena (Buddhist Power Force, BBS), a racist Buddhist outfit that the previous government tacitly supported, began promoting campaigns that led to mosques and Muslim homes and businesses being targeted, and many believed that the ground had been set for a pogrom against the island's Muslim community. The change in government has forced the BBS and similar organizations to the sidelines, but there has long been an eddy of anti-Muslim sentiment in the country that the civil war helped mask and it is entirely possible that campaigns similar to what the BBS unleashed could resurface.

Communal violence, or violence between religious communities, has long been a feature of Indian politics, and Hindu-Muslim riots especially tend to take place with a degree of regularity especially before elections. The return to power of the Bharatiya Janata Party (BJP) in India has emboldened Hindu nationalists who demand that all communities in India, irrespective of their religious affiliations, subscribe to Hindutva (Hinduness or a Hindu ethos). Claiming that India is both a *pitribhumi* (fatherland) and *punyabhumi* (holy land), the Hindutva forces led by the Rashtriya Swayamsevak Sangh (RSS, or National Volunteer Organization) claim that while Muslims and Christians may consider India their fatherland, the country can never be their holy land as they look to Mecca and Rome/West, respectively, for religious inspiration.

Just as the BBS in Sri Lanka was able to operate with impunity when the Mahinda Rajapaksa government was in power, the Hindutva forces appear to be able to operate with relative impunity now that the BJP is in power. The BJP, however, is a political party and needs to maintain public support and govern in a manner that improves the country's economic prospects. The anti-minority Hindutva agenda, if not countered, is bound to undermine this. The two BJP-led governments that ruled from 1998 to 2004 placed the RSS agenda on the backburner while it sought to strengthen the country's security and improve its economy, although it was during its tenure that the infamous 2002 Gujarat pogrom that killed nearly 2,000 Muslims took place. Narendra Modi, who was chief minister of the state at the time and is considered by many to have condoned the violence, is now the prime minister.

Since Modi came to power a number of Christian churches have been attacked and Hindutva forces have also made denigrating statements against Muslims. While it is clear that Modi is intent on making India attractive to foreign investors and is eager to improve the country's economy, he has failed to condemn the anti-Muslim agitprop and anti-Christian violence. Modi has also promoted and tolerated pro-Hindutva personnel to various cultural establishments while trying to keep the RSS and its affiliates out of the political sphere. Many in India feel the country's secular foundations are being slowly challenged, and it is possible that India may see strategic anti-minority rioting in the future—enough to mobilize Hindu voters and keep extremists like the RSS content but not serious enough to undermine the country's economy or cause the international community to chastise India. A democratically strong and economically vibrant India is more likely to promote prosperity in South Asia but that in turn will depend on the extent to which the ruling BJP and its pro-Hindutva yet pragmatic Prime Minister Modi eschew extremism.

Bangladesh, having gained independence amidst massive violence, has also experienced a fair share of post-independence extremist violence—although this has been colored by the rivalry between the Awami League and Bangladesh National Party and has thus mainly been Muslim-on-Muslim violence. The country appeared to be getting radicalized when the BNP was in power, partly because of the impunity some radical Islamist groups allied with the BNP seemed to enjoy. Indeed, between 1999 and 2005 Islamists perpetrated unprecedented violence, causing widespread fears that Bangladesh was on the cusp of becoming a failed state and a bastion for jihadist forces with links to Al Qaeda and similar outfits bent on perpetrating global terrorism. While subsequent crackdowns have diminished the Islamists' ability to destabilize the state, the political instability in the country provides such extremist groups space to revive their agendas.

When combined with the Nepali civil war between the government and Maoist rebels from 1996 to 2006 that killed over 15,000 people and the ongoing violence in Afghanistan in which ethnicity, regional identities, foreign interference, and Islamic extremism have coalesced to unleash violence, it is clear that South Asia has grappled, and will continue to grapple, with extremism. How the region tames this tendency, which is easier said than done given how political elites manipulate ethno-religious and societal cleavages for petty political gain, will partly determine how well the region progresses.

Every region of the world faces numerous challenges and South Asia deals with more than its fair share. The myriad hurdles, in addition to what has been noted above, include malnutrition, poverty, caste discrimination, gender-based violence, pollution, the spread of superbugs, and climate change. Indeed, a specific and common list pertaining to the countries covered in this book may run into scores. But the progress the region has made over the past few decades has come despite such hurdles, and there is, therefore, no reason to doubt the resilience of South Asia's peoples. In an increasingly interconnected and shrinking world, it is important that South Asia succeeds in meeting these people's aspirations; for were it to fail, it will not merely have consequences for those in South Asia but the world at large.

## Notes

1  Jose Lopez-Calix, Pakistan: Path to Rapid Growth and Job Creation, World Bank Policy Paper Series on Pakistan, at www-wds.worldbank.org/external/default/WDSContentServer/WDSP/IB/2014/ 04/07/000456286_20140407142433/Rendered/PDF/862530NWP0Worl0th0and0Job0Creation.pdf. Accessed March 30, 2015.

2 Afghanistan has the highest fertility rate in South Asia, with 5.4 births per woman while the Maldives, which is not covered in this book, has the lowest at 1.7. The other countries covered in this volume rank as follows: India 2.5; Bangladesh 2.4; and Nepal 2.3. See Central Intelligence Agency, *The World Factbook*, at www.cia.gov/library/publications/the-world-factbook/rankorder/2127rank. html. Accessed March 30, 2015.
3 United Nations Development Program, *Sri Lanka National Human Development Report 2014*, p.vi,athttp://www.lk.undp.org/content/dam/srilanka/docs/localpublications/Sri%20Lanka%20National% 20Human%20Development%20Report%202014123123.pdf. Accessed April 1, 2015.

# Glossary

| | |
|---|---|
| *Adivasi* | original inhabitants; tribal peoples |
| *Dalit* | crushed or oppressed; former Untouchables or Scheduled Castes |
| *dhammadipa* | island containing Buddha's teachings |
| *hartal* | general strike |
| *Hindutva* | Hindu-ness; the idea that "to be Indian is to be Hindu" |
| *jati* | endogamous kinship group; "sub-caste" |
| *khadi* | homespun cloth |
| *madrassa* | (pl. *madaris*) a school attached to a mosque |
| *Mahavamsa* | Great (Sinhalese) chronicle |
| *mandir* | temple |
| *Mureed* | one who follows a *pir*; someone initiated into a Sufi order |
| *Pir* | term for a traditional leader, often associated with a Sufi religious order, but sometimes also for leaders of tribal and kinship groups |
| *satyagraha* | soul force; nonviolent civil disobedience |
| *Sharia/Shariat* | Islamic law, including diverse approaches to jurisprudence |
| *Sinhadipa* | Island of the Sinhalese |
| *Sufi* | an adherent of Sufism, a broad term referring to a traditional approach to Islam that emphasizes internal and esoteric spiritual awareness. Well-established Sufi orders can have millions of members, and are sometimes seen as liberal in comparison to Wahhabis, who see Sufi practices as religiously suspect |
| *swadeshi* | self-sufficiency; idea of economic nationalism |
| *swaraj* | self-rule |
| *Ulama* | religious scholars |
| *varna* | color; "caste" categories (*Brahmin, Kshatriya, Vaishya, Shudra*) |
| *Zakat* | religious obligation of alms-giving; a portion of wealth that Muslims give annually |

# Index